A Texan Plan for the Texas Coast

NUMBER THIRTY-ONE
Gulf Coast Books
Sponsored by Texas A&M–Corpus Christi

John W. Tunnell Jr., General Editor

A Texan Plan for

Texas A&M University Press • College Station

the Texas Coast

JIM BLACKBURN

with GIS mapping by Christina Walsh and Priya Singh

First edition

This paper meets the requirements
of ANSI/NISO Z39.48-1992 (Permanence of Paper).
Binding materials have been chosen for durability.
Printed in China through Four Colour Print Group.

Library of Congress Cataloging-in-Publication Data

Names: Blackburn, Jim, 1947– author.
Title: A Texan plan for the Texas coast / Jim Blackburn.
Other titles: Gulf Coast books; no. 31.
Description: First edition. | College Station: Texas A&M University Press, [2017] | Series: Gulf Coast books; number thirty-one | Includes author's poems about the Texas coast. | Includes bibliographical references and index.
Identifiers: LCCN 2017007158 | ISBN 9781623495787 (book/flexbound (with flaps): alk. paper)
Subjects: LCSH: Gulf Coast (Tex.)—Environmental conditions. | Coastal zone management—Texas—Gulf Coast. | Economic development projects—Texas—Gulf Coast. | Sustainable development—Texas—Gulf Coast. | Community development—Environmental aspects—Texas—Gulf Coast. | Gulf Coast (Tex.) —Poetry.
Classification: LCC F392.G9 B55 2017 | DDC 976.4—dc23 LC record available at
https://lccn.loc.gov/2017007158

A list of titles in this series is available at the end of the book.

This book is dedicated to "my girl" of forty-eight years, Garland Kerr, to whom I sent the following poem just before leaving my room to argue the whooping crane case before the Fifth Circuit in New Orleans.

Got the feather that you gave me in my pocket
Just like having your picture in a locket
I'll reach down and feel
And know you are real
And come after them like a rocket.

Contents

Acknowledgments

Writing a book such as this is a humbling experience. It is impossible to complete such an effort without inspiration, assistance, support, and nourishment from many different people and entities. This book is dedicated to my wife, Garland Kerr, my partner for over forty years in marriage and in life, the love of my life. I doubt that this book would have been written without Garland, and I know she was one of the keys to getting it done. So to start with, thanks, G.

Another key to this book was Ann Hamilton, the "tough old bird" who has been my partner in the fight to protect the whooping cranes, as well as in reading and reviewing early drafts of this book. Ann first read the draft of these many chapters when we traveled to Africa together, me pestering her all the time for feedback. "Is it okay?" "Is it okay?" To her credit, she never turned and told me where to place my chapters, although I am sure it was tempting. Ann—thank you from the depths of my heart, you tough old bird.

Two other key people in the evolution and development of this book are Mary Carter, my law partner for many decades, and Elizabeth Winston Jones, my partner in envisioning two of the key concepts set out in the book, the Lone Star Coastal National Recreation Area and the Texas Coastal Exchange. Mary and I worked through many experiences representing the citizens and groups of the coast that helped form the key role of litigation in this vision for the future of the coast. And Mary has always been my first editor, helping me choose softer, more appropriate pathways for expressing my feelings. Elizabeth and I have lived and continue to live through the trials and tribulations of developing creative concepts and watching them being born—almost, maybe next year, maybe this year—a sometimes slow and agonizing process, one where a friend and partner is truly appreciated and necessary. Thank you both.

I must also recognize Dale Cordray, my wonderful assistant

with whom I have been working for over sixteen years. Dale is a good soul, a person who makes others feel happy to be in her presence. She has tried her best to bring order to the chaos I create, and I am grateful for her help, assistance, and loyalty all these many years. Dale created many loose-leaf versions of this book, each of which I worked on, pored over, and then sent back to her to do again, which she did with a smile. Thanks, Dale.

This book is a vision of the future of the Texas coast, a vision made clearer by the wonderful maps compiled by Christina Walsh of Houston with the assistance of Priya Singh, a student in the professional master's program in the School of Natural Sciences at Rice University. Christina put up with hours of my describing the types of maps that I wanted to present, and she and Priya would then go out and find the data sources and pull the maps together. Some maps were quite hard to compile. I think you will agree that these maps reflect well upon Christina and Priya. Thank you both.

Additionally, in chapter 3, "Water Assets of the Coast," I was assisted substantially by Christy Flatt, another professional master's student at Rice University. Christy spent a semester compiling various water data for the coast and put them together in an extremely well-organized and well-presented manner. I am sure she learned more about water in Texas and on the coast than she bargained for, and I benefited from it, which I really appreciated.

I want to acknowledge the many people who are part of this book and with whom I have shared many of the experiences that created some of the visions and concepts set out in these pages. I must thank Team 11, my fishing buddies—John Chapman, Jack Schwaller, and John Fenoglio—with whom I have spent many, many hours fishing and bullshitting, and the owners of Team 11, our wives—Garland, whom you have met, Isabelle Scurry Chapman, Sue Schwaller, and Sally Fenoglio. We have had many adventures together, often joined by our friends Shelly and Bubba Kaufman of Austin, Diane Jones of Marshall, Cheryl Overend of California, Carol Keeney of Houston, and Dale Cordray of Houston. Friendship is a key to many things in life, including the realization of the vision of ecoplay as set out in chapter 7. It's nice to have great friends to play with among our ecological jewels of the coast.

Many people took time to review various facts and to help me get them straight. First, to my old friend Bud Payne of

Weslaco for taking the time to help me understand the dynamics of the Valley Land Fund competition, "Thanks Medley." My thanks also go out to John Kirksey and Julie Hendricks of Kirksey and Associates; Susan Rieff, formerly of the Lady Bird Johnson Wildflower Center; Robert Potts of the Dixon Water Foundation; Tenna Florian of Lake Flato Architects; and Michael Bloom of R. G. Miller Engineers. These firms and individuals are excellent in their profession. They are among the best we have to offer in Texas.

Another nod goes to the best legal team I have ever worked with, the lawyers who worked on the whooping crane trial for The Aransas Project (TAP)—Charles Irvine, Jeff Mundy, David Kahne, Mary Conner, and Patrick Waites—as well as Mary Carter, who kept our firm alive during that time. I also want to acknowledge Mark Rose, our policy adviser from whom I continue to learn, and the D. M. O'Connor Interests, who supported us along with all the groups and individuals who joined TAP. I also want to acknowledge Molly Cagle, a fierce and excellent opponent for whom I have great respect.

Rice University is noted throughout this book, and I want to say a word or two about this great institution. Rice has been a rock in my professional life. I came to Rice as a graduate student straight out of law school and learned the science of the environment, knowledge that opened a whole new realm of possibilities. I began teaching at Rice in 1975 as a lecturer and am now a professor in the practice in civil and environmental engineering. Rice has treated me well, as have numerous leaders of the civil and environmental engineering department such as Dr. Herb Ward, Dr. Phil Bedient, Dr. Pedro Alvarez, and Dr. Rob Griffin. They have been unwavering in their support of me, and I truly appreciate them. And, as is mentioned in the book, the Rice Faculty Club, a wonderful eating and meeting place, has been the site of a number of interesting and important introductions, meetings, and ideas. Thank you, Rice, for being there and for providing an umbrella under whose protection ideas can grow.

Similarly, Houston Endowment deserves recognition for providing the funding that allowed me and others to develop, understand, and explore several of the key concepts set out in this book. In particular, aspects of chapter 4, "Hurricanes and Flooding"; chapter 5, "Climate Change"; chapter 6, "Ecosystem Services and Ranching"; and chapter 7, "Birds and Ecoplay," utilize information and ideas developed at the Severe

Storm Prediction, Education, and Evacuation from Disasters (SSPEED) Center at Rice over the last six or seven years. Elizabeth Love has been excellent to work with in her role as our project officer, supporting us and encouraging us to do bigger and better things, as have Ann Stern and Lisa Hall. I should also thank the great Houston visionary Jesse Jones, whose financial legacy established the Houston Endowment and ultimately provided the SSPEED Center with support. I appreciate this great leader more today than ever when I think of how our coast is facing challenges similar to the financial failures of the late 1920s through which Jesse Jones led the Houston financial community. I hope this book will help guide our ship through the shoals of climate change, the carbon economy, and other issues discussed herein.

The director of the SSPEED Center, Phil Bedient, deserves special mention. I met Phil the first day he set foot on the Rice campus, and we have been friends ever since. Phil and I have worked well together over the years, and I appreciate his willingness to listen to and support most if not all of my somewhat unorthodox ideas. I also want to thank and acknowledge our Texas Coastal Exchange team at the SSPEED Center. It is a pleasure to work with nice, sharp people, including Elizabeth Winston Jones, Henk Mooiweer, Megan Parks, Frances Kellerman, and Larry Dunbar. Similarly, I want to acknowledge Victoria Herrin and Suzanne Dixon of the National Parks Conservation Association, who took the idea of the Lone Star Coastal National Recreation Area and ran with it, along with John Nau, Cynthia Pickett-Stevenson, Cullen Geiselman, Bill King, and Elizabeth Winston Jones, the founders of the Lone Star Coastal Alliance, who, along with the "chief," former secretary of state James Baker, have worked to bring forth this recreational and economic asset that could be and should be a key aspect of the future of the Texas coast.

On the topic of Rice University, two men deserve special recognition for their importance in helping me learn to think critically and meaningfully about science and society. First, Dr. H. C. Clark, the geophysicist, my mentor in all things geological. H. C. and I first worked together forty years ago at the Rice Center for Community Design and have been great friends and professional allies more or less since that time. I owe a tremendous amount to H. C., but most of all I appreciate his friendship and support and wise counsel for these many years. We have been through a lot together, and it was all good. And then Dr. Ron Sass, the biogeochemist, my mentor in climate change and another close friend. Ron and I have become friends in the last fifteen years, and he has been a true delight to get to know. There are not many people I can talk to about either climate change or the deepest issues about life in general. Ron is open to both and always seems to have a nice word and an insight that fills a gap or a need. When I think of these two, I smile, and that is good.

Regarding funding, I want to acknowledge Joe Swinbank of Sugar Land. His funds were used to support much of the GIS work and the purchase of many of the photographs in this book. Joe appreciates creativity such as that set out in chapter 6, and I appreciate him for that. I also want to acknowledge the support of my planning firm, Sustainable Planning and Design, for underwriting certain other expenses in the production of the book along with my law firm, Blackburn and Carter. Thanks to all.

I also want to acknowledge the Reverend Duane Larson, a theologian who provided a key insight to me regarding the Earth and the Trinity that is discussed in chapter 10. I have to admit that I forgot about a lunch meeting with Rev. Larson, totally my fault, and when I called him to make amends and asked how he was at forgiveness, he responded with a smile. Graciousness rather than bitterness is a gift that I enjoyed that day. I also want to again call out and thank Cynthia Pickett-Stevenson, a true steward of Galveston Bay, who leads by example as well as by intelligence.

There are many others I want to recognize. The Fennessey Ranch and its manager, Sally Crofutt, do a wonderful job of trying to understand and combine ecotourism with ranching. The Nature Conservancy and its leader in Texas, Laura Huffman, do a great job of maintaining excellent private conservation areas, trying to restore them, and learning about what works best for our future. I particularly want to thank Dr. Jorge Brenner of the Conservancy for taking me to the Mad Island Christmas Bird Count, an event chronicled in chapter 7.

This set of acknowledgments would not be complete without the inclusion of my friend and fishing guide Al Garrison. Al taught me how to fish the Texas coast, how to use my eyes, how to see the fish. Al loves the marshes of the coast, as do I. Thanks, Al. You and the knowledge you have conveyed to me are much appreciated. I also want to tip my hat to two premier outdoor writers on the coast—Shannon Tompkins of the *Hous-*

ton Chronicle and David Sikes of the *Corpus Christi Caller-Times*. Both are excellent reporters and stewards of the Texas coast. And let's not forget Captain Mickey Eastman, whose coastal fishing show, which airs Thursday through Sunday on KILT 610 starting at about four in the morning, is the heart of Texas coastal fishing action.

Christmas Bird Counts are also an important part of my coastal life and this book. Here, there are countless individuals to thank, including the late Dr. David Marrack, who taught me basic birding, and Victor Emanuel, who started the Freeport count as a young man and who has grown to be one of the best birders in the world. While I am at it, I want to acknowledge the birds of the Texas coast, the best in the United States in my opinion, and the source of inspiration for my poetry.

And now to the heart of this book—my editors. One of the joys of this book was to again have the opportunity to work with Dr. Shannon Davies, the Edward R. Campbell '39 Director of Texas A&M University Press. Shannon is special to me and to many other Texas writers. She inspires me to do better, and she helps me to be better. She is all a writer could ask for in an editor, or, as is now the case, in the "big boss" of a press. I particularly want to thank Shannon for keeping my poems as the last chapter. I also want to thank Stacy Eisenstark, the acquisitions editor for the natural environment at the press, and the point person for review of this document. Stacy was excellent in her insight and probing questions back to me, raising issues and insights that made this book much better. Similarly, my two peer reviewers offered many great comments that made this book better as well, so thanks to Dr. David Yoskowitz of the Harte Research Institute in Corpus Christi and to Dr. Shannon Van Zandt of the landscape architecture department of Texas A&M.

I would also like to thank the photographers whose works of art illustrate and highlight points in the book. Kathy Adams Clark is a major bird-photography talent who contributed many of the images in this book. Kathy, I am in awe of your ability and your patience in capturing these birds, which are not cooperative with me when I look at them, much less when one is trying to capture their images for the rest of the world to enjoy. Kudos.

I also want to thank Geoff Winningham for his willingness to help on this book, and for sharing with us his excellent landscapes of the coast. Geoff is also at Rice and shares my love for the coast. Similarly, I want to thank Jim Olive, my long-time friend and collaborator on *The Book of Texas Bays*, for allowing a few of his images to be used in this book. No one does fishing like Jim. Thanks also go to Greg Lasley for the caracara award-winning photo, James Nielson for his shot of me in my kayak, and Michael Paulsen for the two ibis on a marsh mud bank. I also want to thank amateur photographer Al "Bubba" Kaufman for capturing green jays attacking a barred owl, and, snaring me in my habitat as well, Cheryl Overend for capturing our field trip to Fennessey Ranch.

I would like to acknowledge the role that my extended family played in who I am today. My father, Bernard Blackburn, spent massive amounts of time teaching me about the outdoors and taking me hunting and fishing in South Texas, instilling in me a sense of stewardship I maintain today. I can still see him walking from log to log down the middle of Little Spring Creek at a place called Mud Flats at the edge of Cocodrie Swamp, coming back with a stringer of bass that he caught on a black popping bug with a fly rod, a huge smile spread across his face. I also see him with the same smile with two smallish perch from a family outing in Chicot State Park, always happy, always having fun, as he graciously drove into town and bought catfish for our fish fry.

I spent most of my summers when I was younger with my grandparents in Glenmora, Louisiana, where my grandfather Bun Graves took me fishing in Cocodrie Swamp for bluegills, taking me to Jayhawkers Landing and Big Bend to cast from the bank in the late afternoon sun, making me swim in Spring Creek to retrieve the new lure that he had just bought for me, a lure that represented real money. I also remember my other grandfather, Cody Blackburn, a lumber company foreman who cut the virgin cypress in Cocodrie Swamp, a man who loaded me up in his car, picked up his friend, an African American man I called Mr. Jones, and let me run loose on the banks of the Calcasieu River, never thinking twice about it, he and Mr. Jones sitting on a high clay bank, legs extended over the edge, talking and passing the time, laughing and joking with me as I tried to figure out how to catch a catfish.

I am eternally grateful to my Uncle L. E. Blackburn, who used to take me fishing and hunting all over Louisiana in his red Willys Jeep named Henrietta, a man with his own mind, a man who had a KKK cross burned in his front yard, a man who allowed me to see the most spectacular duck migration

I have ever seen in Gueydan, Louisiana, where the sky was covered from end to end with strings of migrating ducks. Uncle Charles Blackburn would take me floating on the Calcasieu River near Hineston, looking for smallmouth bass. And perhaps no figure played a larger role in my formative years (other than my dad) than did my Uncle Bun Graves, known as Bill in Port Neches, where he lived and worked in the plants, a man who taught me to hunt the marsh and love the swamp, kicking up the woodcocks and squealers, catching bass on a fly rod float-fishing down Spring Creek. Uncle Bun and Aunt Bobbye would take me for a week in the summer when I was young, hauling me down to the beach, using a big dragnet to catch whatever we could seine up, taking me fishing for bass on Hildebrand Bayou and Village Creek in southeast Texas, taking me duck hunting in the marsh. Then later Uncle Bun would play his fiddle and mandolin; he was a man who enjoyed life, a man who left a vivid imprint on an impressionable young boy.

I also want to acknowledge the role of religion and spirituality in my life. When I was young, I attended almost every form of Baptist church that existed, including Sunday school, morning and evening services, training union, prayer meetings, and vacation Bible school. My grandfather Graves was a serious man of the church, as was my grandmother Claire Graves. That is serious with a capital S. My parents raised my sister, Ann, and me in the church, passing on what they had learned, providing us with immersion in their faith. Today, I don't attend organized religious services and have found my own form of spirituality, which is set out in chapter 10. But without that foundation, without that background, I don't think I would think as I do today, and that makes it important to acknowledge and appreciate. While I am at it, let me acknowledge my sister, Ann Blackburn, my partner in all those many years of churchgoing, and for whom I have the greatest affection. Family counts, and she's the best.

Finally, I want to acknowledge optimism and hope, two key attributes that I have maintained through many decades of hard cases and punishing Texas politics. For a while I drank too much in an attempt to cushion these blows, but after a while, I came to realize that feeling and experiencing life is more important than numbing it. Out of that realization came recognizing and facing fear and doubt, understanding that life is a gift and that we have a choice in our perception and pathways moving forward. I hope that the pages of this book contain insights and concepts that will help us today and those who come after us to find a good path through the twenty-first century, a way fraught with problems yet with a route to a better economy—one that incorporates, protects, and enhances, rather than dissipates and destroys, our ecological assets, one that is circular, one that will last much better over time than what we have today. That is the hope—that is the vision—of this book.

INTRODUCTION

Welcome to the Texas Coast

The Texas coast is my place, a place of soft mud and hard-headed people. It is a place of natural wonder, of neotropical songbirds and endangered whooping cranes, a place of marshes and shrimp, a fisherman's paradise. It is also the global center of the oil, gas, and plastics businesses and home to major real estate development in and around Houston. This region is facing long-term problems that threaten its ecology as well as its economy and social structure. It lacks resilience on all levels. Yet on a good day, I see solutions to these challenges, solutions applicable throughout the United States and the world. And today is a good day.

We are living in a time when the Earth is filling up with humans and human impacts, yet we have value sets, policies, and thinking that were developed during a time when the world was relatively empty of people and impacts. My

Figure I.1. At its aesthetic best, the Texas Coast is a serene place with marshes that are nurseries for shrimp, blue crabs, and flounder and that provide habitat for birds of all types. Photograph by Geoff Winningham.

favorite economist, Herman Daly, wrote about the distinction between empty-world thinking and full-world thinking. The empty world is what our parents and especially their parents and grandparents were born into—a world that was relatively empty of humans and human impacts, a world where there was always a perceived frontier.

Today there is a different type of frontier. If we are to flourish over the next century, we will need to adapt to the realities of the "full world." We will need to "settle" this new frontier.

The Texas coast will be affected by these "full world" realities. If we are opportunistic and apply ourselves, this transition to the full world will open up opportunities for actions and strategies that can lead to long-term coastal protection and even enhance the coast over its current situation, moving from minimization of impact to regeneration. But like many aspects of life, realizing these opportunities will require leadership and creativity and bold action.

This new frontier—the full world—is one where resources are limited, where every gallon of water counts, where every ton of carbon dioxide is tracked, where the successful companies are those that combine economic, ecological, and social

thinking. Today, our systems and our thinking are still firmly rooted in a time of expansion, whereas our reality is becoming quite different. Our challenge will be to sustain and maintain an economy that creates optimism and maintains our quality of life, and our values generally, as the game changes. That is true about the Earth, and it is certainly true about the Texas coast.

The Texas coast is different in some aspects from other areas of the United States as well as different parts of the world. We on the Texas coast cannot depend on government regulation to solve these problems (if it could). Texans don't like regulation and are unlikely to pass new government regulations to protect the coast. If we are going to save this wonderful resource for future generations, it will be because we are creative and nimble, something that government regulation often is not. We in Texas may be in a better position to accept this change than those in many other parts of the world simply because we are so obstinate about government and so accepting of independent thinking and entrepreneurship.

By understanding and talking about money and economics as well as water, ecology, climate change, eco-play, and spiri-

Figure I.2. This photograph from the White Ranch in Jefferson County shows the intersection of cattle ranching with the industrial barge canal that is the Gulf Intracoastal Waterway, indicating the mix of the ranching and industrial legacies that are part of the Texas coast. Photograph by Geoff Winningham.

tuality along with the future of the oil and gas business, carbon neutrality, and a circular economy, a path to a healthy Texas coast can be discerned as we head into the future. Money and economic thinking have key roles to play in the long-term protection and restoration of the Texas coast. I realize this after years of disputes and after years of working with various proponents of our coastal assets, both green (natural) and gray (built). In many respects, the future is about the green and gray coming together, merging, cooperating, problem solving together. I often think that as goes Texas so goes the Earth, because if we can find solutions here, they should work anywhere in the world. And if we fail here, it likely foretells setbacks elsewhere. This view of the world through a Texas lens assumes that in order to address our most pressing global issues, we must find solutions that work for the most difficult and intractable regions. And Texas is such a region.

The problems of the Texas coast are those that come from placing a linear economic system based on use and consumption upon a natural system that works in a different way, a natural system with rhythms, cycles, and limits. When resources and assets were not limited, these issues were not as pronounced, but they are emerging as we face resource and pollution absorption limits. As a society, we are forcing the square peg of our economic model into the round hole of the natural system of the Texas coast, and not surprisingly, they do not match well heading into the future.

Over the years that I have spent working on the Texas coast, I have come to appreciate that we citizens of the coast and of Texas need to think differently about the coast and its future. There is a series of private-sector actions that can keep us from reaching a negative tipping point before our economic system migrates to theories and applications that are more in sync with natural systems, rather than working against them.

Several specific problems can be identified. Our bays are slowly being starved of freshwater—freshwater that is diverted to water lawns that are ill suited to our climate. We are breaking up our big ranches because our agricultural economies don't work so well right now, although there is a future where these economies could become transformed. Perhaps most importantly, our coast is threatened by neglect, by lack of use and understanding, and by a population that is from somewhere else, a population that is not comfortable exploring and enjoying the excellent recreational resources that the coast has to offer. It should also be noted that these problems of the Texas coast have solutions, but I get ahead of myself.

I am an environmental lawyer and planner and your guide to the future of the Texas coast (and perhaps a few other places as well). I started law school before the major environmental laws of the United States were passed in the early 1970s. I grew up with the United States as it came of age as a protector of the environment through governmental regulation, mainly in the form of federal environmental statutes. I have had the good fortune to be an environmental litigator, planner, teacher, and writer. I have witnessed the positives and negatives of governmental regulation to achieve environmental protection. And I have listened to the people of the Texas coast talk with passion and fury against governments and regulation.

After law school I went to Rice University in Houston and received a master's in environmental science, making me one of the few lawyers in the country at the time with such a background. There were also very few environmental science and engineering graduates at that time, and I spent much of the 1970s doing environmental planning, first for the Woodlands, a major new town development north of Houston, and then for an urban design and planning "think tank" called the Rice Center for Community Design. At this same time, I started teaching at Rice, first in the School of Architecture and then in civil and environmental engineering.

The federal Coastal Zone Management Act (CZMA) was passed in 1972 and was applauded by President Richard Nixon as an example of new federalism, meaning that it was not mandatory like the federal Clean Air Act and Clean Water Act that had preceded it. This federal statute singled out the coastlines of the United States for special consideration because over 50 percent of the population lived within fifty miles of the Atlantic, Gulf, and Pacific Coasts and the Great Lakes and because coastal estuaries, wetlands, barrier islands, and other systems were of such great ecological importance. Under the CZMA, coastal states were given the choice of whether to participate in the federal program. However, there was monetary support for planning and for implementation if states chose to join the federal program.

When the time came for Texas to consider developing a coastal plan, I was working for Rice Center, and we wanted to participate in this potential coastal planning process. The

Texas Constitution and statutes give the General Land Office (GLO) of the state of Texas responsibility for managing state-owned lands, which include the bay bottoms along the coast as well as Texas territorial waters out to three leagues (about nine miles). Bob Armstrong, who was then commissioner of the GLO and a popular statewide elected official, took the lead in trying to put a Texas-style program together. However, it soon became clear that the Texas legislature was not interested in "managing the coast," and Texas became one of only two states nationwide to fail to join the federal CZMA program in the 1970s. That was the beginning of my immersion into the antiregulatory bias of many Texans, a bias that emerged on the national scene with the election of President Ronald Reagan in 1980.

Around that time, I began to teach nationwide for the US Army Corps of Engineers. The Corps is a fixture on the Texas coast as well as across the United States and has a pronounced role on the coast. Through this nationwide teaching experience, I began to see what other states were doing with coastal management. I also came to understand the very difficult provisions of the Clean Water Act, under which the Corps had authority over the issuance of permits to fill wetlands. I have watched over the decades as this program has swung from one set of regulations and court rulings to another. Today, these Corps regulations are among the major provisions applicable to development along the Texas coast, joining the Clean Air Act and pollution control provisions of the Clean Water Act. Without federal environmental law, there would be no environmental law on the Texas coast.

After President Reagan was elected, the environmental interest and grant making of many federal agencies waned, and I found myself practicing law out of my home in Houston while also teaching at Rice and for the Corps. Over the years, I have represented many different individuals and groups trying to protect the Texas coast, and I came to know the Texas coast from a very intimate perspective. If someone or some group was willing to spend money on an environmental lawyer—on me and my firm—to try to protect habitat for birds, amphibians, fish, shellfish, or mammals, it meant that they cared about that resource, that the resource was something special. Some of my clients were commercial or recreational fishermen, some were property owners protecting their land, some were environmental groups, and some were just citizens with a personal connection, be it spiritual or ethical, to the land.

In this manner, I encountered the best of the Texas coastal ecosystems, ranging from the cypress swamps, salt marshes, and oyster reefs of the upper Texas coast to the cactus and thorn-brush scrub and algal flats next to the Laguna Madre, meeting millions of multihued, neotropical migratory birds and endangered species such as ocelots, jaguarundis, whooping cranes, piping plovers, and Kemp's ridley sea turtles along the way. I also met some very interesting humans.

The issue of Texas' participation in the CZMA was revisited in the early 1990s when a share of offshore oil revenues became available through the Coastal Impact Assistance Program (CIAP), which made millions of dollars in federal grants available to coastal states and counties, but only if the states were participating in the federal Coastal Zone Management Program. To get this money, Texas was willing to consider regulation. On this occasion, I was asked by Garry Mauro, then commissioner of the Texas GLO, to help his staff draft a proposed Texas Coastal Management Act that would meet federal guidelines for acceptance into the federal program while creating a Texas-style program.

A Texas-style program was one that did not create a new coastal zone permit program but rather added coastal considerations to permit programs already in existence. This time a coastal management statute was passed by the Texas legislature, but only after being worked over by industry lobbyists. I did attend the ceremony in which Ann Richards signed the act into law, but that enactment came to represent a Pyrrhic victory, as it has never resulted in much management or much protection of the Texas coast. In fact, this program is seldom if ever noted or mentioned in the early twenty-first century other than as a required box to check off when obtaining a permit under other laws, offering eloquent, albeit it mute, testimony to the effectiveness of the "gutting" of the Texas coastal program by industry lobbyists.

Without a strong coastal management act, over the years it has fallen on private parties and private action to pursue the protection of the Texas coast, primarily through environmental litigation, and I have been involved in one way or another in much of the key environmental litigation on the coast since 1980. At times we were successful in our lawsuits, but sometimes we failed to achieve our primary goal of stopping some impactful action. However, even when we failed to achieve our primary goal, almost every one of these fights led to collateral beneficial change that increased the protection of the Texas coast.

That experience of collateral change replicated again and again has led me to question the definition of "winning" in fights about ecological and economic systems and thinking. My internal wiring has changed with respect to these concepts over time, sometimes to the chagrin of my environmental friends. On the other hand, I question whether many environmentalists or social change advocates have a realistic concept of "winning." These fights seldom if ever end with a stake through the heart of the other side or with the other side conceding "you win." The victory is often subtle, perhaps even to the point of not feeling all that good.

One of the keys to understanding Texas is understanding the importance of a good fight and personal commitment. Often in this hard place you are not respected unless you represent the potential of harming the other side and the willingness to do so regardless of consequences. A lawsuit in federal court certainly raises potential harm of some type to those sued, and at the least, such an action offers the possibility of leveling the political playing field, which is skewed toward vested economic interests in Texas if not everywhere. I have also found that being involved in these fights opened lines of communication that have led to some very beneficial working agreements for the betterment of the coast. Often you learn a lot about the other side from being eye to eye and toe to toe for a period of years, which is what these legal fights often entail. These fights are acts of will and intent, and they are change agents. I am fortunate to have been a part of that process and to have learned from it.

But litigation alone is inadequate for the future. We need new ideas, perhaps a new philosophy, a vibrant view of the future that is responsive to challenges and based on creative thinking. It needs to be different from the way we have been thinking. Albert Einstein once said, "The world we have created today as a result of our thinking thus far has problems that cannot be solved by thinking the way we were thinking when we created them." We in Texas as well as the world in general need to upgrade our thinking. Unfortunately, it's not quite as simple as buying the newest technology or the next version of Windows.

Most people living in the Houston area and Texas, not to mention the United States generally, know relatively little about the Texas coast, which extends from Mexico to Louisiana. This coast is a working coast, with refineries and chemical plants and commercial waterways in many areas. It is also a relatively undeveloped coast with tremendous natural resources, including world-class birding and fishing. At least in part, these resources are still viable because they are not as stressed as those in many other coastal regions of the country. As can be seen in figure I.3, much of this coast is still held in relatively large tracts, with almost 80 percent in privately owned farms and ranches. This land ownership pattern has protected the Texas coast in the past, and maintenance of this pattern is one key to the future.

Another key aspect of the Texas coast is the protected areas also shown in this figure. These were lands that were purchased by either the federal or state government or private nongovernmental organizations. They were not carved out of the large bank of federal land that existed in much of the western United States, because Texas came into the nation as a republic with significant state-owned or private, but not federal, lands. If the government or nonprofits bought and paid for these lands, it was because they were evaluated and noted as having ecological importance, enough so that money was spent to save them. The expenditure of significant federal, state, and private dollars on land preservation on the Texas coast is often overlooked yet is a compelling statement about the ecological value of this coast. Stated another way, spending money on these preserved lands clearly articulates the value of the ecological resources of the Texas coast.

A less discussed problem is the resilience of our Texas coastal economy, a system that is facing major challenges in the twenty-first century. Since the discovery of the Spindletop oil field near Beaumont in 1900, the Texas coast has been home to first a growing, and now well-established and powerful, oil and gas and chemicals industry. Harris County and Houston are where many major oil and gas companies have their international or US headquarters, and industrial development can be found in clusters from the Louisiana border to Corpus Christi. The remainder of the coast is dominated by farming and ranching, with major ranches still existing in Willacy, Kenedy, Kleberg, Refugio, Victoria, Calhoun, Jackson, Matagorda, Chambers, and Jefferson Counties. Unfortunately, many farmers and ranchers are having a hard time these days, and the oil and gas industry is facing a coming storm about

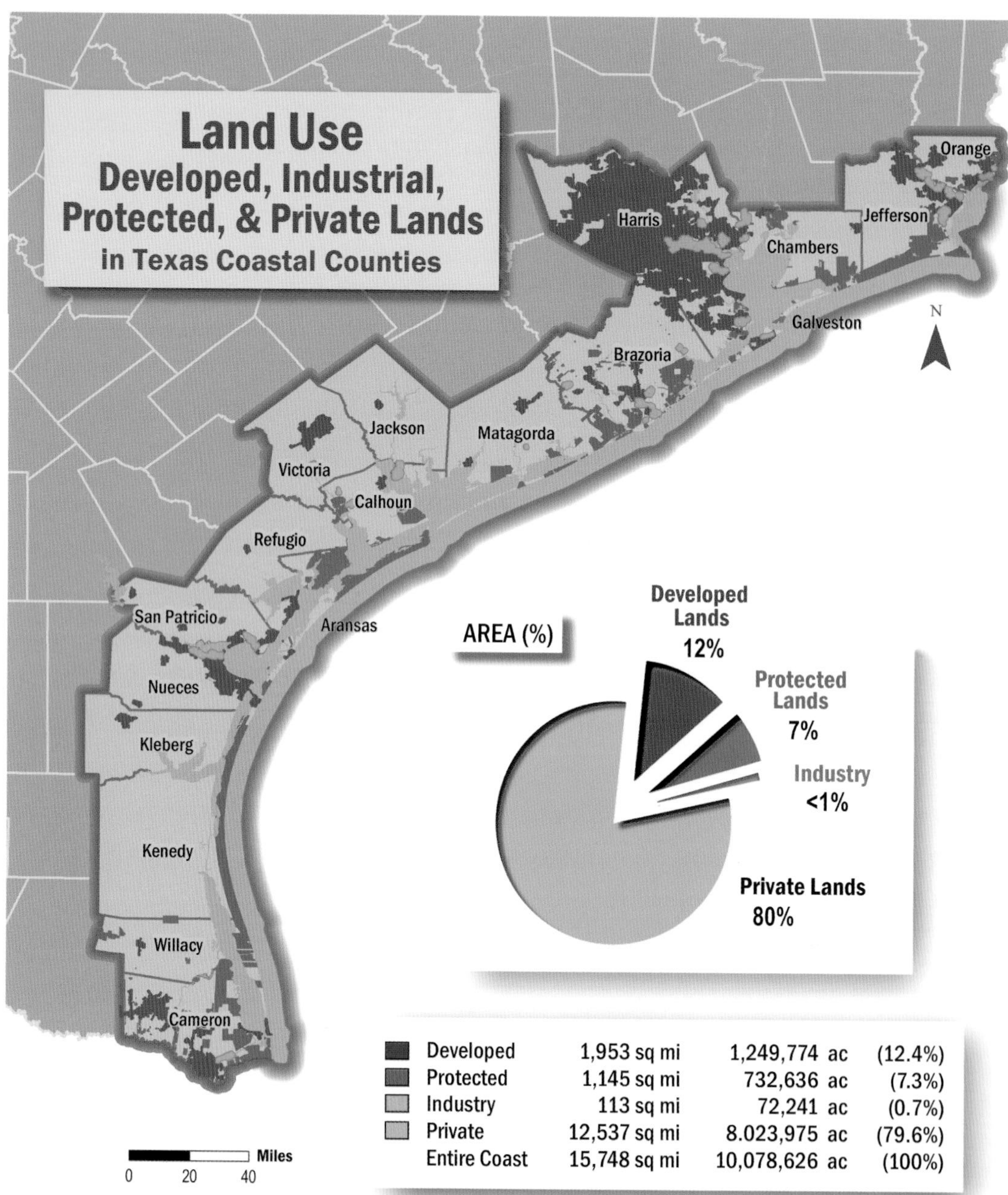

Figure I.3. A large portion of the Texas coast is in private hands, neither urbanized nor preserved. Keeping these large ranches and farms together is one of the keys to the long-term future of the Texas coast.

carbon dioxide emissions and climate change. However, there are solutions ahead that may wed these industries to ecology in ways not previously considered, making economic resilience both a necessity and a possibility. The key point is that our concept of a viable economy will change in the future, and the economic future will belong to those who see and adapt to these coming changes.

There is also the challenge of physical resilience, of withstanding floods and hurricanes worsened by a changing climate and storms of increasing fury. If there is a key concept for the Texas coast, it is resilience—physical, economic, and ecological resilience. It is about understanding vulnerability and about being smart enough and open enough to identify trends and act on them before it is too late. It is about doing things differently.

From a resilience standpoint, it is important to think not only about water and flooding but also about water availability. Water supply will be a challenge in the future, both for human use and for the natural system. Water is both a green and a gray infrastructure item. Just as an economic system can be throttled by an inadequate water supply, so can an ecological system. We must have both, and therein lies the challenge and the key. We must plan and provide for the natural system, and we must care enough about the health of the bays, the marshes, the oyster reefs, the bottomlands, and the prairies so that we want to plan and provide for them. Once there is widespread recognition and concern, solutions will appear from the economic if not the regulatory sector.

This book is about a different future for the Texas coast, one based on thinking a bit differently than we have to date. It is about reflection and openness; it is about appreciation and opportunity. And it is most of all about change. For in order to survive, the Texas coast and the people who live here will have to change. And that may be the hardest of all.

For purposes of this book, the Texas coast is defined by the set of counties shown in figure I.4. The concept behind this boundary is that each county has direct contact with tidal waters. These counties could be called the tidelands of the Texas coast, although I have never heard them referred to in that manner, probably because the daily tidal exchange along the Texas coast is relatively small, with often only a foot to a foot and a half difference between high and low tide.

This book is divided into three key parts. In the first part,

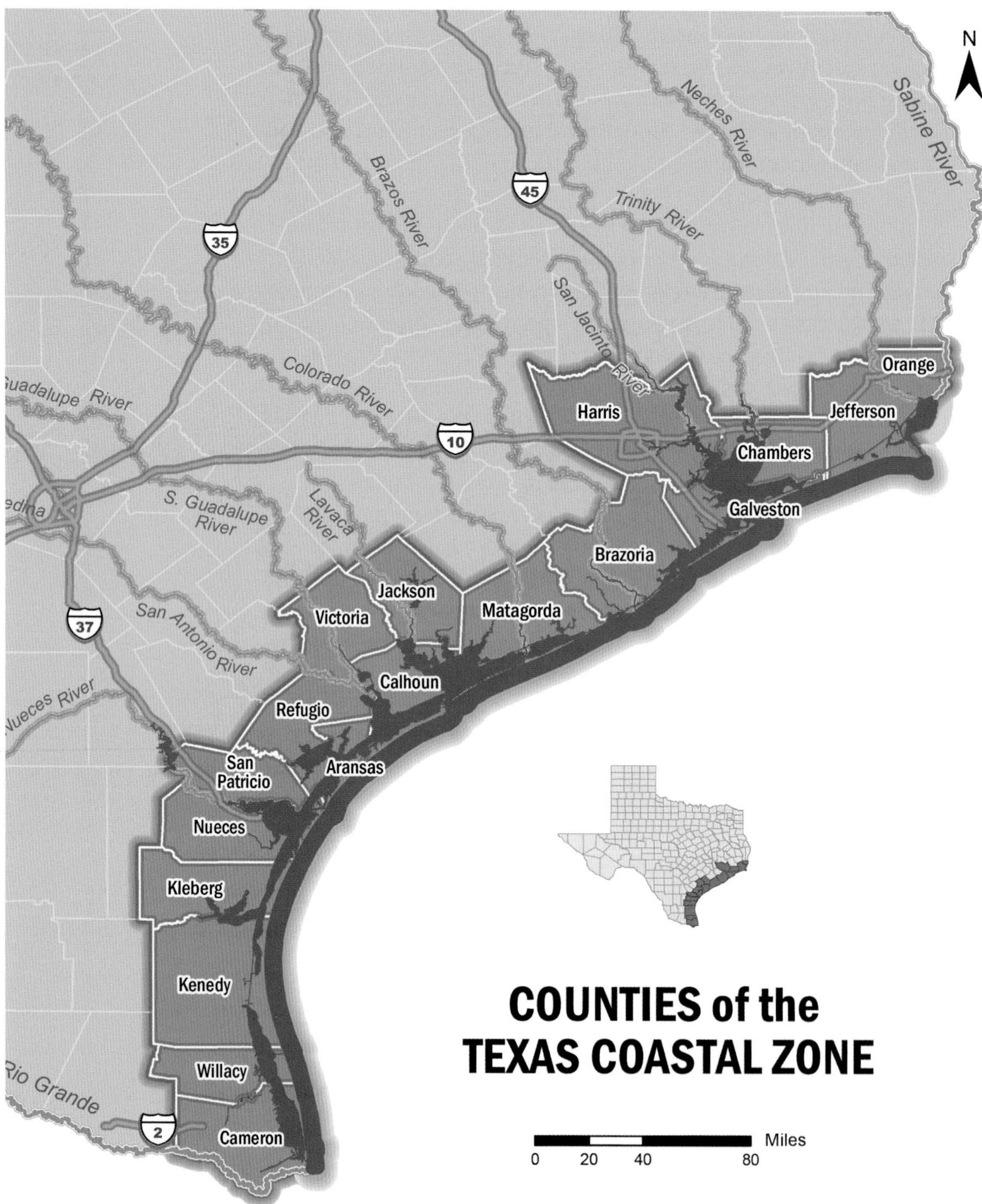

Figure I.4. The eighteen counties that are touched by the daily tide along the Texas coast. These will be the focus of the remainder of this book.

the resources—the assets—of the Texas coast are discussed. Here, there are three chapters: one dealing with our green assets, one dealing with our gray assets, and one dealing with water, which is both green and gray. The second part is about risk and the hazards of the coast. This part is divided into a chapter on hurricanes and flooding and another addressing climate change, a very real future threat to the Texas coast. The third part is about solutions that range from economic tools such as water pricing and the buying and selling of ecosystem services, to supporting legacy ranches and the oil and gas industry, to ecoplay involving fishing and birding, to litigation and spirituality and entrepreneurship and best practices certification. The book then offers a view of a future made by care, concern, and action, one that combines ecology and economics, one that works for all Texans and perhaps for others as well. The last chapter offers a poetic tribute to the coast that I love.

I wish three things from you as a reader of this book. First, I hope you enjoy this view of the Texas coast, both what it is and what it can be. Second, I hope you will be inspired to immerse yourself in one or more facets of the coast. Come visit and experience the wonderful aspects that I have encountered over many decades rambling around this place. And third, I hope you will take some action to work for the future of the Texas coast—a future where our ecological and economic promise can be melded together in a truly creative and wonderful way.

Viewed a certain way, this book presents a plan for the future of the Texas coast. But it is very different from many past plans in that it does not overlay a new system of regulation to implement it. Instead, this is a plan based on market economics and personal commitment and action. It is about protecting the coast with a set of tools that are consistent with the norms that prevail in Texas and on the Texas coast. In that sense it presents a different and perhaps new view of coastal planning.

PART 1

Assets of the Texas Coast

CHAPTER 1

Green Assets of the Texas Coast

Early in the morning I pull up to the edge of Drum Bay in Brazoria County and take my kayak from the racks on the roof of the Toyota Highlander, a vehicle that I once got stuck on the shoreline here, only to return the next morning with a tow truck to find it surrounded by high tide. That was a humbling experience, to discover my car surrounded by bay water, seemingly floating where only a boat should be. Thankfully, the tidal water was only about two inches deep. But such is the nature of the Texas coast—the appearance is often quite different from the underlying truth.

My kayak glides across the smooth bay water, making no sound. The tide is coming in from the Gulf of Mexico through the deepwater channel at Freeport, flowing east within the Gulf Intracoastal Waterway (GIWW), moving through human-made and natural channels to reach the oyster reefs that separate Drum Bay from Christmas Bay. The rising sun provides an orange glow from behind a cloud bank back over the Gulf. The laughing gulls lazily patrol the shoreline, looking for action. It is a peaceful start to a good day on Drum Bay.

Drum and Christmas Bays are at the southern end of the

Figure 1.1. The author on the water in Drum Bay. Photo by James Nielson, Houston Chronicle.

Galveston Bay system, which extends for almost one hundred miles from Drum Bay to the northern tip of East Bay, and for about fifty miles out from the delta of the Trinity River at the top of Trinity Bay to the opening called Bolivar Roads that links Galveston Bay to the Gulf of Mexico. The Galveston Bay system is one of seven major bay systems that make up the water side of the Texas coast, with the Laguna Madre to the south, followed by Nueces–Corpus Christi, Copano-Aransas, San Antonio, Matagorda, and Galveston Bays as well as the Sabine Lake complex moving north and east up the coast. These major bays and many secondary and tertiary ones can be seen in figure 1.2.

Figure 1.2 also shows the major river systems that fuel

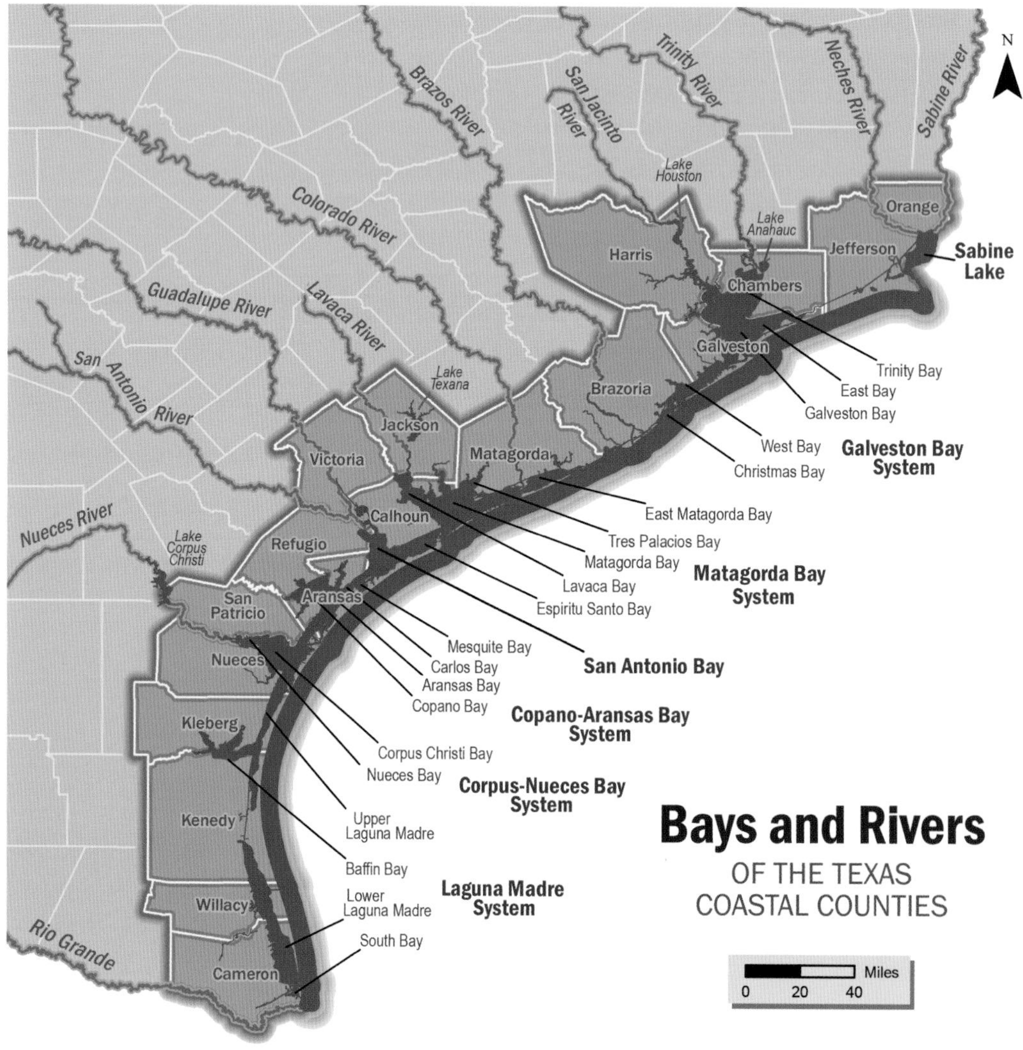

Figure 1.2. The bays and rivers of the Texas coast.

these bays with the freshwater inflow that makes them come alive with fish and shellfish and birds. This freshwater inflow provided by rivers, bayous, creeks, and streams throughout the Texas coast is critical to the health of our bays and the fisheries of the Gulf of Mexico. This water flowing into our bays is not "wasted," as is often thought (if not stated) in water management circles. Instead, this inflow is the source of the carbon, nitrogen, and phosphorus that fuel the microscopic plants and animals of the bay that form the basis of the coastal food chain. This inflow sweetens our bays from a salinity standpoint, providing habitat and living conditions necessary for oysters, blue crabs, shrimp, and juvenile finfish. Without it, our coastal bays would die just as surely as a person would die without water.

Let me repeat—without freshwater inflow, our bays would die. Perish. Cease to perform their ecological functions. There are many threats to our coastal bays and other natural resources. The loss of freshwater inflow is at the top of the list of coastal problems. If it is not addressed, we will lose the most important characteristic of the coast—the living ecosystem that supports commercial and recreational fishing and bird-watching.

The rivers that provide these freshwater inflows are each unique. The Rio Grande provides the border with Mexico and rises in the mountains of Colorado, a once mighty river that went dry in 2000 when the mouth silted over. Although humans have diverted and dried up the Rio Grande, the Laguna Madre historically derived little inflow from the Rio Grande, which empties directly into the Gulf of Mexico, although some inflow comes down the major drainage outlets for the Rio Grande Valley, and some inflow comes into Baffin Bay from creeks that are more often dry than not. Because of the natural absence of freshwater inflow, the Laguna Madre has evolved under different conditions than the remainder of the bays on the Texas coast, making it ecologically distinct from the other Texas coastal bays. It is a hypersaline lagoon rather than an estuary like the other bays, which are places where freshwater and saltwater come together.

The Laguna Madre is divided into two parts, the Lower Laguna and the Upper Laguna. The two are connected by the "land cut," a section of the GIWW that cuts across shallow algal salt flats that link the mainland to North Padre Island except during exceptionally high tide events. The Laguna

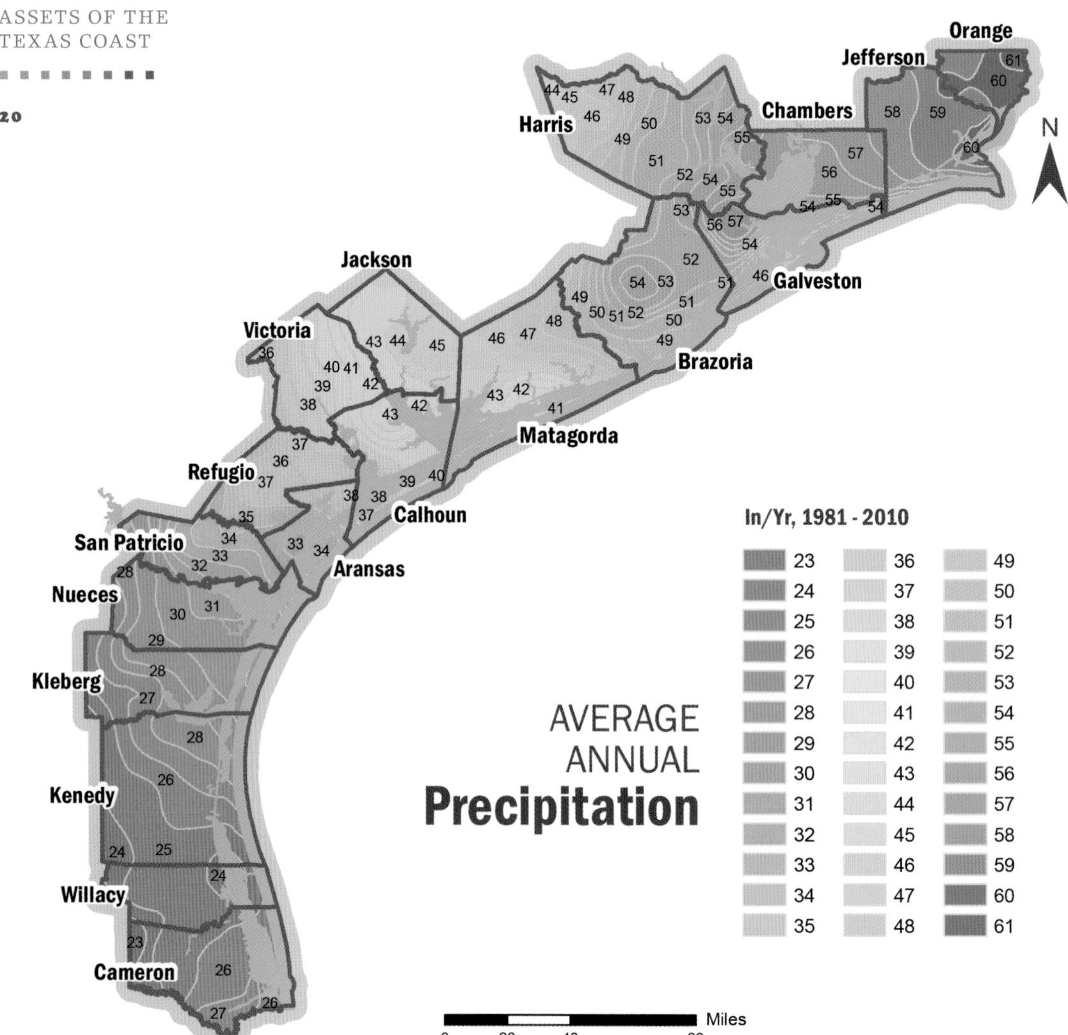

Figure 1.3. The average annual precipitation of the Texas coast varies from a high of sixty-one inches per year in northeastern Orange County to a low of twenty-three inches in western Cameron County.

Madre is fascinating, a system of seagrass and salt-tolerant species, many of which are unique to the Laguna Madre on the Texas coast. This book will not do justice to the uniqueness and importance of this ecosystem.

The amount of inflow from the various river systems that provide significant bay inflow increases from south to north, just as precipitation increases from south to north, as shown in figure 1.3. This rainfall pattern accounts for many of the differences in vegetation along the coast as well as for some of the differences in inflow patterns.

In addition to precipitation, these river systems are also

influenced by the location and extent of their drainage area, their so-called watershed. Figure 1.4 shows the watersheds of the various rivers, with the Nueces being contained in the area southwest of San Antonio, and the San Antonio and Guadalupe River inflows being gathered largely southeast and east and north of San Antonio. In turn, the Nueces River feeds Nueces and Corpus Christi Bays, and the San Antonio and Guadalupe Rivers feed San Antonio, Espiritu Santo, Carlos, and Mesquite Bays. The drainage area for Copano and Aransas Bays, which lie between Corpus Christi Bay and San Antonio Bay, is much more limited, being restricted to inflows from the Aransas and Mission Rivers within the Nueces–San Antonio coastal drainage basin, comprising mainly Refugio and Goliad Counties.

The larger drainage systems start with the Colorado River system, which rises in far West Texas and flows across the state through Austin south to the community of Matagorda, where it flows into Matagorda Bay. Between the Guadalupe and Colorado River systems lie the Lavaca and Navidad Rivers, smaller rivers that flow into Lavaca Bay at the northwestern tip of Matagorda Bay. The Brazos River rises in eastern New Mexico and flows south of Dallas and through Waco to its direct outlet to the Gulf of Mexico in Freeport. It does not directly feed a bay system. Similarly, the San Bernard River also flows directly into the Gulf as the major drain of the Brazos-Colorado Coastal Basin. Nonetheless, freshwater from the Brazos and the San Bernard as well as numerous smaller streams such as Caney Creek, Cedar Lake Creek, Jones Creek, and Oyster Bayou all feed coastal estuarine areas, supporting important fish and shellfish production.

The two largest inflows are provided to the Galveston Bay and Sabine Lake complexes by the San Jacinto–Trinity and Sabine-Neches River systems. The annual inflow from these river systems together far eclipses that of the other major watersheds, based on both the significant drainage areas and the significant rainfall within those drainage areas. Inflows to the Galveston Bay system and Sabine Lake are two to ten times greater than inflows to bays farther south.

These watersheds provide the primary organizing system for Texas surface water rights and for water administration. In fact, river authorities (governmental entities with authority to impound, manage, and distribute water) are found in almost all of these watersheds. These river authorities have signifi-

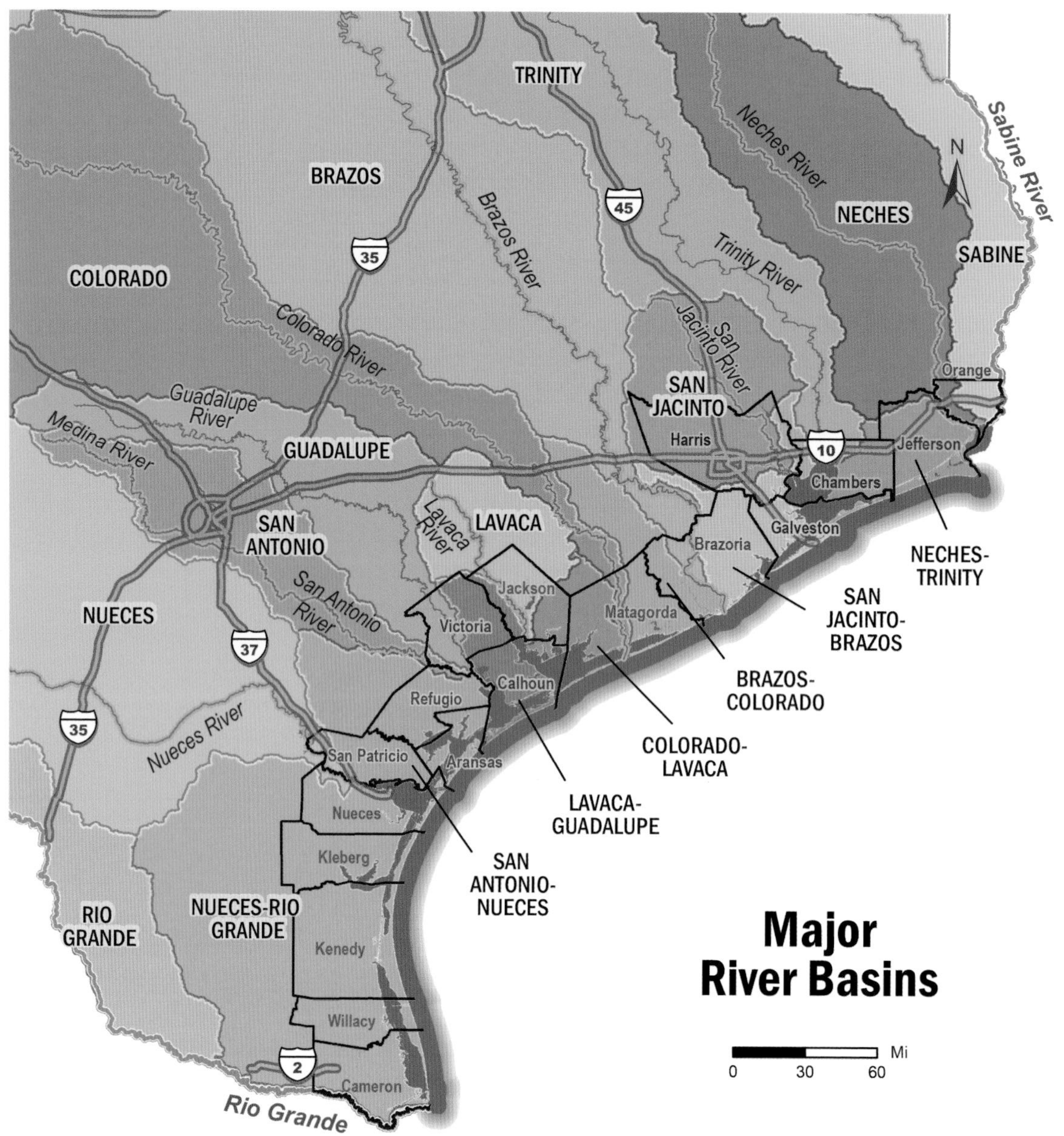

Figure 1.4. The major river basins of the Texas coast, including several that are so-called coastal basins (indicated by hyphenated names), which are not drained by a major river but rather drain overland into the adjacent bays.

cant power and influence over the use of water within these watersheds, although the actual allocation and management of surface water is the responsibility of the Texas Commission on Environmental Quality (TCEQ), a statewide agency with a plethora of names going back to the early 1900s. Unfortunately, over the past century, much more water has been permitted to be withdrawn than exists during times of drought, leading to the very real possibility that river flow and bay inflow will be reduced to a trickle if not to zero during times of drought.

Looking toward the shore as I approach Christmas Bay, I am struck by how flat the coast is. At the water's edge lie the marshes, root systems covered by the rising tide, green stalks extending up for about a foot or two, defining the horizon—grass to the right, open water and then more grass to the left. No mountains, no hills, no terrain. The only elevational relief is provided by the top of a tugboat pushing barges south on the GIWW, a ghostlike image floating above the grass-lined horizon, reminding me that the Texas coast is a working coast.

As I paddle I smile, thinking of my friend Dr. H. C. Clark, the geophysicist who has tried to teach me geology for the almost four decades that we have worked together, patiently reminding me to think in "geologic time," which means very slow and very distant. The Texas coast is made of mud and

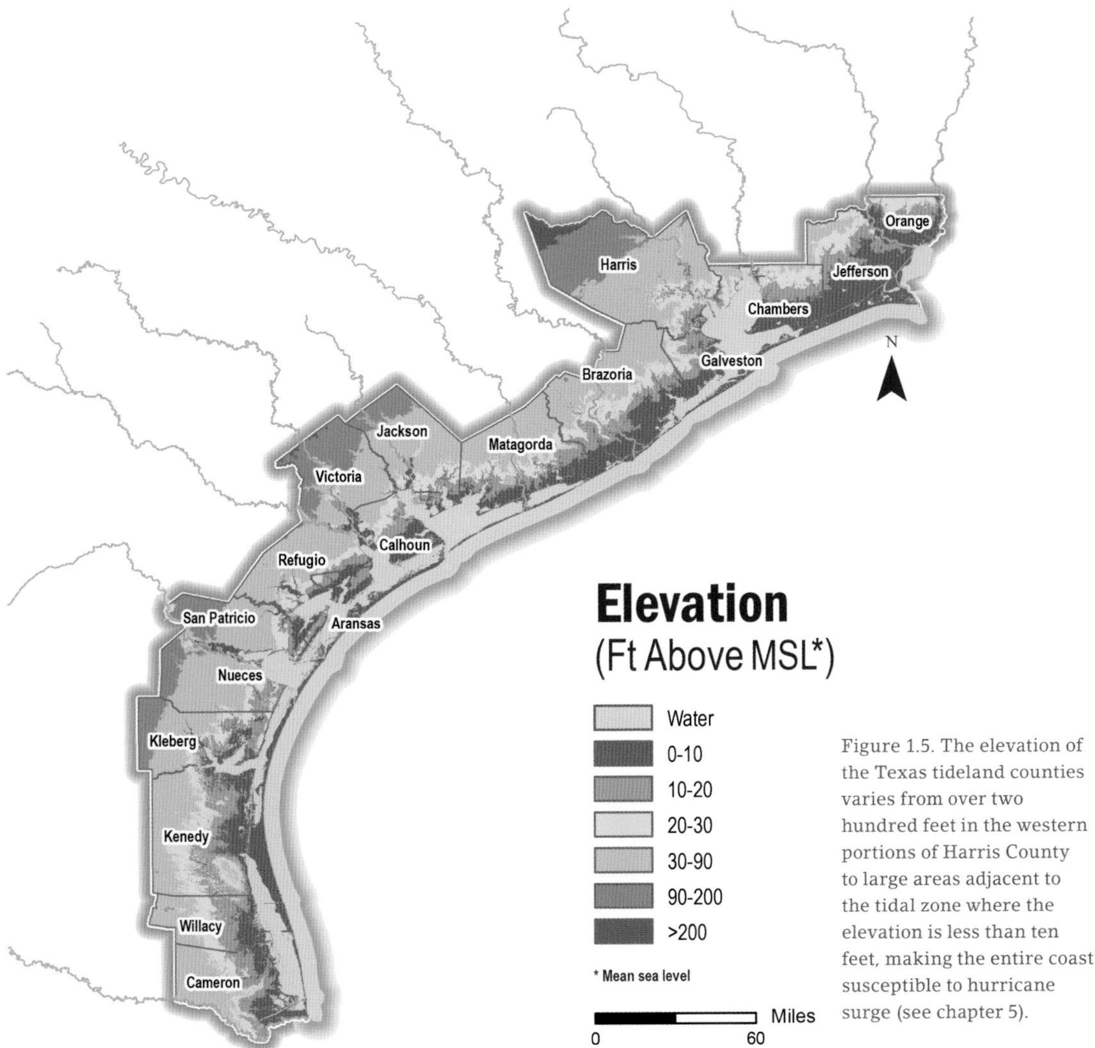

Figure 1.5. The elevation of the Texas tideland counties varies from over two hundred feet in the western portions of Harris County to large areas adjacent to the tidal zone where the elevation is less than ten feet, making the entire coast susceptible to hurricane surge (see chapter 5).

sand. It is a deltaic plain of the Pleistocene epoch, a virtual child from the time perspective of a geologist. The Texas coast was formed after Pangaea, a supercontinent containing all of the current continents, divided about 175 million years ago, splitting North America away from Africa, Europe, and South America. One geologic break occurred roughly along a line from Waco to San Antonio known as the Balcones Escarpment, meaning that the rocks in Texas are generally west of that line and that the land to the east has been built over time as sediment, sand, and mud have been deposited by the forces of erosion and flooding.

As such, the Texas coast has been built from relatively new (geologically speaking) deposits of material weathered from rocks to the west. The Gulf of Mexico sits over a basin of mud and sediments, with essentially similar terrain existing beneath and beyond the Gulf waters. The barrier islands such as Galveston, Matagorda, San Jose, Mustang, and Padre are

Figure 1.6. The relative flatness of the Texas coast means that you encounter it at eye level, on its terms rather than yours. Photo by Geoff Winningham.

platforms of sand at the interface of land and water, islands that are constantly in motion from a geological perspective.

There are no rocks to provide elevation, no hills and no mountains adjacent to the Texas coast. As can be seen in figure 1.5, the elevation of coastal counties rises slowly, with much of the first tier of counties below twenty feet in elevation. I believe that the absence of elevation is one of the greatest psychological impediments to more widespread use of the Texas coast. The Texas coast meets you at eye level. You have to enter it to enjoy it, as opposed to many of the rocky, craggy coastlines where you look out from a perch above it all. That is not the experience on the Texas coast. The elevation here ensures that the land and the water merge with you.

Like many Texans, I grew up hunting and fishing on the coast but never thought much about its elevation. As a young boy, I remember walking into the marsh with my uncle to hunt ducks and floating in a johnboat along the marsh edge, fishing

Figure 1.7. A pair of white ibis searches for food on a mudflat adjacent to a stand of the salt grass *Spartina alterniflora*. The mudflat was revealed by a north wind that pushed over a foot of water out of the bay and into the Gulf. Photo by Michael Paulsen, Houston Chronicle.

for flounder and redfish. I was fortunate. I had a guide to teach me to feel comfortable, to feel at home in these areas. Decades later, paddling along in my kayak, I believe my early immersion into the Texas coast was a cornerstone of my love and appreciation of it, "immersion" an apt expression because one literally immerses oneself in and into the Texas coast.

On this morning's paddle, I cruise by stands of marsh grass, which is technically known as *Spartina alterniflora* and is common on the upper and middle coast. As one moves farther south, marsh grass gives way to algal flats, scattered mangroves, and *Salicornia*, a lovely succulent springing from the sand. On the upper coast, the vegetation gradates as one moves away from the waterline, first with grasses that require saturated soils, then to those that are adapted to living with or without saturated soils, and finally to those that can survive inundation and saturation only for shorter periods. Farther

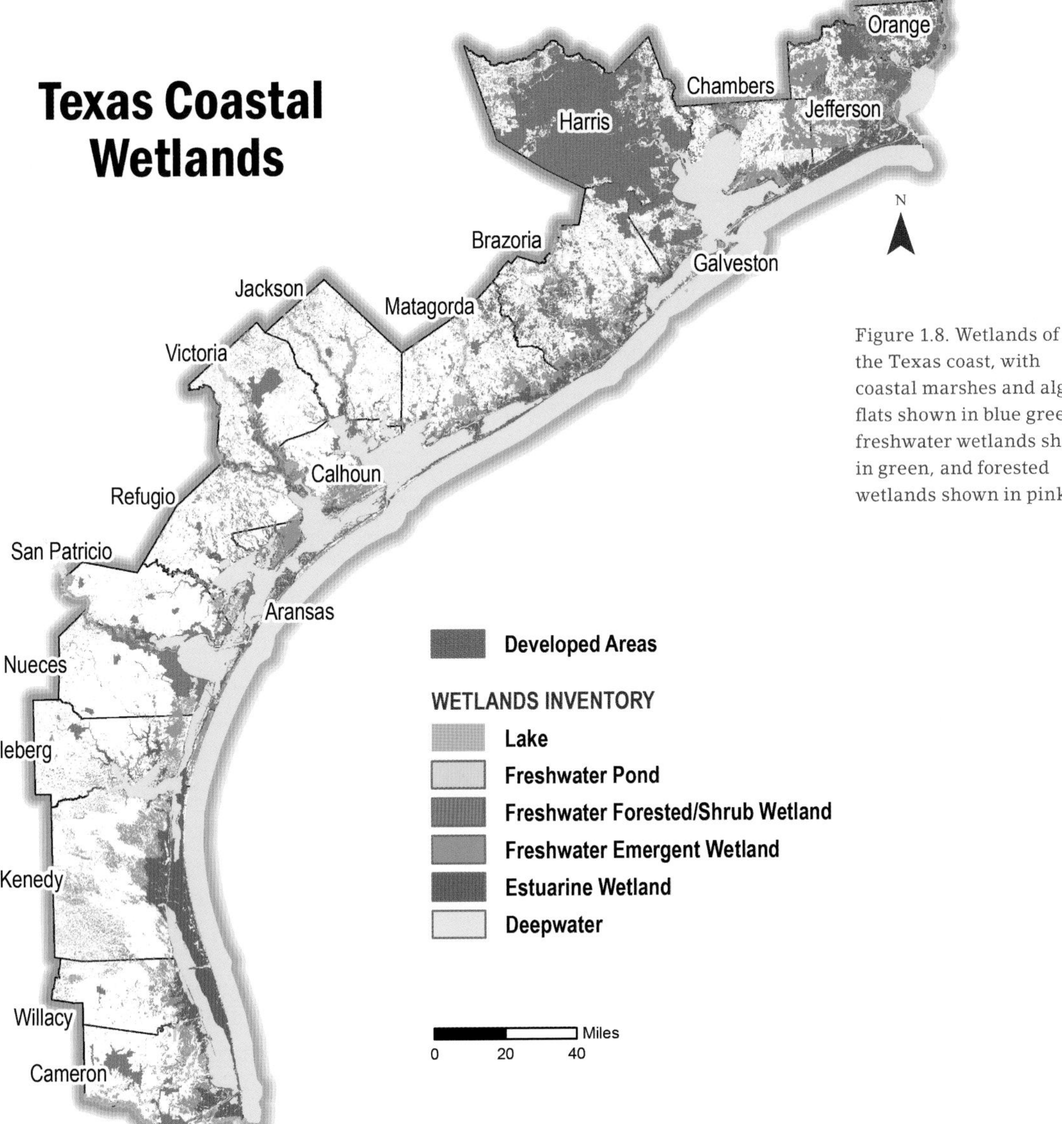

Figure 1.8. Wetlands of the Texas coast, with coastal marshes and algal flats shown in blue green, freshwater wetlands shown in green, and forested wetlands shown in pink.

USGS DEFINITIONS: WETLANDS: Permanent shallow waters that commonly support aquatic beds and emergent plants (erect, rooted, nonwoody plants that are mostly above water) are classified as wetlands.

Freshwater wetlands are defined to include, "but not be limited to marshes; swamps; bogs; ponds; river and stream floodplains and banks; areas subject to flooding or storm flowage; emergent and submergent plant communities in any body of freshwater including rivers and streams, and that area of land within fifty feet (50') of the edge of any bog, marsh, swamp, or pond." Various wetland types are further defined on the basis of hydrology and indicator plants, including bog (15 types of indicator plants), marsh (21 types of indicator plants), and swamp (24 types of indicator plants plus marsh plants). USGS: https://water.usgs.gov/nwsum/WSP2425/definitions.html

Figure 1.9. Oystercatcher removing an oyster from a shell on a reef, a beautiful sight when you are paddling alongside. Photo by Kathy Adams Clark.

south, there is slightly more topography and less rainfall, and the adjacent wetlands often give way to salt-tolerant plants that can survive only very short-term saturation.

Throughout the Texas coast, native prairie is found adjacent to coastal marshes and wetland systems and is often interspersed with potholes and poorly drained areas that fill with water during the cooler, wetter periods. Similarly, riparian forests along our major rivers and bayous may be either wet systems (e.g., swamps), such as are found along the Trinity, Neches, and Sabine River systems, or drier floodplains that can survive inundation for longer periods (bottomland hardwoods), such as the Columbia Bottomlands of the Brazos, San Bernard, and Colorado River systems. Collectively, the distribution of these wetlands along the Texas coast is shown in figure 1.8.

As I paddle toward Christmas Bay, the oyster reefs appear as obstacles, barriers rising above the calm, flat water. The incoming tide marks a path through the reefs, the water surface literally showing the flowing water as the tide pushes through pathways that can be hard to see when the reefs become submerged. Because of the absence of inflow, the Laguna Madre has its own hypersaline oyster. However, the reefs known for fishing and for producing tasty morsels are found from Nueces Bay northward. Oyster reefs are great ecosystems, harboring many different types of organisms. They provide a feeding platform for fish-eating birds that pick off morsels as the water rises and recedes within the reef, and a meal for the beautiful orange-billed oystercatcher. Fishermen know that oyster reefs are also feeding areas for speckled sea trout and redfish. A bay with an oyster ecosystem is a bay that is alive and functioning.

It is worth mentioning that oyster reefs can be very unkind to the bottom of a kayak. My kayak is plastic and has survived countless encounters with these reefs, with scrapes all along its bottom as evidence. However, once when I was paddling with a friend who had a beautiful wooden kayak, he became horrified that he might damage his beautiful craft as we approached the maze of oyster reefs separating Christmas and Drum Bays. There are certainly pathways here that will avoid kayak bottom blues, but be aware that a close encounter with a reef is a very real possibility and that a plastic boat will emerge better than a beautiful varnished wooden boat.

As I enter Christmas Bay, I can see the delicate structure of the subsurface seagrass that used to be much more prevalent in the Galveston Bay system, grass that increases in abundance southward down the coast, culminating in the vast submerged meadows of the Laguna Madre. Again, much like the oyster reefs, the seagrass beds create an ecological system with habitat and shelter for juvenile shrimp and finfish and feeding areas for fish-eating birds and predator fish. Seagrass has a distinct beauty, lacy leaves moving with the tide, a green meadow visible through clear shallow water.

Once I led a group of kayakers on Christmas Bay near the outlet of Cold Pass adjacent to San Luis Pass. It was a cold day and the north wind had blown much of the water out of the bay system, as it often does. On this day, a muddy point that was covered with short, dark green seagrass had become exposed, leaving thousands of small shrimp, crabs, and other organisms literally out of the water. As is typical of nature, the point was filled with shorebirds, most notably godwits, gulls, and sandpipers, capitalizing on the free meal, an opportunity provided by a strong north wind, seagrass, and shallow water.

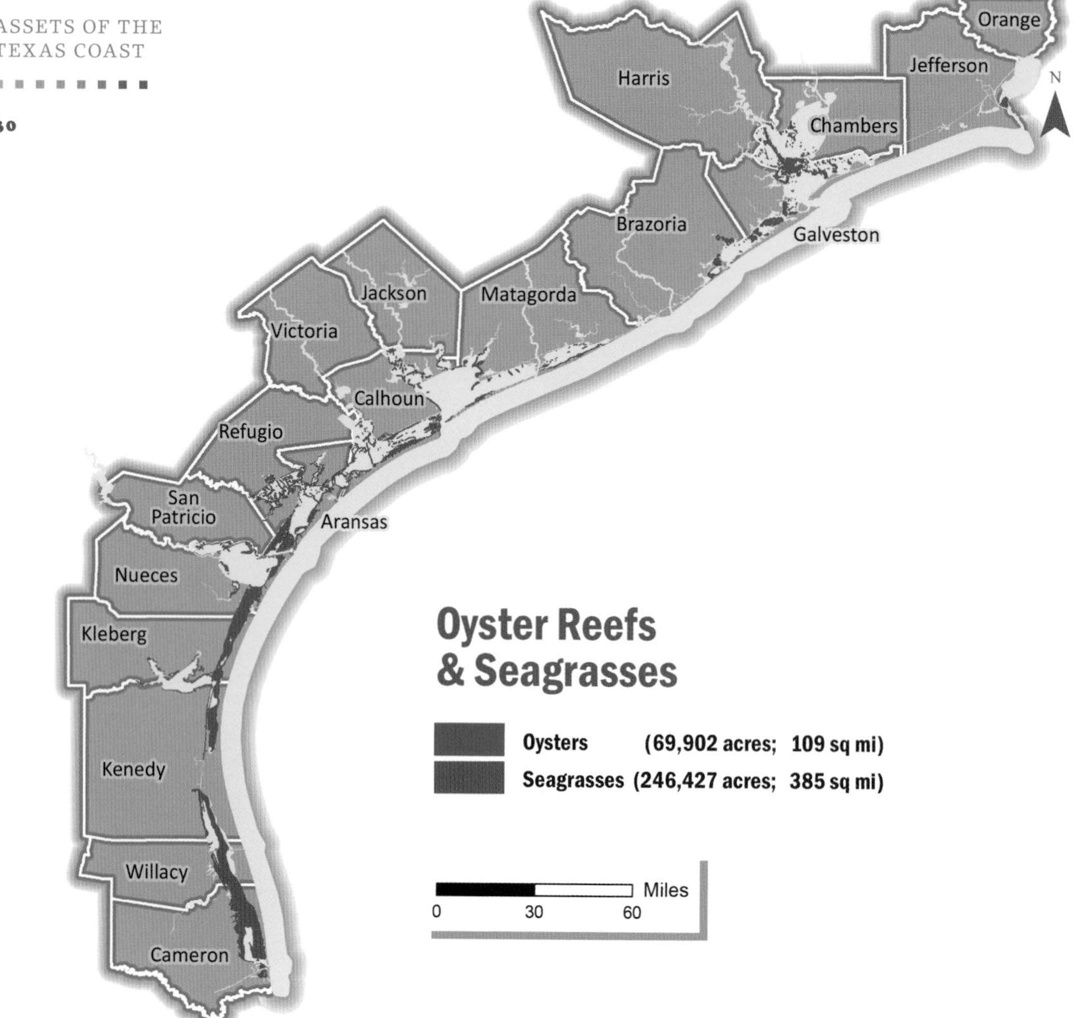

Figure 1.10. Oyster reefs are found predominantly in estuaries with lower salinities up the coast, whereas the submerged seagrass is found in saltier and clearer bay systems down the coast.

I still remember that sight years later, a true glimpse into the opportunistic side of nature, a system that responds with great speed to an unexpected opportunity. The distribution of seagrass and oyster reefs on the coast is shown in figure 1.10. Generally, oysters decline and seagrass increases from north to south.

As I paddle along Rattlesnake Point (well named), I see a sign stating that the land here is part of the Brazoria National Wildlife Refuge, part of a wonderful system of land that has been converted over the years on a willing-buyer, willing-seller basis (i.e., without the use of the power of condemnation) from private landowners to public or nongovernmental organization ownership. Together, the land area along the

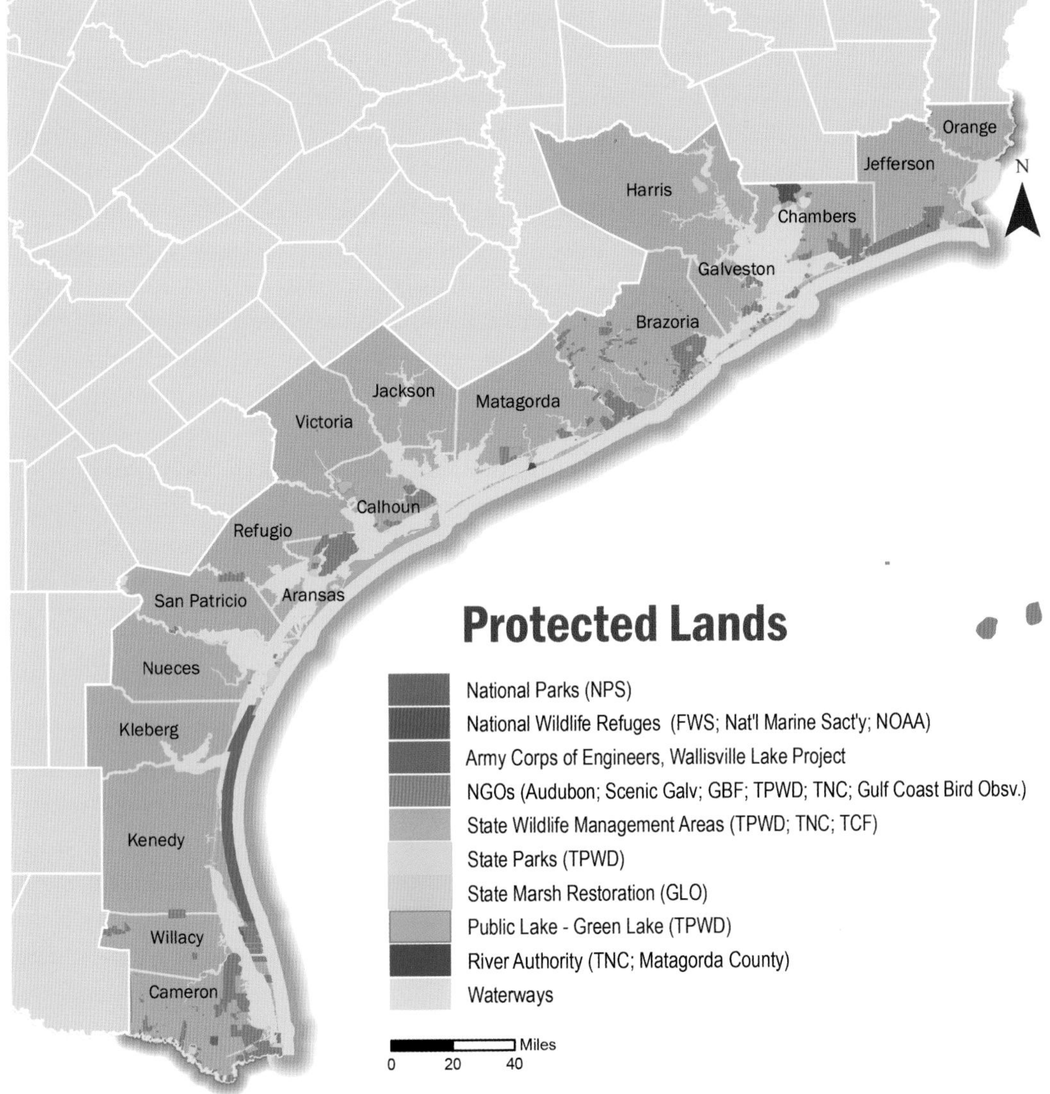

ACREAGE TOTAL for Protected Lands & Green Lake: 732,636 Acres

PROTECTED LANDS - STATE: 135,388 acres
PROTECTED LANDS - NGO: 59,754 acres
PROTECTED LANDS - FED: 529,672 acres
(Flower Garden Banks not included): 35,973 acres

PROTECTED LANDS - OTHER:
GREEN LAKE (public lake) 6,050 acres
Protected, LCRA (River Authority) 1,772 acres

Figure 1.11. Preserved land under various ownership along the Texas tidelands represents almost 733,000 acres.

coast that is protected in this manner is substantial, extending from the Texas Point National Wildlife Refuge at Sabine Pass down to the Las Palomas Wildlife Management Area at the mouth of the Rio Grande. This system of protected land is a greenbelt that runs down the coastal lowlands and floodplains and is one of the best-kept secrets on the coast. These jewels are addressed in more detail in chapter 7. In total, almost 530,000 acres of land are owned by the federal government, just over 135,000 acres are owned by the state of Texas (excluding bay and Gulf bottoms), and almost 60,000 acres are owned by private nongovernmental organizations. Together, these conserved lands represent about 7 percent of the coastal counties.

As I paddle back to the put-in, the birds are in evidence everywhere. A pair of roseate spoonbills flies over, bright pink against the blue sky. I startle a great egret wading along the water's edge. A white ibis sticks her head up and a willet flies up, fussing at me, white wing bars flashing in the sun. The oyster reefs are almost covered now by the incoming tide, and both an oystercatcher and a snowy egret are prowling the crevices, searching for morsels. A flock of brown pelicans sails by, and the bait fish are moving, generating the "nervous water" that is famous among fishing guides, nervous perhaps because of feeding predators like speckled trout stalking them from below.

Closer to the landing, the noise begins to increase. The rookery island is ahead, a sand spit covered with low shrubs that are literally filled with nesting birds. Tricolored herons are in the tall grass at the tips along with gulls and a few terns. The shrubs are full of white- and pink- and black-feathered bodies, showing their breeding plumage, looking for and pairing off with mates. The egrets, the spoonbills, the night herons, and the cormorants all share the homestead, which they use every year, a place that is literally for the birds. Many of these rookery islands are owned or maintained by local Audubon Society chapters and can be found throughout the coast.

The birds of the Texas coast are in many respects its most unique natural resource. The abundance and diversity of habitat and its location as a migratory crossroads have led to an extensive variety of bird species. An automobile route along the Texas coast called the Texas Coastal Birding Trail has identified various stopping points with high bird usage and a good chance of catching sight of many different species (see chapter 7). And no coastline can compare with the Texas coast when it comes to the species diversity recorded during the annual Christmas Bird Counts that occur throughout the United States. The Texas coast generally has several counts in the top ten in the United States and has more counts with more birds than any other state (see chapter 7).

The superlatives continue regarding threatened and endan-

Figure 1.12. Nothing is nicer on the eyes than a roseate spoonbill navigating the skies over the Texas coast. Photo by Kathy Adams Clark.

gered species. The whooping crane was almost extinct in the late 1930s before the Aransas National Wildlife Refuge was set aside by President Roosevelt. Today, the flock is still in jeopardy but has recovered to over three hundred birds from a low of sixteen. The brown pelican was endangered for decades but has recovered to the point of delisting; however, the piping plover, another coastal resident, remains endangered. Further, there are several types of sea turtles on the Texas coast, most of which are classified as rare except for the endangered Kemp's ridley sea turtle, which nests on most Texas coastal beaches and eats crabs in the bays. One of my most exciting coastal moments came when I was drift fishing in my kayak and a sea turtle surfaced nearby and stayed in my vicinity for several minutes, surfacing every so often, puttering along, neither of us minding the other.

On this kayaking trip, I didn't fish, but the fishing here is superb with the right wind and tide conditions. The marshes, seagrass flats, and shallows are full of juvenile shrimp, finger mullet, and various types of finfish, all enjoying the nursery provided by the plants, oyster reefs, and lower salinity.

Christmas and Drum Bays and every other bay on the Texas coast have been designated essential fish habitat under the Magnuson-Stevens Fishery Conservation and Management Act because of the critical role these nurseries play in maintaining the fisheries of the Gulf of Mexico. Without healthy nurseries—nurseries with the right inflows and habitat conditions—the fish population of the Gulf of Mexico would plummet. There would be no redfish or flounder or speckled trout or black drum or croaker or even piggy perch and hardheads. Without the base of the food chain intact, the predators have nothing to harvest for their survival.

Such is the nature of the Texas coast. It is a wonderfully balanced collection of ecosystems—systems that maintain certain types of plants and animals based on rainfall, river and creek flow, topography, geology, and soils. Each ecosystem differs based on the way the ingredients are mixed. The green infrastructure of the Texas coast is like a beautiful natural food buffet organized by a master chef, varying from the Valley on the south end to the Golden Triangle on the north, providing perhaps the greatest ecological diversity to be found in the United States.

The last few strokes push my kayak into the sandy shoreline. I stretch my legs and push my body up from the sitting position that I have held for a few hours. I'm getting older now, but the feeling at the end of the paddle is still overwhelmingly good. When I experience the natural wonder of the Texas coast, I am truly alive. And I leave Drum Bay with a big smile and an absolute intention to return again and again.

CHAPTER 2

Gray Assets of the Texas Coast

I learned the Texas coast from four main sources—the upper coast from my Uncle Bun (Bill) Graves of Port Neches, the lower coast from my dad, Bernard Blackburn, who learned about it to take me hunting and fishing, and the midcoast from my wife's brother-in-law Walter Duson, originally from El Campo, and a fishing guide from Matagorda named Al Garrison. These men taught me how to enjoy myself—how to feel comfortable—in the surf, the salt marshes, the oyster reefs, and the navigation channels of the Texas coast. They and my fearless fishing buddies of Team 11 and our wives have opened a landscape to me that keeps on offering surprises, adventures, and dividends.

One week several decades ago, I sailed down the Texas coast with Walter, my wife's sister Lizabeth Kerr, and my wife, Garland Kerr, using the Gulf Intracoastal Waterway (GIWW) as our highway. We slept on the sailboat either anchored alongside the channel at night or docked in a marina. In this manner, I learned about the "back side" of the Texas coast, the system of waterways that send commerce back and forth from Texas ports as well as eastward to Louisiana, the Mississippi River, and beyond, connecting the industrial centers of the Texas coast with each other and with the deepwater channels that bring seagoing vessels laden with oil and container boxes into our cities and the hinterlands beyond.

This sailing trip revealed an amazing spiderweb of connections that I have continued to learn about, explore, and litigate over the past several decades. The spine of the spiderweb of connections is the GIWW, which extends from the Sabine River almost to the Rio Grande, stopping at the Port of Brownsville at the tip of Texas. Connected to this waterway are numerous navigation spurs that link industrial development with raw material and product markets as well as provide a means for moving aggregate, and in the past, oyster shell, throughout the coast.

There are any number of vantage points where you can drive to the edge of the GIWW and watch the barges and tugs go by. Up close, you can see that a filled barge pushes a wave of water before it, propelled forward by diesel engines of several thousand horsepower that generate a frothy wake behind them where the gulls and terns dive for small fish caught up in the turbulence.

The GIWW has a long history on the Texas coast. According to the Texas State Historical Association, the segment of the GIWW from Christmas Bay to Galveston Island was authorized by Congress in 1892 and was joined with a privately owned canal system that connected Christmas Bay to the Brazos River by 1902. The GIWW was authorized from Galveston to New Orleans as a canal 9 feet deep and 100 feet wide in 1905, with the tab to be picked up by the federal government. However, it took until 1941 to complete the section down to Corpus Christi, and it was not completed to the tip of Texas until 1949. Today, the waterway is maintained at 12 feet deep and 125 feet wide, although bank erosion has extended it beyond those boundaries.

As you move down the GIWW, one constant is the presence of spoil islands, areas in which the material dug from the bay bottom for the canal was disposed of in the past and which

Figure 2.1. A tugboat pushing a load of aggregate down the Gulf Intracoastal Waterway rises above the marsh; when seen at a distance it can appear ghostlike as it moves across the marsh horizon. Photo by Kathy Adams Clark.

may possibly be used again for disposal in the future. The term "dredge spoil" is an old one that has come into disfavor by port and waterway types who have been fighting the negative connotation conveyed by the word "spoil." Today, we talk about the beneficial use of dredged material, and there are many positive ways that this material can be disposed of and used, such as diking off disposal cells, draining the dredged material, and then planting marsh grass.

The maintenance dredging of the GIWW and most of the Texas deepwater ports is the responsibility of the US Army Corps of Engineers, which is funded to construct these projects by Congress through various water resource and development acts and its local partner, the Texas Department of Transportation. Over the years, billions of federal dollars have been spent creating and maintaining waterways along the Texas coast.

Unlike certain ports on the East and West Coasts of the United States, the ports of Texas are shallow, suitable in their natural state for only the shallowest-draft commercial vessels. Starting in the early 1900s, various ports along the Texas coast decided to engineer their way to commercial navigation. Over the years, numerous deepwater channels have been constructed to link the navigation corridors of the Gulf of Mexico with inland ports, ports that thrive today because of federal funding for navigation improvements and maintenance dredging.

Deepwater ports can be found throughout the Texas coast. The Sabine-Neches Waterway provides deepwater navigation through Sabine Pass to the Ports of Beaumont, Port Neches, Port Arthur, and Orange. The Houston Ship Channel connects the Ports of Houston, Texas City, and Galveston with the Gulf through the pass known as Bolivar Roads. The Port of Freeport has its own deepwater channel that comes inland at the former mouth of the Brazos River, which was relocated around Freeport in 1929. The deepwater channel adjacent to Pass Cavallo in Matagorda Bay leads to industrial development in Point Comfort, and the deepwater channel at Port Aransas leads into Corpus Christi Bay and the Port of Corpus Christi. The Port of Brownsville is the southernmost deepwater port, coming in through the Brazos Santiago Pass between South Padre Island and Boca Chica. A shallow cut exists across from Port Mansfield to allow recreational fishing access into the Gulf of Mexico.

Figure 2.2. Tankers at anchor waiting to enter the deep-draft Houston Ship Channel just off the eastern tip of Galveston Island. Photo by Kathy Adams Clark.

Today, much of the navigation commerce is related to the import of oil from various suppliers around the world. Oil comes to the Texas coast from South America, Africa, and the Middle East. It often comes in supertankers that are too deep for most Texas ports, which are limited to maintained depths of forty to fifty feet. These "mother ships" are off-loaded through a process called "lightering" into smaller tankers, which then navigate the deepwater channels to the major refining centers of the coast. Container transshipment is an emerging deepwater trend, with the development of new container ports at Bayport near Houston and at Ingleside near Corpus Christi. The most recent trend is to build liquid natural gas export facilities because of the current glut of low-priced natural gas from the fracking fields, with major facilities proposed for Brownsville, Corpus Christi, Freeport, and Sabine Pass.

The GIWW is the yin to the yang of these deepwater ports. The bigger ships bring raw materials into and export finished products out from the Texas coast, and the barges move chemicals and aggregate within the coast, creating interdependencies that are key to understanding the developed fabric of the Texas coast. Spinning off the GIWW are numerous smaller industrial complexes that are linked to this barge transportation network, including Adams Bayou in Orange County, Cedar Bayou in Harris and Chambers Counties, Chocolate Bayou in Galveston County, the San Bernard River near Sweeney, the Colorado River at Bay City, the Port of Victoria, and the Port of Harlingen on the Arroyo Colorado. At the end of each of these deepwater and barge ports is heavy industry, usually petroleum refining or chemical manufacturing, which in 2015 was expanding to take advantage of cheap natural gas as a feedstock. The navigation channels of the Texas coast are shown in figure 2.3.

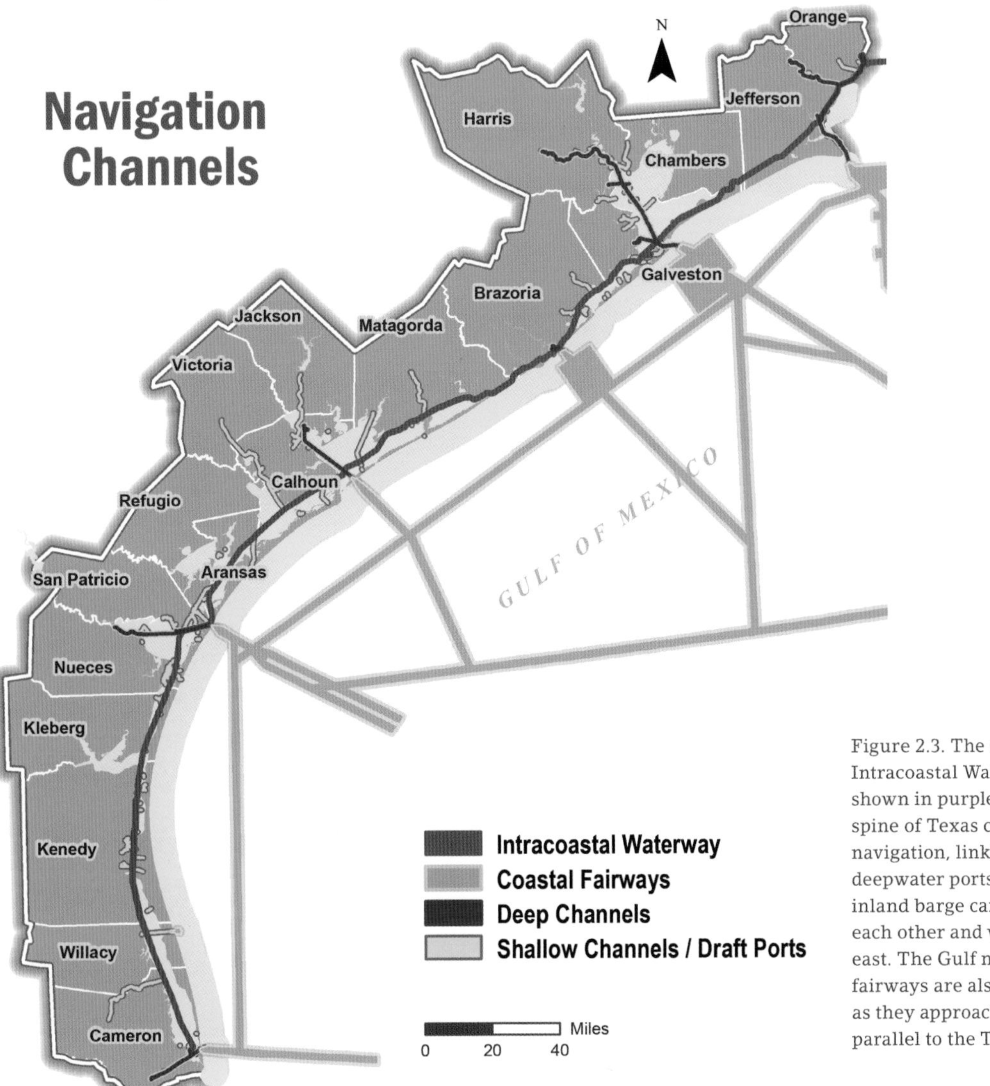

Figure 2.3. The Gulf Intracoastal Waterway, shown in purple, is the spine of Texas coastal navigation, linking deepwater ports and inland barge canals with each other and with points east. The Gulf navigation fairways are also shown as they approach and run parallel to the Texas coast.

Another piece of the infrastructure puzzle of the Texas coast is the rail system, which connects with the ports at almost every notable juncture. Unlike the navigation and road systems, the rail system was built and is maintained by private companies. Today, there are two major rail providers on the Texas coast, BNSF and Union Pacific. These two systems provide a lattice for moving raw material such as Dakota Bakken oil and Wyoming coal into the coast and exporting various types of products, most notably chemicals and plastics. At each point where rail and port systems come together, significant industrial development has likely occurred. In some cases, there is only industry and no surrounding community, as in the development at Chocolate Bayou, which is visible at night as a glow from the west end of Galveston Island. The intersection of rail and navigation along with industrial development is shown in figure 2.5.

This rail and port infrastructure and the industry it supports are also part of an extensive energy production and distribution system along the coast. The refining and petrochemical industry is supported by a system of pipelines that

Figure 2.4. Industrial development is right on the coast, often adjacent to prime natural resources such as these marshlands near Freeport. Photo by Kathy Adams Clark.

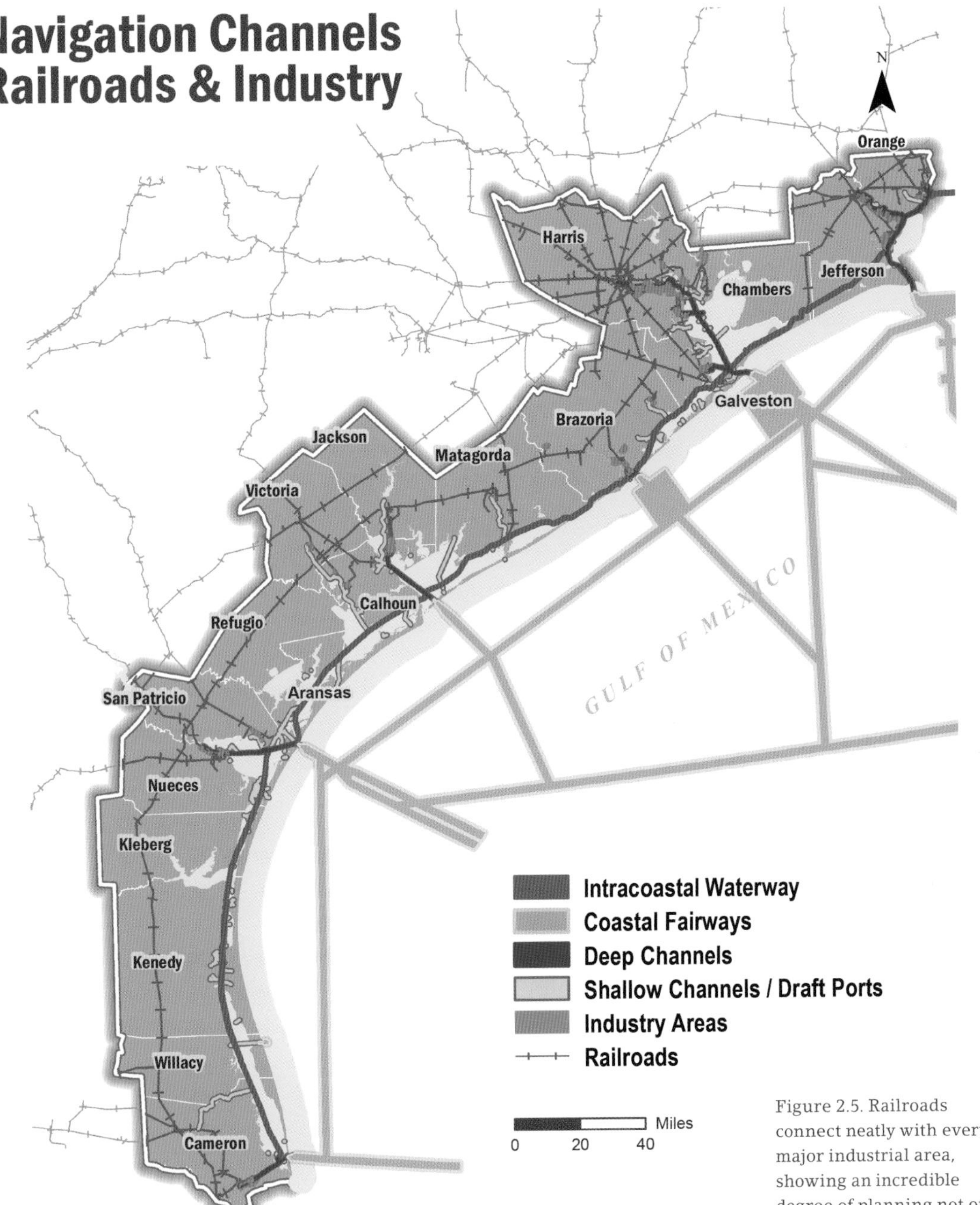

Figure 2.5. Railroads connect neatly with every major industrial area, showing an incredible degree of planning not often associated with the Texas coast.

offer alternative feedstock sources to the crude brought in by heavy crude tankers from Venezuela, Saudi Arabia, and other exporting nations. This system of major crude pipelines, shown in figure 2.6, is supported by myriad chemical pipelines that crisscross the coast.

The Texas coast is also full of electricity-producing facilities. Many of the refineries and chemical plants have cogeneration facilities where electricity for both the plant and the

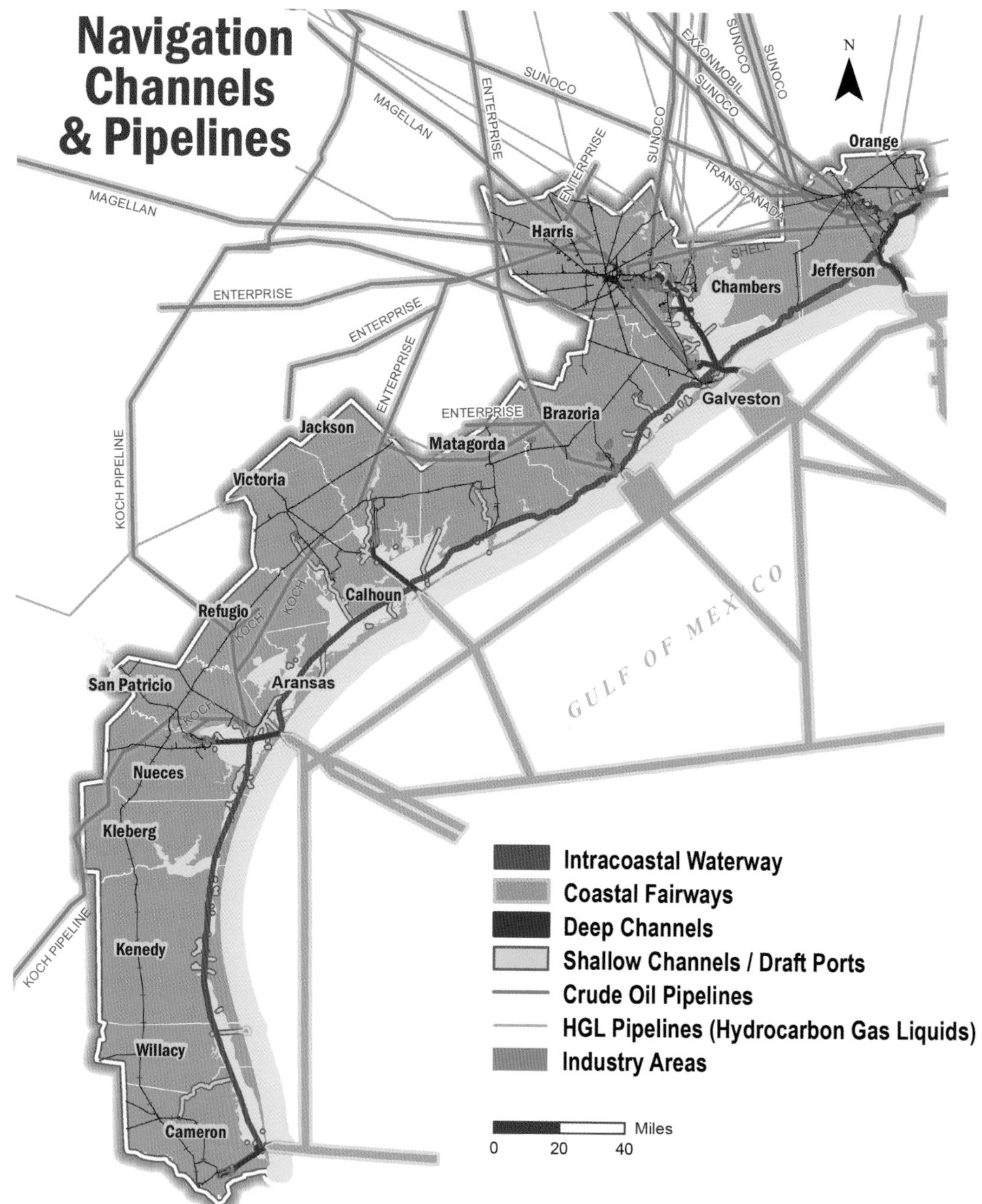

Figure 2.6. Crude pipelines also connect back into the major coastal industrial centers.

grid is generated. There are also two nuclear units just outside Bay City and three major wind farms around and south of Corpus Christi, along with several natural gas and two major coal-fired facilities. Figure 2.7 shows the energy production units of the coast along with the transmission grid that connects them to the major demand centers.

On another day, I drive south down the coast from Houston

to Port Aransas to speak to a class at the Marine Science Institute at the University of Texas. The coastal drive is a favorite of mine, whether I am going to Corpus or the Valley or just to Matagorda. I start out on US 59, the high-speed gateway southwest out of Houston. Along the way, I cross the major coastal rivers, the Brazos at Richmond, the Colorado at Wharton, the Guadalupe at Victoria. I like to check the flows in the rivers; the crops being planted, harvested, and used by wintering waterfowl; the condition of the ranches; the green of the mesquite and the parched brown of the late summer grasslands. I like to greet the spring as the wildflowers and mesquite announce the end of winter (see fig. 2.8).

Going to Port Aransas, one must take a ferry across the

Figure 2.7. Significant amounts of energy are produced and distributed within the Texas coast, including two nuclear power plants at Bay City and several wind farms in South Texas.

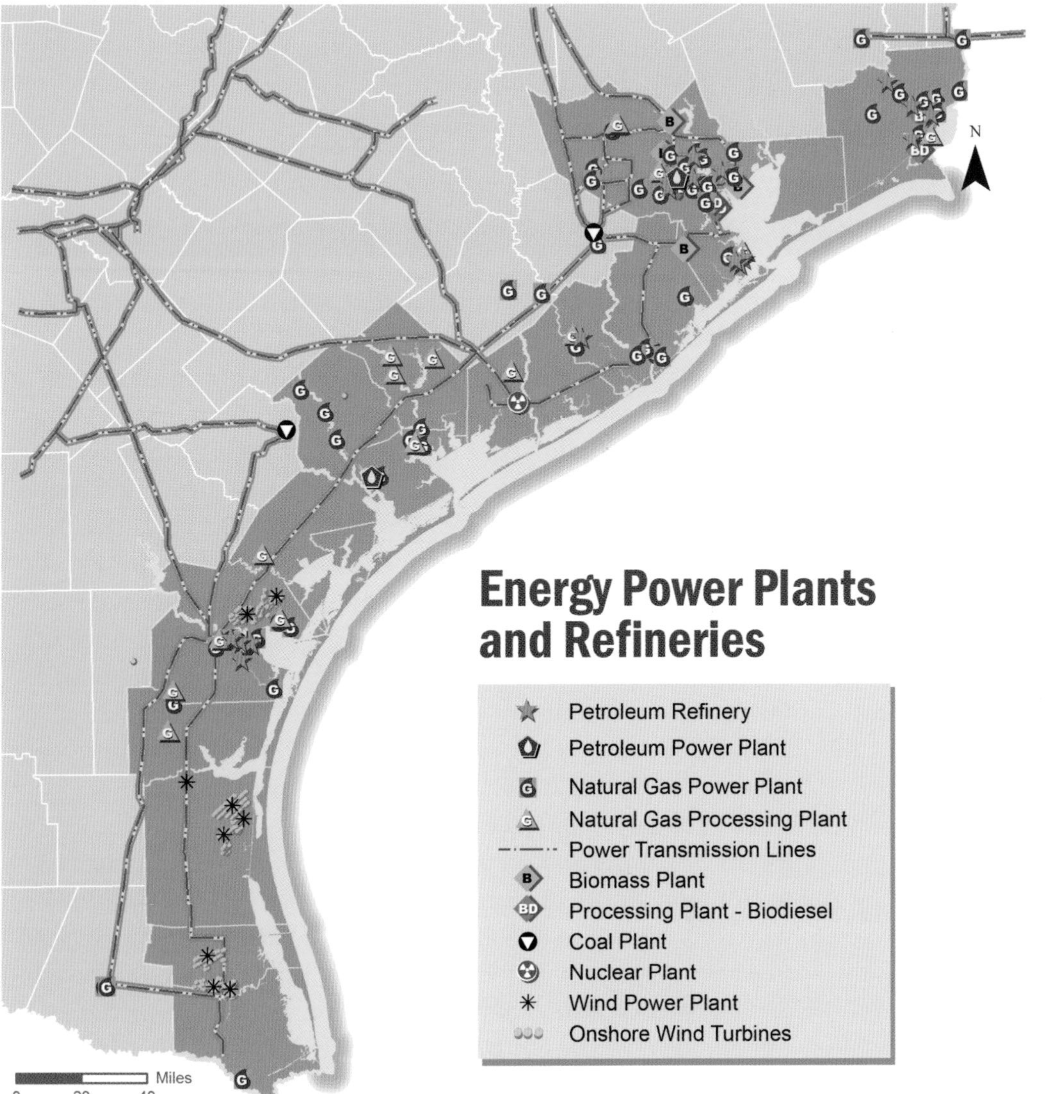

Figure 2.8. Wildflowers come to life in the early spring in South Texas. Photo by Larry Ditto/KAC Productions.

Corpus Christi Ship Channel, which is also part of the GIWW at this location. There are only two ferries along the Texas coast, the one at Port Aransas and the one on US 87 from Galveston to the Bolivar Peninsula across Bolivar Roads. Both ferries cross deepwater navigation channels at locations where there is not enough room for the major bridges that are required, bridges like the Rainbow Bridge from Port Arthur to Bridge City across the Sabine-Neches Waterway or the Fred Hartman Bridge across the Houston Ship Channel at Baytown, an engineering masterpiece. Today, we also have bridges at most crossings of the GIWW rather than the drawbridges that used to keep traffic tied up for significant amounts of time. Among the newer bridges, Matagorda has one of the nicest, offering a magnificent view of the marsh and East Matagorda Bay.

The road system traversing the Texas coast is anchored by US 77 from Brownsville to Victoria, US 59 from Victoria to Houston, and I-10 from Houston to Orange. Texas Highway 35 is known as the Coast Road and extends from Houston to Alvin, Angleton, Bay City, Palacios, Port Lavaca, Rockport, and Corpus Christi. There is really no comparable road on the upper coast, where SH 87 used to extend from Galveston to Sabine Pass and connect to the Louisiana coast, but in recent decades it has been rendered unusable because of coastal erosion in the segment between High Island and Sabine Pass. Now, to get from Galveston to the Louisiana coastal highway, one must take the ferry to Bolivar and SH 87 to High Island, then travel north to Winnie and east on Texas Highway 73 to Port Arthur, and then take 82 into Louisiana.

Some of the more interesting Texas coastal roads are the tertiary ones, the smaller two lanes that open up areas that are not traveled as much. One such road is FM 521, which runs from the small community of Bailey's Prairie west of Angleton on SH 35 south to Brazoria and then turns southwest through the heart of the Columbia Bottomlands, a double-canopy forest, then connects through Wadsworth just north of Matagorda and meets SH 35 near Palacios at the top of Tres Palacios Bay. This road opens up the wetlands between Galveston and Matagorda Bays as well as between East Matagorda Bay and Matagorda Bay. The key roads of the Texas coast are shown in figure 2.9. Houston clearly stands out as the large confluence of road infrastructure, as does San Antonio farther inland.

The Texas coast has substantial urban and industrial development, although it is not as densely developed as many coastal areas of the United States and the world. An initial indicator of the development status of the Texas coast is the map of the urban areas shown in figure 2.10. These are areas that are more densely developed, primarily cities and towns, although large areas of developed Harris County are unincorporated due to the extensive use of special governmental districts called Municipal Utility Districts, reflecting a distrust of city policies and government in general, another defining characteristic of the Texas coast.

A striking aspect of this map is the amount of undeveloped land: thirteen of sixteen coastal counties have less than 10 percent of their land "developed," often for very good reasons such as low elevation and flooding. On the other hand, this "undeveloped" area is not unused, as it supports farming and ranching activities as well as oil and gas exploration and development, wind farms, and abundant wildlife.

The disparity in population along the Texas coast tracks this developed land dichotomy. Harris County has by far the largest population, with 4,441,370 people estimated as of July 2014. That represents a whopping 68 percent of the population of the eighteen coastal counties. The second-highest population is Cameron with about 417,000, followed by Nueces

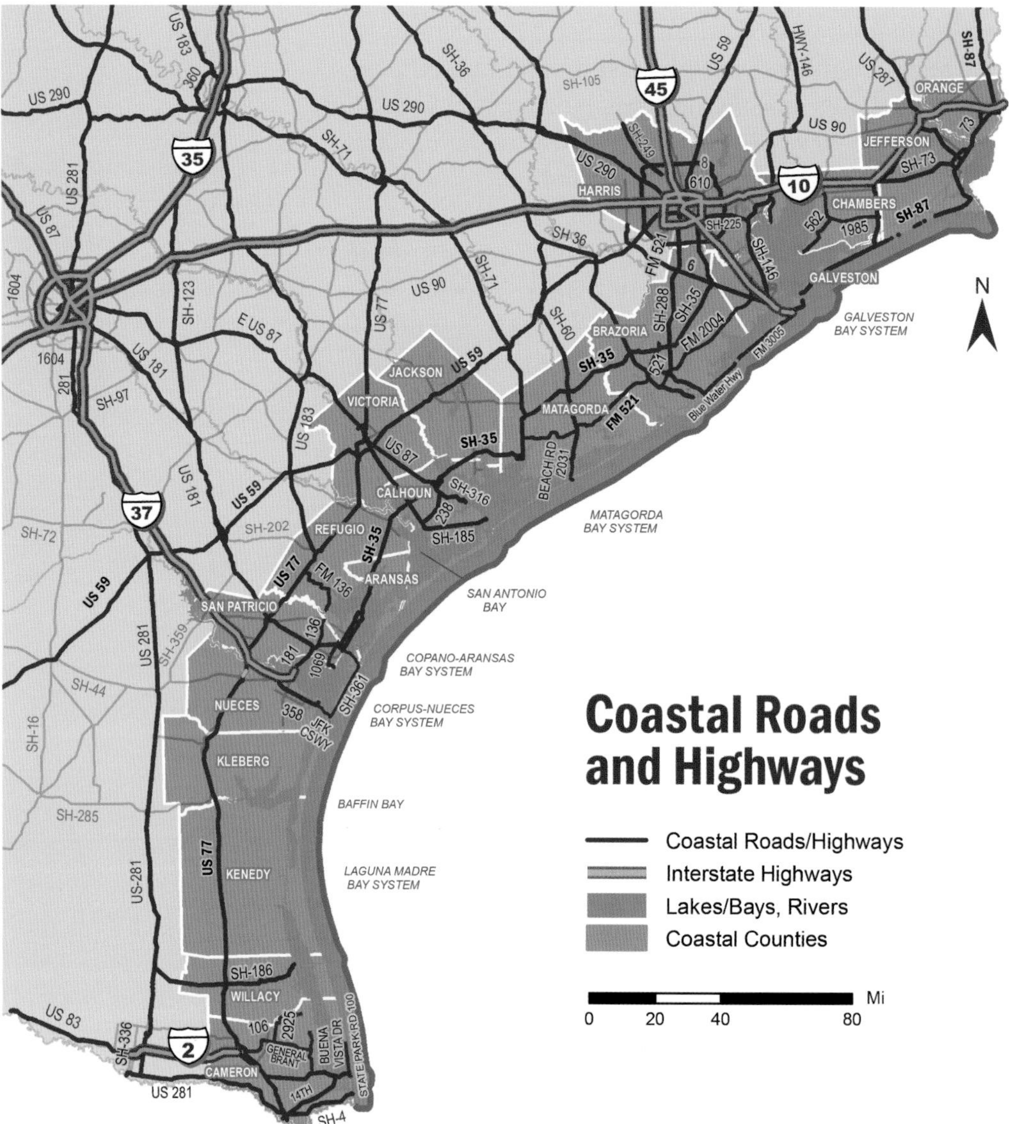

Figure 2.9. The major roads within and connecting to the Texas coast bring anglers, bird-watchers, employees, and beach vacationers to destinations up and down the coast.

with about 356,000, Brazoria with about 338,000, Galveston with about 314,000, and Jefferson with about 252,000. At the low end, Kenedy comes in with about 400 people, Refugio with about 7,300, Jackson with about 15,000, and Calhoun with about 22,000, with the other eight counties in between.

Along the Texas coast, there is development and then there is "coastal development." By the latter I mean water-oriented subdivisions. Of these, there are two types—beach development and bay development. They are quite different. Beach development is about access and view, with homes on elevated slabs to avoid surge flooding, and one or more balconies for the view. When I was a kid, many of the beach homes were "fishing camps," which were not much more than a camping trip with a hard roof and walls rather than a tent. To the extent any of these were left on the upper Texas coast, they were removed from Bolivar by Hurricane Ike and from Freeport by Alicia as well as by Ike.

Today, beachside development is decidedly high dollar. Bolivar has been rebuilt since Ike hit in 2008, and the new Bolivar development is state-of-the-art flood proofed—elevated as much as twenty feet above sea level with serious bracing above concrete piles, all in an effort to keep the foundation and structure in place during the next big storm. New houses here cost more than $500,000 for beachfront and can certainly go higher. The west end of Galveston Island is even more high priced, with some of the mansions on pilings looking somewhat silly in the shimmering heat of a summer afternoon. In addition to the beachfront. there are several canal

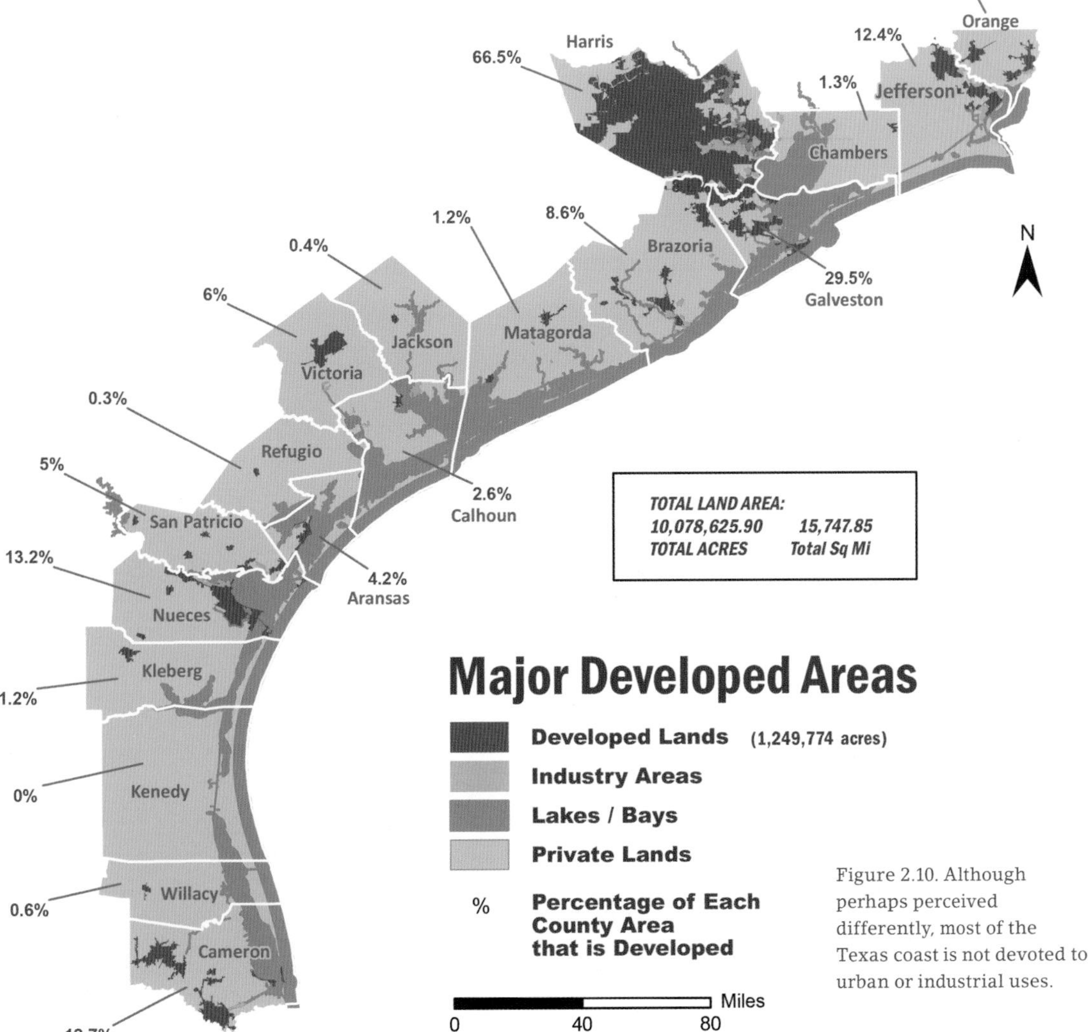

Figure 2.10. Although perhaps perceived differently, most of the Texas coast is not devoted to urban or industrial uses.

subdivisions back on West Bay as well as the town of Jamaica Beach with both beach and bay-side development. Farther south across San Luis Pass and onto the Blue Water Highway, the beach development begins again at Surfside near Freeport and is somewhat more pedestrian, with homes more in keeping with the risk, not inexpensive yet not outlandish, except for a few of the newer ones.

There is not much coast-oriented housing between Freeport and Matagorda. There are a few condos on the beach at Matagorda, but most of the housing occurs along the San Bernard River and the old Colorado River channel, and back in the town of Matagorda. One must go much farther south to find the next substantial beach development, to Port Aransas, the most interesting and quaint of the Texas coastal towns because of its layout, scale, and style. From the ferry to the historic Tarpon Inn, from the interior bungalows to the beachfront condos, from the fishing piers to the University of Texas Marine Science Institute, Port Aransas is a complete beach town. It is quite different from the neighboring North Padre Island, which is also nice not so much because of its canal home developments but rather because of the huge expanse of accessible public beach made possible through the Padre Island National Seashore.

One cannot drive along the beach from North Padre Island

Figure 2.11. Beach houses on the west end of Galveston Island, showing setback behind small dunes and elevated first floors. Photo by Kathy Adams Clark.

to South Padre Island because of the Mansfield Channel, an artificial cut through the barrier island that allows Port Mansfield access to the Gulf of Mexico. Instead, one must take Highway 77 south to the Rio Grande Valley, passing through Harlingen and Port Isabel to reach and cross the Queen Isabella Causeway to the town of South Padre Island. This is the glittering jewel of the Texas coast, with the clearest water, the best surf, and the most elaborate collection of high-rise condos on the Texas coast. I grew up near here and fondly remember huge sand dunes where there are now condos of ten-plus stories along several miles of beach, accompanied by back-side development along the crystal-clear Lower Laguna Madre, a fishing paradise.

The bay-side development of the Texas coast is equally different and somewhat similarly distributed. Port Isabel is a quaint coastal town with a commercial fishing fleet and excellent recreational fishing in the Lower Laguna Madre. Port Mansfield is a small collection of fishing guides and offshore oil service facilities with virtually no development to its north for fifty or so miles (that's the King and Kenedy Ranch lands) until you reach Baffin Bay and the seafood at the King's Inn. If you are in the area, stop in and get some really good food, but be advised that there are not many places to spend the night.

Corpus Christi is perhaps the most beautiful city on the Texas coast. The city is laid out on Corpus Christi Bay from its confluence with Nueces Bay on the north all the way to its southern edge—the Upper Laguna Madre interface—and its boundaries cross the Kennedy Causeway to North Padre Island. Corpus is a major industrial center, with refineries and chemical plants along the southern periphery of Nueces Bay and the northern periphery of Corpus Christi Bay. Corpus is a hub for South Texas oil and gas transport and oil and gas deals and is home to some of the best trial lawyers in the state.

Going north out of Corpus Christi, one crosses the high bridge over the Corpus Christi Ship Channel, looking down on the lights of Whataburger Field (home of the Houston Astros AA affiliate), and then comes a really nice crossing of Nueces Bay and some lovely created and natural marshlands where there can be excellent bird-watching. Coming up from Nueces Bay, one enters San Patricio County and the bay-side community of Portland, another hidden jewel on the north side of Nueces Bay. From there, State Highway 35 continues northward to the developed western shoreline of Aransas Bay.

Figure 2.12. Padre Island National Seashore stretches for almost seventy miles from Corpus Christi south to the Mansfield Cut, a magnificent stretch of undeveloped beach accessible by four-wheel-drive vehicles and hardy souls. Photo by Geoff Winningham.

Ingleside and Aransas Pass form the lower part of this developed shoreline, and Rockport and the Lamar Peninsula represent the northern part, all on the western shore of Aransas Bay and the eastern shore of Copano Bay. The development along this stretch is more impressive from the water than from the land, as the growth in housing has been intense along the Aransas Bayfront, with the shoreline filled by canal developments and only a small gap between Aransas Pass and south Rockport. The newer homes on the south side of Rockport join the older development of Key Allegro, a wetland point that was filled for development decades ago when wetlands could be easily destroyed, something that requires a federal permit today. Fulton Beach is a staid old Bayfront community looking out over restaurants and bait houses. It has a classic Texas coastal look and is an excellent place to stop for a while, particularly during the fall when the whooping crane tours begin and wintering waterfowl arrive. Little Bay in Rockport may be the best place on the coast to see redhead ducks at a reasonable distance.

For the most part, coastal development adjourns from the

Lamar Peninsula northward until Galveston Bay. San Antonio Bay is essentially not developed, and Matagorda Bay is only lightly developed. The only community of any size on San Antonio Bay is Seadrift, a town based on a bay commercial fishing industry that no longer prospers along the Texas coast. On the other side of Calhoun County, Port O'Connor is a lonely outpost at the point where Matagorda Bay and Espiritu Santo Bay come together, a recreational fishing destination of note. The downturn of commercial fishing has also hit hard in Port Lavaca and Palacios, nice bay-side communities on the north shore of Matagorda Bay that are in transition. The town of Matagorda exists where the Colorado River enters Matagorda Bay, and the community of Sargent exists where Caney Creek empties into the northern edge of East Matagorda Bay. Together, these two Matagorda Bay communities represent fewer than one thousand permanent residents, although weekend and summer populations may increase tenfold.

Moving north into Brazoria County, one begins to encounter significant development in pockets throughout the Columbia Bottomlands and in the industrial towns of Lake Jackson,

Clute, and Freeport. These are not bay-side communities, however, as there is no water view except in a few housing developments along lower Oyster Creek and Bastrop Bayou. True bay development comes back into focus as one approaches Galveston Bay, with subdivisions such as Tiki Island and Bayou Vista adjacent to I-45 as it crosses West Bay and goes into Galveston, a city that was the jewel of the Texas coast before the Hurricane of 1900 killed 6,500 people and destroyed homes, businesses, and the future of Galveston. Although rebuilt and bold and ambitious, Galveston is a star that has lost its luster. There is a quality coastal setting in Galveston and there are some wonderful people and places, but it has just never seemed to get its act together in a way that understands the challenges and problems of barrier island development and accepts and acknowledges them. The leadership of Galveston is perhaps the greatest of the deniers of these risks, including sea level rise, and the community has suffered and will suffer because of it.

Moving north along the shoreline of Galveston Bay into northeastern Galveston County, one encounters the new center of Galveston County government and new bay development. Texas City, behind its levee and with its refineries and chem-

Figure 2.13. Fulton Beach as seen from Aransas Bay. Photo by Kathy Adams Clark.

Figure 2.14. Galveston Bay coastal development offers beautiful views of wetlands and fish-eating birds at work. Photo by Kathy Adams Clark.

ical plants, is an industrial zone, but not so with Kemah and League City, cities that have one foot in Galveston Bay or Clear Lake and the other in the suburban development of Houston. New development abounds, a trend visible on the north shore of Clear Lake, where waterfront towns such as Seabrook, El Lago, Taylor Lake Village, Nassau Bay, La Porte, and Morgan's Point enjoy the development that has spread south from the Houston Ship Channel and east from NASA headquarters and the space industry. This is perhaps the most dangerous real estate on the coast in that it is low lying, holds a lot of people, and is not protected from hurricane storm-surge flooding; in addition, the residents and would-be residents are not provided good information about the hazards.

Heading east toward Trinity Bay, one crosses the Hartman Bridge and enters Baytown at the edge of the eastern development of Houston. Along Cedar Bayou one finds classic coastal development along with some beautiful sites that are protected from ship channel air pollution by the prevailing breeze that blows inland off the bay. There is some development on the western shore of Trinity Bay, including the community of Beach City, but then development stops at the Lost and Old River marshes and swamps at the Trinity River.

Anahuac is the county seat of Chambers County, overlooking the upper end of Trinity Bay. Chambers County extends southward along Trinity Bay to Smith Point and eastward along the top of East Bay, but that land is extremely low and not much development has been attempted. Farther east, coastal access declines. US 87 used to connect the Bolivar Peninsula and High Island northeastward to Sabine Pass and Port Arthur, but that road eroded into the Gulf of Mexico years ago and was never replaced. Today, it is not possible to drive along the Gulf from the Bolivar Peninsula to Sabine Pass. Instead, one must go east from Interstate 10 across Jefferson County to Port Arthur, a town that has been boarded up and abandoned by business and is now largely a minority community left behind as prosperity, and whites, moved to the midcounty region. This is one of the centers of environmental justice concerns in the state, a topic for another book.

There is not much coastal development in the Golden Triangle area. The water's edge is marshy and low. Beaumont is an older industrial city on the north end of the Sabine-Neches Waterway, but there is no true coastal development here. Most of Beaumont and this part of the world go to Bolivar for their beach and bay recreation. Approaching the Louisiana border

Figure 2.15. The Fred Hartman Bridge, one of the most beautiful in Texas, spans the Houston Ship Channel and leads into Baytown, home of a major ExxonMobil refinery and chemical plant on the north bank of the channel. Photo by Kathy Adams Clark

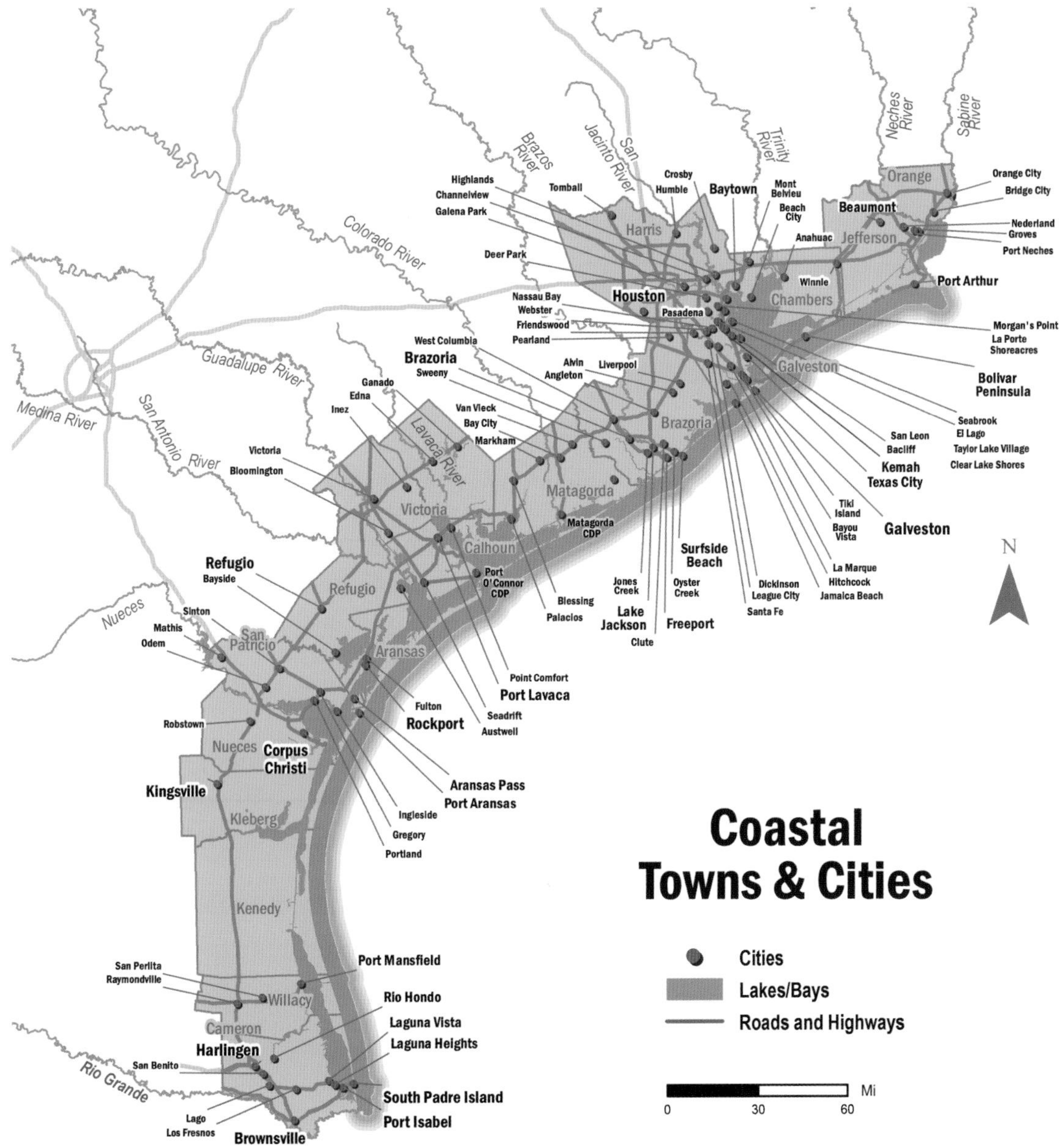

Figure 2.16. Various cities and towns of the Texas coast.

and Orange, one encounters bayous with cypress and tupelo gum trees, more like Louisiana than Texas, complete with alligators and that lovely green algae that floats menacingly in the slow-moving waters, hiding whatever lies beneath (and there always seems to be something lurking nearby). A map showing many of the cities and towns discussed above is presented in figure 2.16.

The Texas coast is soft and fat, and it is hard and tough. It is white rubber boots and running shoes. It is cold beer and fancy red wine. It is fried shrimp and broiled snapper. It is a very real mixture of all that is good and bad about Texas.

CHAPTER 3

Water Assets of the Coast

WITH THE ASSISTANCE OF CHRISTY FLATT

During the writing of *The Book of Texas Bays*, my friend and photographer for that book, Jim Olive, flew the coast to take photos, and he came back with a shot that has stuck with me ever since that time. It is a picture of the mouth of the Rio Grande almost completely closed off by silt, and in fact the river silted shut about a month after Jim shot that photo. Now, think about that. During my lifetime, during our lifetimes, Texas and Mexico have managed to dry up a river that has flowed for millions of years.

That thought really bothers me, and unfortunately, the problem is not limited to the Rio Grande. It extends to every major river system flowing into the coast. And whereas the Rio Grande has no bay, almost all the other river systems do, except the Brazos. The hard, cruel truth is that our Texas bays

Figure 3.1. The mouth of the Rio Grande just before silting closed it in 2001—proof that Mexican and US water usage can cause a river to stop flowing to the Gulf of Mexico. Photo by Jim Olive.

and estuaries will die without freshwater inflow. Period. They will become fundamentally altered without adequate freshwater inflow from rivers and streams. They will lose productivity, meaning fewer shrimp and crabs and oysters and trout and redfish. No inflow means no inshore fishing. Similarly, Texas coastal industries, development, and agriculture also need freshwater. No water means no industrial production, no municipal water supply, and no irrigated agriculture. No water is no bueno.

Water is unique. It is both a gray and green infrastructure item. It is the giver of life to humans and the human economy, as well as the natural system and the natural economy. Without it, we literally and figuratively will die. Yet we have little respect for this life-giving element, a problem that will haunt the coast as well as Texas in general until we change.

When I first started practicing environmental law in Texas, I was warned about the water lawyers, a crusty old bunch who did not like newcomers or new ideas. And our water system reflects that personality as well. Historically, our legal and institutional system has focused on making water available for industry, municipalities, and irrigated agriculture. However, water for freshwater inflows to the bays and estuaries was simply never considered necessary. Indeed, water was considered to be wasted if it made it to the bays, and the bays have no water rights under the current Texas system. Instead, all permits for water rights are issued for industrial, municipal, or agricultural uses, with a few other minor classifications. As of 2016, the bays are legal nonentities when it comes to water rights.

Many of us have tried for the past thirty or forty years to get freshwater inflows dedicated to Texas bays. I have worked on and litigated inflow issues in Nueces, San Antonio, Matagorda, and Galveston Bays. Stuart Henry, an environmental lawyer in Austin, represented the San Marcos River Foundation in a failed attempt to have water rights issued for San Antonio Bay. Myron Hess of the National Wildlife Federation has devoted much of his professional career to public-interest water law issues. And several groups including the Coastal Conservation Association, National Wildlife Federation, Texas Parks and Wildlife Department, Matagorda Bay Foundation, and The Aransas Project have opposed permits allowing water to be taken from the Colorado and Guadalupe Rivers because they would harm bays and estuaries. Some progress has occurred over the years, but it has been slow.

The important point is that all of us need to understand more about water, yet the system surrounding water is complicated, almost as if designed to make it hard to fathom. One key to understanding the future of the coast is to have at least a basic knowledge of the water institutions and rules applicable to the Texas coast. As the old saying goes, whiskey's for drinkin' and water's for fightin', and we wouldn't be fighting over it if there were a lot of it. When we are not in drought conditions, all seems good. The rivers and wells are flowing, the stock tanks are full, and the bays get inflow. It is when drought hits that the problems, and the fights, begin.

Also, in thinking about water, remember that water is a true infrastructure item, but it is part of both the green infrastructure and the gray infrastructure. Water is the building block of ecological systems and is the key for the ecological health of the bays. Water is also an absolute necessity for human development. So, as you read about water, keep this dichotomy in mind. It really defines the difficulties surrounding water because it is a key to both the human and ecological systems.

As a final opening thought, consider that water is an ancient and basic gray asset. Our laws and practices regarding water are based on the past, not the present. If there were ever a subject that proved the distinction between empty-world thinking and the needs of a full world, water is it. In the following paragraphs, the basic structure of water allocation and an outline of water problems are set out. Throughout, keep in mind that damage occurs when water does not get to the bays, yet we did not understand that until the late 1960s. We are evolving our understanding and our system of water. We need to evolve the pricing of water. Our water system can and should be better, and there are some creative ideas to help it move in the right direction.

Surface Water

Surface water (rivers, lakes) has been and continues to be the go-to water supply source for Texas. It has been that way from the time settlers first arrived with concepts of water rights that they brought first from Spain and Mexico and later from England. These two legal systems were spliced together after the drought of the 1950s to create the surface water system that exists today, a system that allows withdrawals by permits issued by the Texas Commission on Environmental Quality (TCEQ) and also grants rights to owners of riverfront property to use water adjacent to their land for domestic and livestock purposes without a permit.

The state of Texas owns the water in all watercourses, which are defined by the presence of a bed and incised (cut) banks. Surface water is public property, although we aren't as sophisticated, or perhaps as caring, about public property rights as we are of private property rights, an area ripe for future research and focus. All surface water rights are issued on a river-basin-by-river-basin basis. A computer program called a Water Availability Model, or WAM, has been developed specifically for each major river system. These WAMs allow the state to keep track of permitted water rights, and along with the permits themselves, they allow the state to understand which water rights have priority over others when surface water is limited.

During times of drought, some of these water rights are not worth much, if anything, because the only thing that matters in the drought is priority—which permit was issued first, which use has priority. Nonetheless, the state continues to issue new permits for water that is not available 100 percent of the time—a true recipe for disaster, or at least a major fight. On the other hand, the permittee is given fair warning that the water may not be available when it is needed most, although most politicians and appointed officials have trouble cutting off water to people's homes.

The watersheds of the various coastal rivers were shown in chapter 1, in figure 1.4. Generally speaking, the amount of water available for appropriation is highest in the easternmost rivers and decreases as one moves west and south down the Texas coast. Books have been written just on surface water rights in Texas. Suffice it to say that rights become hotly contested as flows diminish, a situation that will likely worsen as more people and development demand more water and as the prospects of more severe droughts increase as our climate changes (see chapter 5).

The state legislature has created certain governmental subdivisions of the state of Texas with authority to undertake various functions related to water. These entities are known as river authorities. Almost every major river basin has one or more river authorities with jurisdiction over that geography, although their jurisdictional boundaries do not always conform to watershed boundaries. These river authorities are authorized to receive water rights permits and to develop, sell, and distribute water within their jurisdiction, as well as provide other services such as sewage treatment and electrical generation as provided by their enabling statute.

River authorities are deeply involved in water rights matters within the state and within their jurisdiction. In many respects, they are the organized force for water development within the state, working closely with the Texas Water Development Board (TWDB), the state agency that oversees and often funds water development. In many cases these river authorities own or operate reservoirs and are often proponents of various surface and groundwater development projects, as are other special governmental entities and some cities or city-owned utilities. The jurisdictional area of Texas river authorities covering coastal counties is shown in figure 3.2.

Groundwater

By contrast, groundwater is owned by the owner of the land surface above it, as established by the Texas Supreme Court as recently as 2012 in *Day v. Edwards Aquifer Authority.* The so-called *Day* case clearly established that the landowner had a property right "in place" relative to groundwater, meaning the landowner had a property right in the groundwater even if there was no well claiming that water. This case arose out of the regulation of groundwater by a groundwater conservation district, an effort that on the Texas coast goes back to the late 1970s in Harris and Galveston Counties where the land surface was sinking from overpumping. Later, various legislative acts created or allowed the creation of several other individual groundwater control districts on the Texas coast. Today, there are many separate groundwater conservation districts, each of which is trying to understand its vulnerability to claims of unconstitutional "taking" of property if it denies or substantially limits the right of a landowner to pump groundwater. The groundwater districts of the Texas coast are shown in figure 3.3.

These various groundwater districts are each different with respect to their funding sources and budgets as well as their rules and regulations regarding groundwater withdrawal and development. Some districts are restrictive, attempting to protect springs and seeps and existing water wells, whereas others are more generous in their allowed drawdowns of water levels. The Gulf Coast Aquifer comprises several permeable sand layers in the subsurface that are present through-

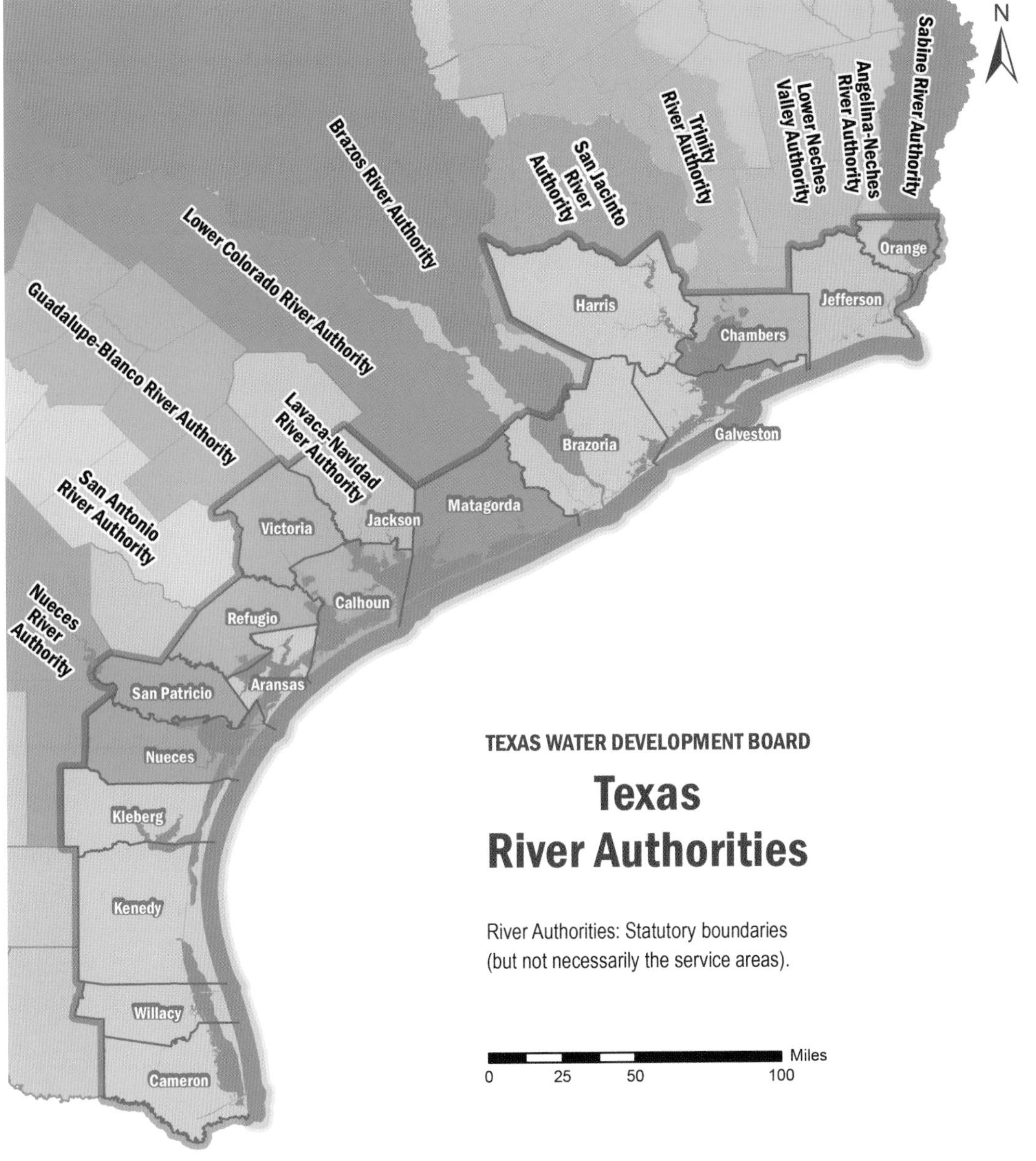

Figure 3.2. In Texas, river authorities are synonymous with water supply development and delivery, but they are also useful for other functions such as wastewater treatment, flood control, and recreation.

out the Texas coast, and it has several freshwater subaquifers, most notably the shallower Chicot and the deeper Evangeline. Our coastal aquifers are sloped from west to east and obtain their water from rain falling on permeable sandy areas called "outcrops" or recharge zones, which are usually at least one county inland from the coast. Rainwater falls on the recharge zone, moves underground, and flows toward the coast. "Safe" groundwater production is limited by the rate of recharge of the aquifer (the rate of flow into the aquifer), the potential for

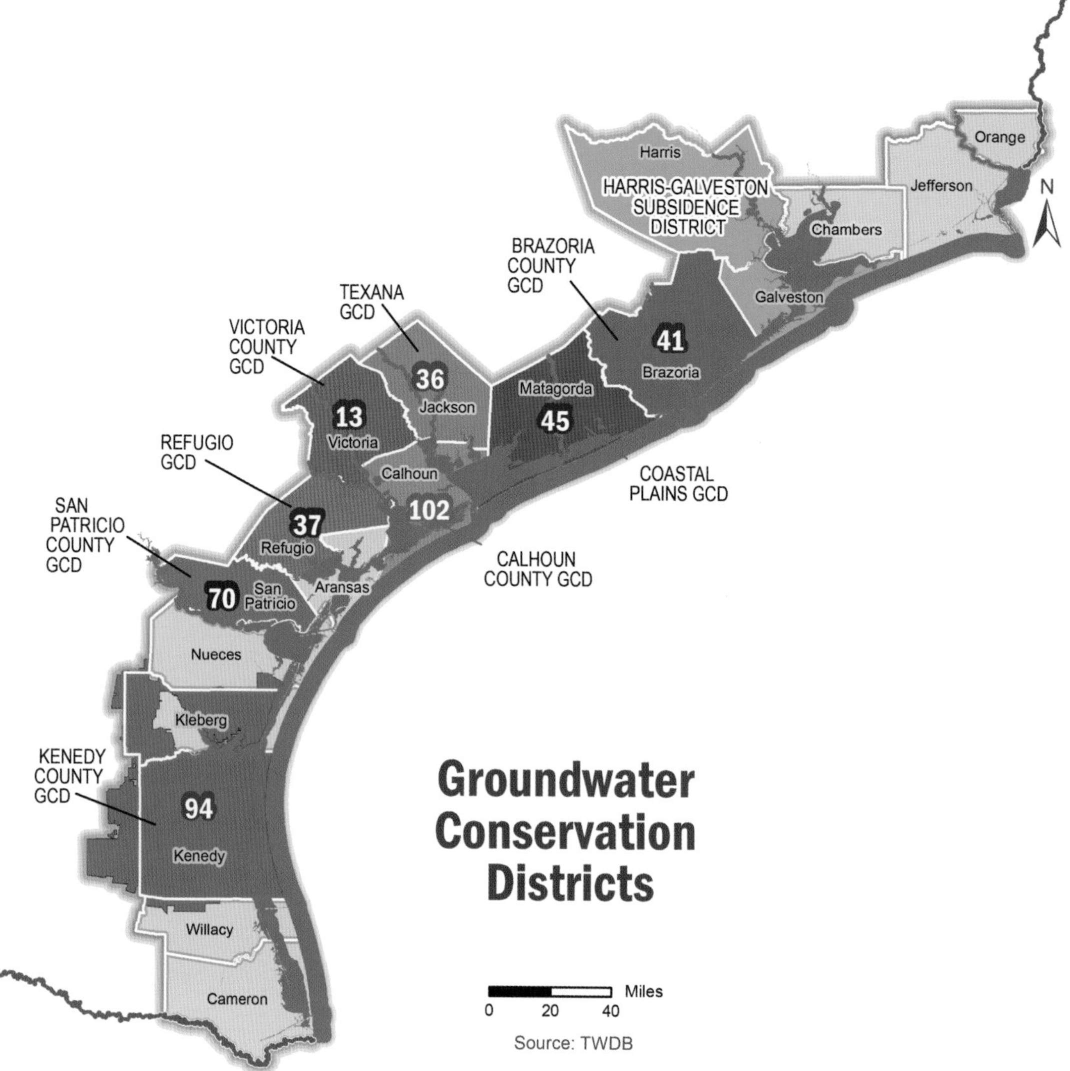

Figure 3.3. Groundwater conservation districts are extremely important in the effort to understand and fairly allocate groundwater, a task complicated by poor or nonexistent funding and the Texas Supreme Court *Day* decision that made groundwater the private property of the surface owner.

land surface subsidence, and the potential to bring saltwater in from beneath the Gulf of Mexico.

Groundwater regulation has been complicated by the Texas Supreme Court *Day* decision because denial of a groundwater development permit can now lead to a suit by the landowner alleging an illegal taking of private property (the groundwater), in violation of state and federal constitutional safeguards. This property-rights aspect of groundwater makes its use and development very different from that of surface water, which is owned and allocated at the discretion of the state through the TCEQ.

Together, surface water and groundwater management systems create a water-use pattern along the Texas coast. Both the rivers and groundwater aquifers feed a system of irrigation and municipal water canals and pipelines that extend throughout the coastal zone, bringing water to cropland, cities, and industry. The various water distribution systems of the coast are shown in figure 3.4.

Some of these systems deserve special attention. Much of

Figure 3.4. The Texas coast has an extensive water distribution system, with major interbasin water transfers from the Colorado and Lavaca-Navidad River basins to Corpus Christi and from the Trinity River basin to the Houston-Galveston area.

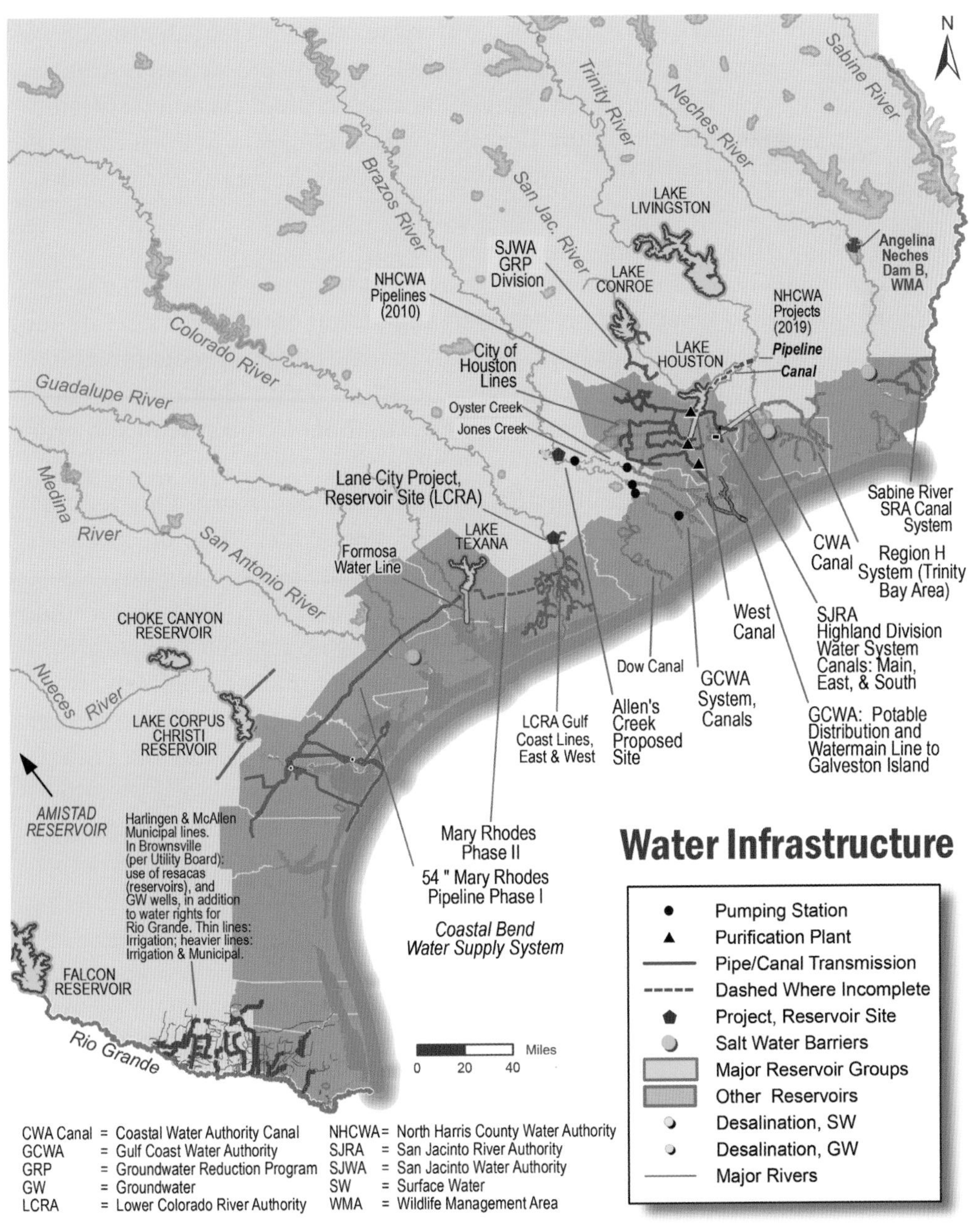

the water for the Houston-Galveston area now comes through interbasin transfers of water stored in Lake Livingston on the Trinity River directly through the canals of the Coastal Water Authority into the east side of Houston, with supplemental amounts from the Brazos River. Another conveyance from the Trinity River to Lake Houston, called the Luce Bayou diversion, is now under development. Corpus Christi receives much of its water from the Mary Rhodes pipeline, which brings water from Lake Texana in the Navidad River watershed and is being extended to collect water from the Colorado River based on a very shrewd purchase of water rights by the City of Corpus Christi. Major irrigation systems are shown in Chambers County (from the Trinity River), Brazoria and Galveston Counties (from the Brazos River), Matagorda County (from the Colorado River), and Cameron County (from the Rio Grande).

Water Planning

The various water systems shown in figure 3.4 have been developed and proposed by individual entities working under the purview of regional planning authorities created by the Texas legislature. These regional planning entities evaluate the projected needs and compare them to the supplies in order to develop a regional water plan that identifies concepts and projects to provide any additional needed water. This regional plan then becomes part of the Texas Water Plan, the key document that guides the allocation of funds for water development within the state of Texas. If a water project is not in the Texas Water Plan, it will not be eligible for state assistance or permitting. As such, these regional plans are extremely important in guiding future water development. The regional water-planning entities with jurisdiction over the Texas coast, Regions I, H, K, P, L, N, and M, are shown in figure 3.5. The regional planning agency compiles a list of proposed projects to meet projected water shortfalls. Inclusion on the list does not guarantee funding or construction; however, if a project is not on the list, it likely will never be built. One thing to note in the geography of these water-planning entities is that they are larger than the coastal area and can, as in the case of regions K and L, contain major noncoastal metropolitan areas (Austin and San Antonio, respectively) that may dominate the water supply needs picture.

Water planning in Texas can be criticized on many levels. Perhaps most importantly, these regional planning efforts are

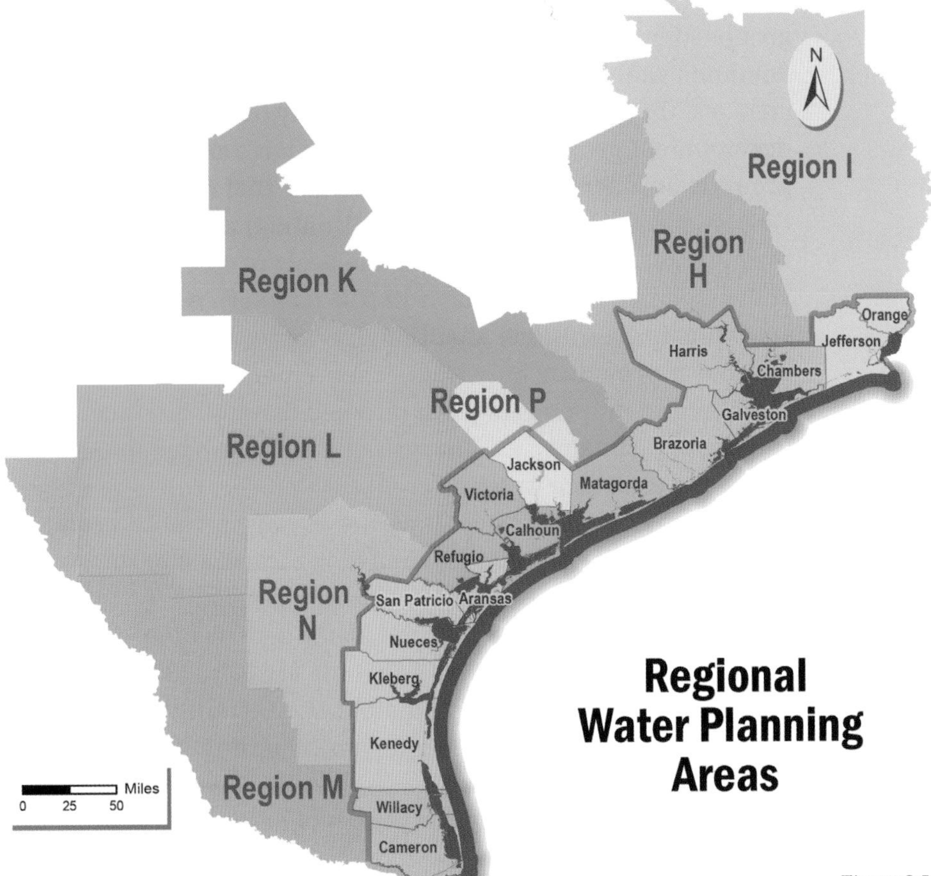

Figure 3.5. Water planning in Texas is done by regional water planning entities and then combined by the Texas Water Development Board into the Texas Water Plan.

often dominated by civil engineering firms that are proponents of large-scale water development projects, both surface and groundwater. Typically, these projects involve constructing reservoirs and pipelines to pump surface water tens if not hundreds of miles to the users as well as developing groundwater fields and pipelines. Because the state of Texas does not charge for the use of its surface water, surface-water development is very cheap and seriously undervalued. Many concepts, such as conservation, often do not get full consideration because we seek to meet a projected demand rather than take action to shape demand. Important concepts such as pricing strategies do not seem to be considered at all. In many respects, market concepts could be very helpful in addressing major water-supply issues, particularly in the context of securing freshwater inflows for bays and estuaries, the most important single issue for the future of the Texas coast.

As a general proposition, each of these regional planning

groups identifies future water demands and evaluates these demands against existing supplies. Then, to address any deficiencies, they generally propose an array of water-development projects that typically include reservoirs and groundwater development. To the extent that other alternatives such as reverse osmosis (desalination) are considered, they are generally dismissed on the basis of cost (an issue addressed in more detail later in this chapter). And while conservation is given some attention, it is generally considered capable of providing only smaller increments of water rather than the larger amounts often pursued through engineering solutions. Ultimately, we always seem to come back to developing more surface water or groundwater, regardless of the impacts and consequences. If we are to have a viable, ecologically productive estuarine system along the coast of the future, that mindset and those practices must change.

Figure 3.6 shows the projected water deficits identified in these various regional plans. For some areas, the shortfall is huge, not necessarily immediately, but certainly by 2060. These deficits are expressed in terms of acre-feet needed but not available by current accounting, with an acre-foot being enough water to cover one acre one foot deep, or 325,851 gallons. Of particular note is Harris County, with a projected shortfall of over 450,000 acre-feet, and Brazoria County, with a shortfall of almost 300,000 acre-feet. Respectively, these areas rely on the Trinity and the San Jacinto (Harris), and the Brazos (Brazoria), three river systems with no more to give. Similarly, Cameron County, at almost 200,000 acre-feet of overdraft, and Matagorda, at about 150,000, round out the top four counties. Interestingly, Nueces County has a deficiency of only 50,000 acre-feet, but its supply was enhanced by the water trade that allowed it to pull water south from the Colorado, a trade that hurt Matagorda Bay because there used to be substantial return flow from agricultural use of that water. Today, that water is totally removed from the watershed, as is the water Houston is receiving from the Trinity River, although some of the Trinity water may make it back into the Galveston Bay system through wastewater discharge by the city of Houston and industrial users.

Freshwater Inflow

Freshwater inflow for the Texas coast is an absolute necessity based on the ecological reality that estuaries are ecosystems formed by the joining of freshwater and saltwater. Estuaries are hybrid systems—neither salty nor fresh—that are among the most productive ecological systems on Earth. University of Texas law professor Corwin Johnson wrote in the late 1960s of the need to evaluate bay and estuarine inflow needs and create water rights for our bays and estuaries. In the late 1970s and early 1980s, the Texas Water Development Board and the Texas Parks and Wildlife Department created early computer models describing the circulation, salinity, and inflow patterns for various bays and estuaries, establishing the minimum inflow needed to maintain bay productivity.

Although the need for freshwater inflow to maintain estuarine systems like Sabine Lake and Galveston, Matagorda, San Antonio, Aransas-Copano, and Nueces-Corpus Bays has long been understood and established, water rights for estuarine

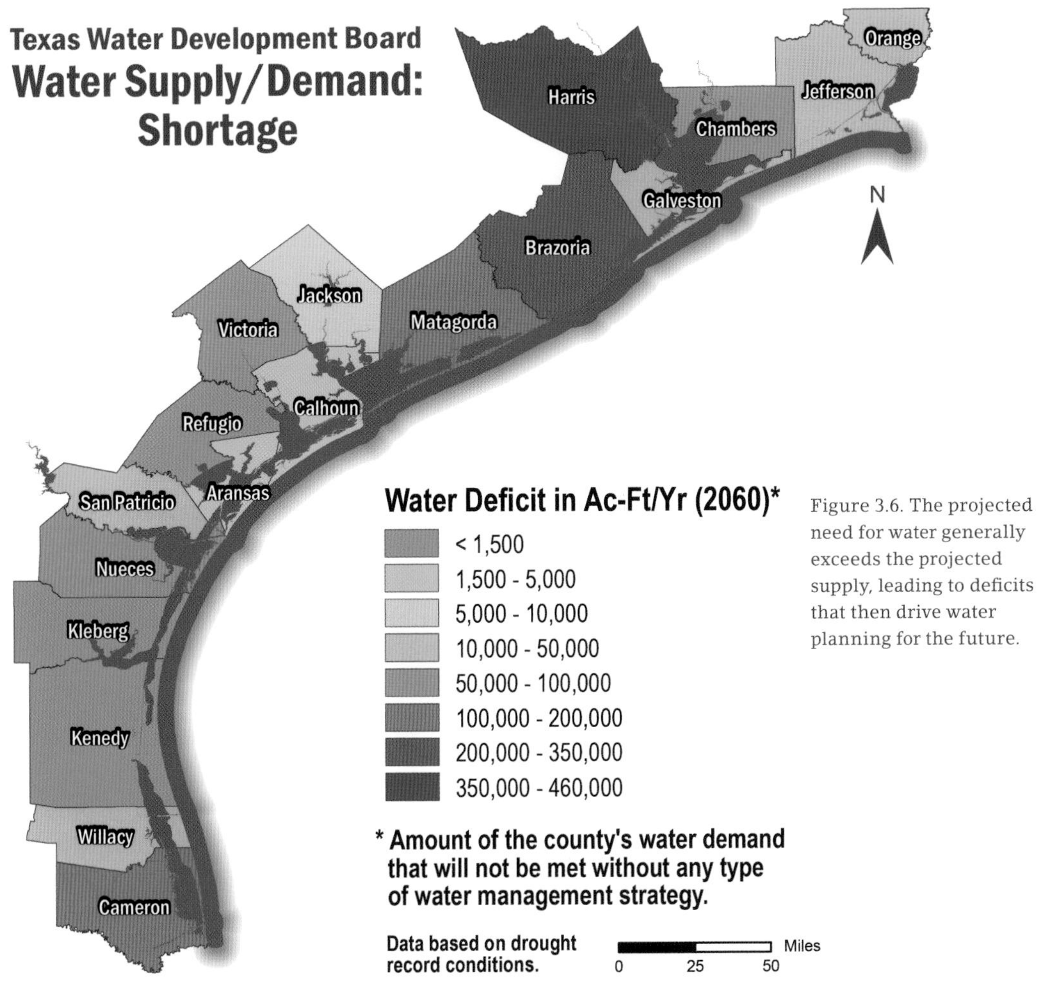

Figure 3.6. The projected need for water generally exceeds the projected supply, leading to deficits that then drive water planning for the future.

inflows are almost nonexistent. A settlement agreement on a water supply permit for the City of Houston obtained 300,000 acre-feet for Galveston Bay, and one provision of a Colorado River water rights permit provides for the maintenance of a salinity level within Matagorda Bay of twenty-five parts per thousand if that permit is used, a requirement that in theory necessitates some inflow from water covered by that permit during certain years. Otherwise, the bays have no water rights, and this is the biggest single problem facing the Texas coast in the future.

It is difficult to make absolute statements about freshwater inflow because there are many ways to look at the issue and many factors that come into play. What we know is that Nueces Bay has been ecologically killed. Here, information from the water availability model (WAM) used by the TCEQ can be useful. Based on historical data, the WAM can predict what inflows would be like under natural conditions by simply adding back the water removed under permits as reported to the TCEQ. This results in a so-called natural flow. Also, one can run the model such that all permits issued by the TCEQ are fully utilized according to their terms and conditions, the so-called full-use model run.

I asked Joe Trungale, an expert computer modeler, to undertake some computer runs to help me understand the difference between the full-use and natural conditions models for various bays. For example, in Nueces Bay, the natural-flow model shows that the bay gets inflow 95 percent of the time over the decades and is naturally near zero only about 5 percent of the time. With the full-use model, the inflow drops to zero about 35 percent of the time. This pattern led to the ecological destruction of Nueces Bay.

Similar analyses of the other bay systems yield an interesting pattern. In all estuaries, the natural flow is significantly reduced with the use of all permits, as one would expect. Stated simply, all river flows are substantially reduced by permitted withdrawals during times of drought, but some river basins are much more heavily impacted (or overdrafted) than others. Trinity Bay appears to be headed for major problems, with inflow dropping to near zero about 50 percent of the time in the future, a truly frightening projection. This is surprising because the sizable Trinity River watershed receives large amounts of rainfall.

Down the coast, the Colorado also looks to be in bad shape,

with zero to low flows occurring about 35 percent of the time with full permit use, offering the potential of a fate similar to that of Nueces Bay unless the dams on the Colorado are managed to protect Matagorda Bay. On the other hand, the Guadalupe looks a bit more promising, with zero to no flows showing up only about 5 percent of the time, reflecting the major role of spring flows from San Marcos and New Braunfels (e.g., the Edwards Aquifer) during times of drought in keeping water in the river, and the bay.

Estimates have been made about the need for freshwater inflow based on studies from the mid-1990s. These inflow studies indicated that Trinity Bay/Galveston Bay needed about 5.4 million acre-feet per year to optimize productivity, while San Antonio Bay needed about 1.2 million acre-feet per year. These studies were based on inflow circulation models and fisheries data indicating which species thrived in which salinity ranges. These early efforts were criticized as simplistic in that they made inflow estimates on a yearly basis rather than seasonally or monthly, but for many years they were the best we had. And they may prove, in the long term, to be more useful than the politically crafted solutions ensuing under Senate Bill 3, as discussed below.

The Senate Bill 3 (SB3) Process

The Texas legislature passed SB3 in 2007 to establish a process for providing freshwater inflow for Texas bays. Both water development and conservation/environmental forces joined the effort to pass SB3, which was initially applauded as a potential breakthrough concept, an early hope that has not been realized.

The SB3 process comprises three key steps: (1) the Basin and Bay Expert Science Team (BBEST) study and report, (2) the Basin and Bay Area Stakeholders Committee (BBASC) study and report, and (3) the Texas Commission on Environmental Quality (TCEQ) final action. The BBEST is charged with evaluating inflow and estuarine health from a strictly scientific standpoint and with making inflow recommendations from that basis. The BBASC brings various interests together to work through other water needs and provide a recommendation that is grounded in both ecological and economic considerations. And third, the TCEQ issues proposed rules for inflow and establishes final targeted amounts for the various bay and estuary systems.

Some of the BBEST studies have been powerful and solid. The Nueces Bay BBEST indicated that Nueces Bay was in "unsound ecological condition" and identified two reservoirs—Lake Corpus Christi and Choke Canyon—as the cause. Other BBEST efforts have struggled to develop relatively simple recommendations, choosing instead to suggest complicated formulations that are difficult to understand and implement. Nonetheless, BBEST studies have been completed for all bays and estuaries on the coast.

The responsibility of the BBASC was to integrate economic and social issues into the BBEST inflow recommendations, which were supposedly based strictly on science as opposed to economics or politics. Generally speaking, the recommendations of the BBEST were reduced by the BBASC for virtually every bay system on the coast, a result that was in keeping with the structure of the legislation. The third step involved the TCEQ formally adopting a target goal for inflow for each of the affected bay systems. Here, even more political inputs occurred, often further reducing the values.

There is no easy way to summarize these results. The science itself is not easy. However, this difficult scientific work was made virtually impossible when economic and political considerations were combined with the scientific investigation. To further confuse the issue, SB3 applies only to new permits that are issued after the adoption of the rules. SB3 inflow requirements do not apply to any water rights currently issued by the TCEQ, so that the full-use scenarios discussed above are not affected by SB3 inflow requirements.

In short, I do not believe that the coast has benefited or will benefit from the excellent work done by the scientists because the structure of SB3 is flawed. I was never impressed with it, and my fears have been realized. The bottom line is that if we are going to obtain adequate inflow for the coast, we are going to have to achieve it without the assistance of the SB3 process. The tragedy is that a lot of people spent a lot of time thinking that this was a beneficial effort.

A Market-Based Potential Solution

In order to change the status quo regarding freshwater inflow for bays and estuaries, a different approach seems necessary, and it is here that the market system may be able to come to the rescue of the Texas coast. At this point, no charge is assessed for surface water withdrawn from the rivers of the state. However, when this water is taken out of the river systems above certain levels, the productivity of the bays is reduced. This reduced production translates into millions of dollars of lost shrimp, crab, and oyster revenue and also translates into thousands of person-hours of recreational fishing being lost, not to mention the guides that have no clients, the rental units that are not rented, the fishing tackle sales that are lost, and the restaurants that must find alternative, nonlocal food sources. If we can talk about water in monetary terms, we may have a chance to develop an alternative approach to allocating it.

The fact is that the surface water we Texans use is *not* "free." There are costs associated with removing water from a river or lake. Our science is clear—cause and effect exists between lowered inflow and lowered finfish and shellfish production in our bays and estuaries, as shown by the demise of Nueces Bay. Even though we know that harm is caused to estuaries from our current and proposed water management practices, Texas does not quantify that loss, much less charge the cost of this resultant harm to the water user. This can and should be done.

In 1997, Robert Costanza and a group of environmental economists published a paper titled "The Value of the World's Ecosystem Services and Natural Capital," wherein dollar values were set for various ecosystems on the Texas coast, including estuaries, wetlands, algal flats, and submerged seagrass. This group of economists placed a dollar value on natural functions such as waste treatment, nutrient cycling, recreation, food production, and habitat usage. These recognized natural functions had not been valued from a dollar standpoint up to that time. These economists estimated values that ranged from about $11,000 per acre per year for estuaries to about $5,500 per acre per year for marshes.

Dr. Costanza's work does not directly translate to the Texas coast because we Texans tend to require practical rather than theoretical examples. On the other hand, no one disputes that there are current economic values being "harvested" from San Antonio Bay, not to mention Aransas and Espiritu Santo. For example, in *The Book of Texas Bays*, the San Antonio Bay shrimp fishery was determined to be worth about $30 million a year, the crab fishery about $1 million, oysters on the half shell about $17 million, and recreational fishing about $6 million (based on 500,000 person-hours at $12 per hour). Collectively, these marketable services generated about $55 million a year, a number that does not include indirect economic values.

The Texas Water Development Board, the Texas Commission on Environmental Quality, and the Texas Parks and Wildlife Department have worked together over decades to produce excellent computer models such as the Texas Circulation and Salinity Model (TxBLEND), which quantifies the relationship between freshwater inflow and changes in bay salinity. These agencies have also developed models that link inflow to natural productivity, such as the Texas Estuarine Mathematical Programming Model (TxEMP). These peer-reviewed, published models are the best we have at this time.

Using the TxEMP model for illustrative purposes produces some interesting results. If one assumes that water in the Guadalupe and San Antonio Basins were managed to provide inflow of 1.15 million acre-feet (the inflow value that TPWD staff determined to be the target value to fulfill the biological needs of the Guadalupe Estuary System), and if a water supply project were to remove 100,000 acre-feet from that 1.15 million through diversion or impoundment, the bay inflow would fall to about 1.05 million acre-feet. According to TxEMP, the difference in natural productivity for brown and white shrimp, crabs, and oysters between what would be produced by the inflow recommended by the TPWD and the inflow after a new diversion is about 14 percent. This does not include the myriad other species found in San Antonio Bay.

If one assumes that this reduction from the optimum occurred in about one out of every three years (i.e., drought occurred once every three years), a 14 percent decline in the reported values for those identified species would result in a projected loss of $130 million in natural productivity over the fifty-year life of the proposed water project. This dollar loss in coastal productivity can then be allocated to each gallon of "new" water created by the hypothetical 100,000-acre-foot project. In the above example, the TxEMP coastal impact analysis results in an impact cost increment of $1,300 per acre-foot. This cost should be added to the projected cost per acre-foot of water production from the new project (which was estimated to be about $800), leading to a net cost of over $6 per thousand gallons. For comparison, it is estimated that the cost of desalination will soon be about $6 per thousand gallons, a cost that is clearly competitive if the "full cost" of that surface water is calculated and charged, a full cost that does not include indirect economic impacts such as rentals, tackle sales, and so forth as computed above.

This example is just that—an example. It is intended to show what can and should be done to guide future water planning. There is no doubt that we can kill a bay by depriving it of freshwater. There is also no doubt that we can develop tools to predict the incremental costs of these harms. It might take a couple of million dollars per bay system to create fully defensible models, but it can be done. The difficult issue is whether sufficient commitment exists to get the price right and send the proper market message to water consumers.

Full-cost pricing of water—pricing based on its actual value—would alter the world of water use and water wastage. We would begin to correctly value the resources we have, and we could make reasoned choices to select among various alternatives, many of which cause little or no ecological damage. But if we do not value the ecosystem, then we also send a message—a message that sends the wrong signal to water consumers.

Over time, we need to harmonize our human consumption of water with the natural hydrologic system to provide water for the bays as well as for humans. Full-cost pricing of water is one idea that might improve our water system. And, as will be discussed in other chapters, there are many others. What is clear is that the current water system is the system of an empty world. We should all remember and recognize that we are no longer living in that empty world.

PART 2

Risks and Hazards of the Texas Coast

CHAPTER 4

Hurricanes and Flooding

With water supply we are concerned about droughts—about too little water. But too much water is terrifying as well and much more immediate in its effect. A drought causes plants, the economy, and humans to slowly wither and perhaps die; a flood is quick and devastating, immediate and harsh. Floods are also natural phenomena, and the natural world has evolved to survive these events. Not so the human world.

Nothing brings home the problems of settlement patterns in the full world more than the impending arrival of a severe weather event like a hurricane, bringing with it the threat of annihilation of low-lying homes and industry. And this conflict between full-world development patterns and severe storms will only get worse, as proven by the experiences with, and lessons learned from, Hurricane Ike and what we know about our changing climate.

I remember Hurricane Ike in 2008 very well. The television weather folks were excited during the second week of September. A storm had formed in the Atlantic several days before and had been steadily moving west, each day's progress mapped and projected, pathways foreseen, warnings issued. From the outset, Hurricane Ike was projected to enter the Gulf, and true to the prediction, it failed to spin north into the Atlantic as hurricanes often do. We all watched, we all waited.

By Tuesday, Ike had cleared Cuba and was heading west, a bad situation for the Texas coast. Projections showed it could hit anywhere from the Valley to the Golden Triangle, but the Texas coast was the sole possessor of the cone of projection. A big one is heading our way. So—what do we do? Do we evacuate? Or do we "hunker down," as Harris County judge Ed Emmett advises us?

Evacuation seemed a poor alternative after the horrible result of the evacuation prior to Hurricane Rita, a storm that came about a month after Katrina destroyed much of New Orleans. No one wanted to stay in Houston for Rita with the Katrina debacle in mind. Luckily for the Texas coast, Rita,

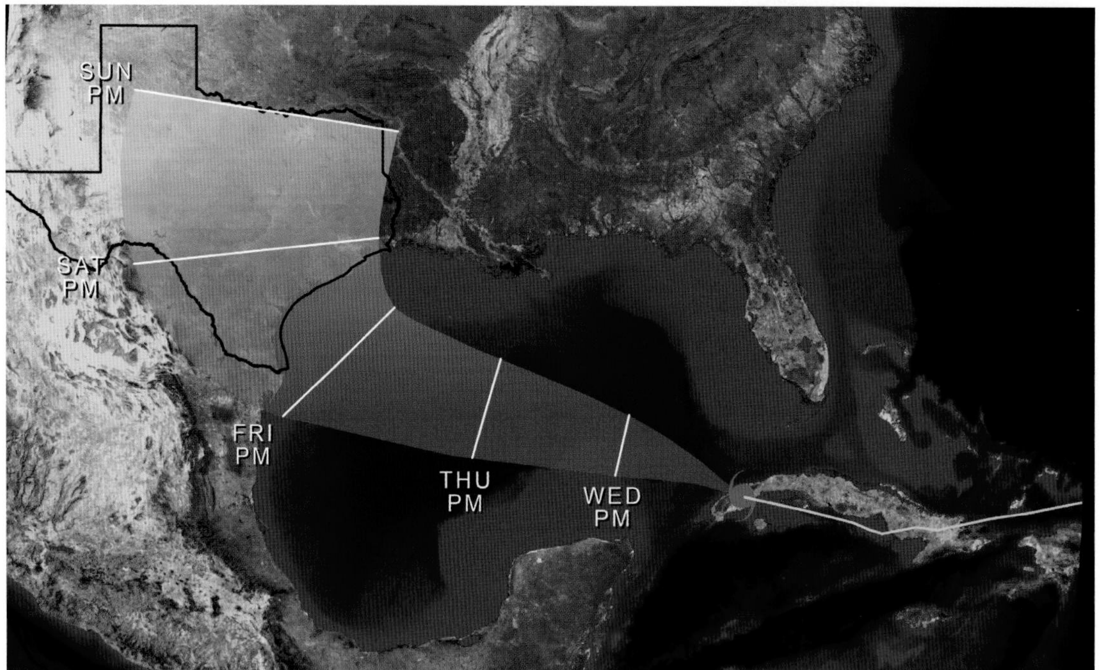

Figure 4.1. Projected path of Hurricane Ike four days before landfall showing the "cone of uncertainty" in the point of landfall. Source: NOAA and NASA, Goddard Space Flight Center, Bryan Carlile, Beck Geodex.

a large category 3 storm at landfall, curved to the east and pounded southwest Louisiana as well as the Golden Triangle area of far southeast Texas. However, over one hundred people died in the Rita evacuation, and stories are legion about those trying to leave who were caught for ten to twenty hours in traffic jams—no gas, no water, no food. So now with Ike, what to do?

In the Houston-Galveston area, evacuation zones were identified in which people were urged if not required by the local government to leave based on the strength of the storm. These zones were based on the Saffir-Simpson scale, which assigns categories based on wind speed. Ike had a surge larger than would have been indicated by its wind speed, a point I will return to later in this chapter. The evacuation zones for Houston and other areas of the coast are shown in figure 4.2, although please note that all of these zones are not expressed in the same way in all areas, which is both confusing and perplexing. With something as serious as evacuation, one might think that the state of Texas would have uniform provisions, but not so.

The home where my wife and I live is not in an evacuation zone, so we decided to stay. With canned goods, water, batteries,

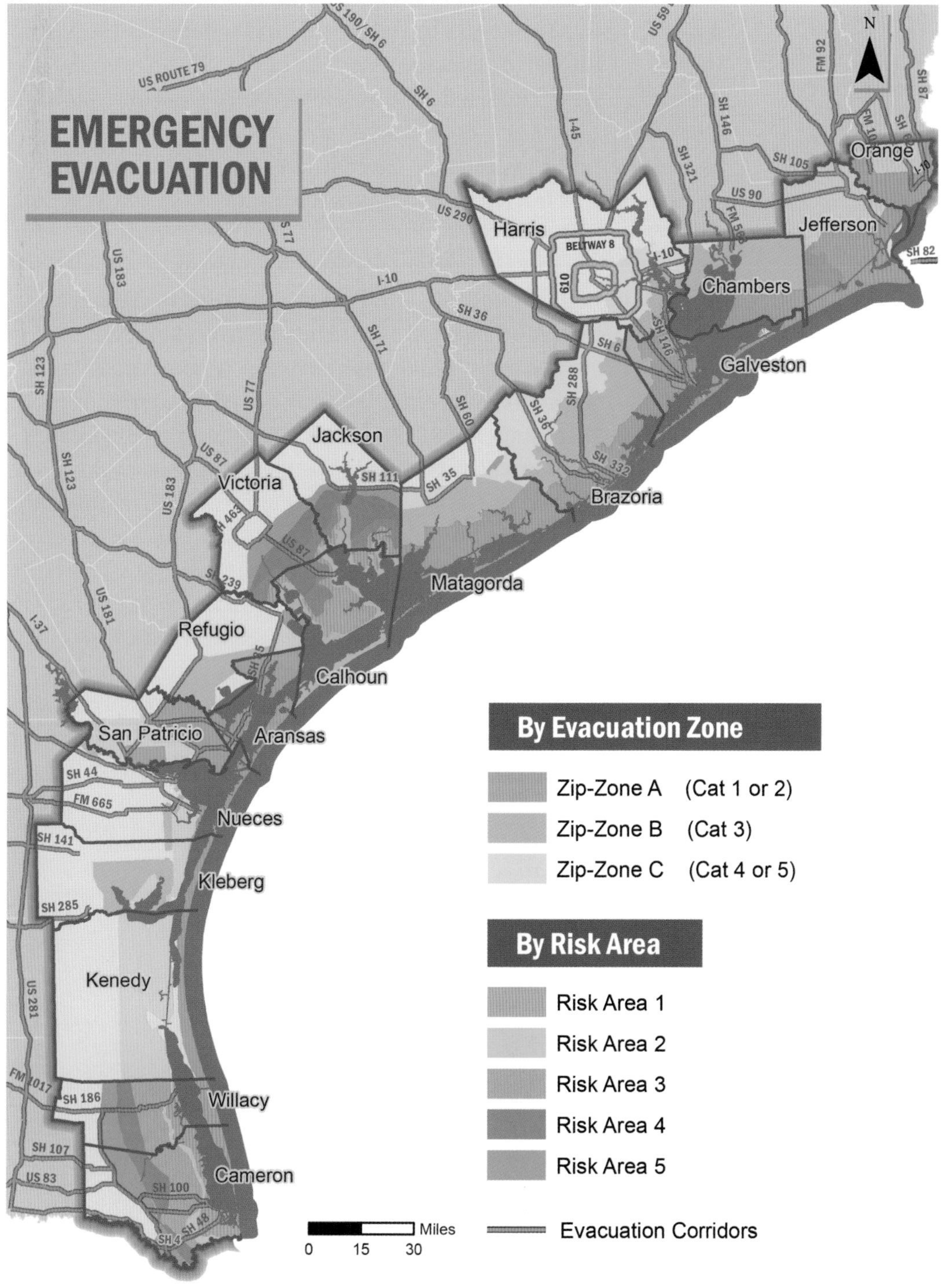

Figure 4.2. Various zones along the Texas coast have different schemes for evacuation, some based on risk areas and some based on zip codes. The bottom line is that residents in the colored areas are at a much higher risk than those living outside the colored zones with respect to hurricane surge and wind damage. The preferred evacuation corridors are also shown.

a radio, a small mattress in the closet, and a nervous cat, we waited for the storm to come. A check of the NOAA website Thursday night revealed that surge levels up the Houston Ship Channel were projected to reach beyond twenty feet, a height never attained in Galveston Bay for the surge flooding that is an aspect of hurricanes, along with high winds and heavy rain.

We awakened Friday morning to televised reports of flooding throughout the middle and upper Texas coast. A forerunner surge formed in front of Ike, bringing five to six feet of high tide into the coast almost twenty-four hours before landfall, flooding the marshes and low-lying areas, moving over coastal highways such as SH 87 on Bolivar and the Bluewater Highway from Galveston to Surfside. Beach houses at Surfside, the west end of Galveston Island, and the Bolivar Peninsula were surrounded by water while stressed and animated television news crews rushed from one emergency to another.

I cannot remember a surge like this in advance of a hurricane. We watched television as the waves broke and the spray rose above the seawall in Galveston. A young woman interviewed on a Houston television channel said she tried to evacuate Thursday night, only to have car trouble. Still in Galveston, she woke up Friday morning and walked down to the

Figure 4.3. Forerunner wave flooding on Friday morning, September 12, 2008, at Surfside. This forerunner wave was about five feet high and flooded much of the upper Texas coast at least eighteen to twenty-four hours before landfall. Photo by Reuters/Carlos Barria.

seawall to gawk at the waves, as did numerous other Galvestonians, all of whom agreed that they had never seen anything like those waves. When the reporter asked the woman for her response to this sight, all she could do was exclaim "Holy shit," summing up the morning eloquently.

In Galveston, Friday morning was the beginning of several days of misery. The seawall, built after the Hurricane of 1900 demolished most of Galveston, protected the beach side of the city from a Gulf surge to a height of about seventeen feet. This Friday morning, however, the threat was from the back side, not the front. The overall water elevation of Galveston Bay increased with the forerunner surge, flooding the drainage system and low-lying areas along Offats Bayou and Harborside Drive, pushing water into the streets and buildings in many parts of the city before noon, a situation that only worsened as the storm moved through.

All day Friday we watched as the storm approached and the danger increased. If you hadn't left Bolivar and the west end of Galveston Island by midmorning Friday, you were not getting out by car, as the roads were impassable by noon and landfall was still fourteen hours away. The bands of rain came into Houston during the afternoon and the more serious squall lines moved ashore. As night fell, it looked like the storm would move a bit farther north than was thought on Thursday. If that happened, perhaps the Houston area would be spared the worst of the storm.

Throughout the night, the storm howled. The eye came ashore at about two in the morning, almost coming up the Houston Ship Channel. The "dirty" side of the storm, with the highest surge and the most rain, was east of Houston, slamming the Bolivar Peninsula and Chambers and Jefferson Counties. The city of Galveston suffered significant flooding damage as water rose to twelve or thirteen feet as the storm came ashore. While most of mainland Galveston County and southeastern Harris County did better than expected, significant surge damage occurred in Bacliff, Shoreacres, La Porte, Seabrook, Kemah, and San Leon. However, the bulk of the Houston region was spared the worst, another bullet ducked.

Over the weekend, the damage toll mounted. Most of the housing on the Bolivar Peninsula was damaged to some extent, and much of it was simply missing, ripped from its foundations and tossed across East Bay. Debris was piled up across northern Chambers County, including human bodies mixed with the roofs, shingles, and timbers from what used to be. Shocking stories of survival emerged. A tiger was found wandering free about the peninsula. Newscasters trying to cover the story came ashore like Marines into areas where they were not welcome, areas the National Guard had taken over to maintain order and prevent looting.

The next week the true horror of the surge became clearer. Bolivar near Rollover Pass was devastated, as was much of the area around Crystal Beach. Oak Island in Chambers County was hit hard. Galveston lost much of its housing stock in the main part of the city, although the west end homes generally made it through because of elevated floor slabs and stronger construction, and also because the bulk of the surge went farther east. Reports started coming in from farther east, places like Bridge City and Orange in the Golden Triangle near the Louisiana border, where the surge pushed up into Sabine Lake, inundating the Invista chemical facility, which stayed shut down for months. And then there was the confusion and anger from residents who had fled and were trying to return to assess the damage. They were either not allowed back in or faced difficulties returning after the storm. Of course there were also the problems of people trying to live after losing their home, a major issue for many residents of Galveston and other north-facing, low-lying areas along Galveston Bay.

The final tally from Hurricane Ike was large, with over one hundred people killed and $24 billion in estimated damages, making it the fourth most expensive in US history after Katrina, Sandy, and Andrew. But there are two aspects of Ike that portend bad news for the future of the greater Houston area. First, Ike was only category 2 when it came ashore and it certainly could have had higher winds and a higher surge. Second, Ike came ashore at Bolivar Roads, the pass between Bolivar and Galveston, meaning that the worst of Ike's surge and wind was east of the greater Houston region. If Ike had come ashore at San Luis Pass at the south end of Galveston Island as forecast Thursday evening, the death toll could easily have exceeded one thousand people, the damage toll would have approached $100 billion, and oil and chemical products from the Houston Ship Channel industrial complex would likely have spread across Galveston Bay, essentially ruining its fishery and ecology.

Shortly after Ike, the Severe Storm Prevention, Education, and Evacuation from Disasters (SSPEED) Center at Rice University (of which I am codirector) received the first of two major grants from the Houston Endowment, a philanthropic foundation, to study lessons learned from Hurricane Ike and to evaluate various alternatives for protecting the Houston region in the future. The SSPEED Center assembled a team of researchers to address various issues including developing sophisticated computer models to evaluate various-sized storms and various storm paths. The results of this research are fascinating, suggesting both worst-case scenarios and solutions for not only the Houston-Galveston region but also for other areas of the coast.

Computer modeling is a key aspect of this work, and the modeling team is led by Dr. Clint Dawson and Dr. Jennifer Proft of the University of Texas Computational Hydraulics Group; Dr. Phil Bedient, director of the SSPEED Center at Rice; and Larry Dunbar, our project manager at the SSPEED Center. It is amazing what can be done with computer modeling these days. The model takes a hurricane from its beginning point and charts its progress across the Atlantic or Caribbean and into the Gulf to landfall, predicting various physical aspects of the storm including the height and extent of the surge. Our team developed a modified version of the

Figure 4.4. Classic image of the home standing alone on Bolivar near Rollover Pass. This portion of the Bolivar Peninsula was populated with houses prior to the landfall of Ike. Photo by Bryan Carlile.

model that cuts the time required on the University of Texas supercomputer from several hours to less than two, which still represents a significant amount of time on a very big and very fast machine.

This computer capability has led to the identification of what the SSPEED Center considers to be a reasonable worst-case storm for the Houston region, one similar to Ike that comes ashore at San Luis Pass at the southwestern end of Galveston Island (rather than at Bolivar Roads) with a wind speed 15 percent greater than that of Ike, making it a solid category 3. The result of this projected storm is shown in figure 4.5, and the damage it portends is truly horrifying. The shoreline of Galveston Bay, Galveston Island, and Bolivar are shown beneath the colored isobars that demonstrate the height of the surge, which reaches upward of twenty-four feet within the Houston Ship Channel, the oil refining and chemical manufacturing center of the United States. Even though the Texas City area is protected by a levee and Galveston by a seawall, both to about seventeen feet, the surge levels of this modeled storm overtop both. There is certainly some benefit from the Texas City levee, but that is not the case with the seawall when it is faced with these levels of surge along with back-side flooding. Simply stated, we on the Texas coast, and in the Houston-Galveston area, have not seen the worst.

No one really wants to consider what would happen if a storm of this magnitude came ashore such that the ship channel was inundated, as shown in figure 4.5. Over 2,200 petroleum and petrochemical product tanks would be flooded to some extent. At least six refineries and well over a hundred chemical plants would have various levels of water within the facility. The direct economic damage is estimated to be well beyond $50 billion, and there would be national security implications because of the role of the Houston Ship Channel in producing gasoline, diesel, and jet fuel. Studies completed for the SSPEED Center by Dr. Jamie Padgett of Rice University indicate that over 90 million gallons of crude oil and hazardous substances would be released into neighborhoods adjacent to the channel and then into Galveston Bay. Such a spill would likely represent the worst environmental disaster in US history, far surpassing the Exxon Valdez oil spill and possibly the Deepwater Horizon event, and potentially rendering the Galveston Bay system unusable for decades for fishing and recreation.

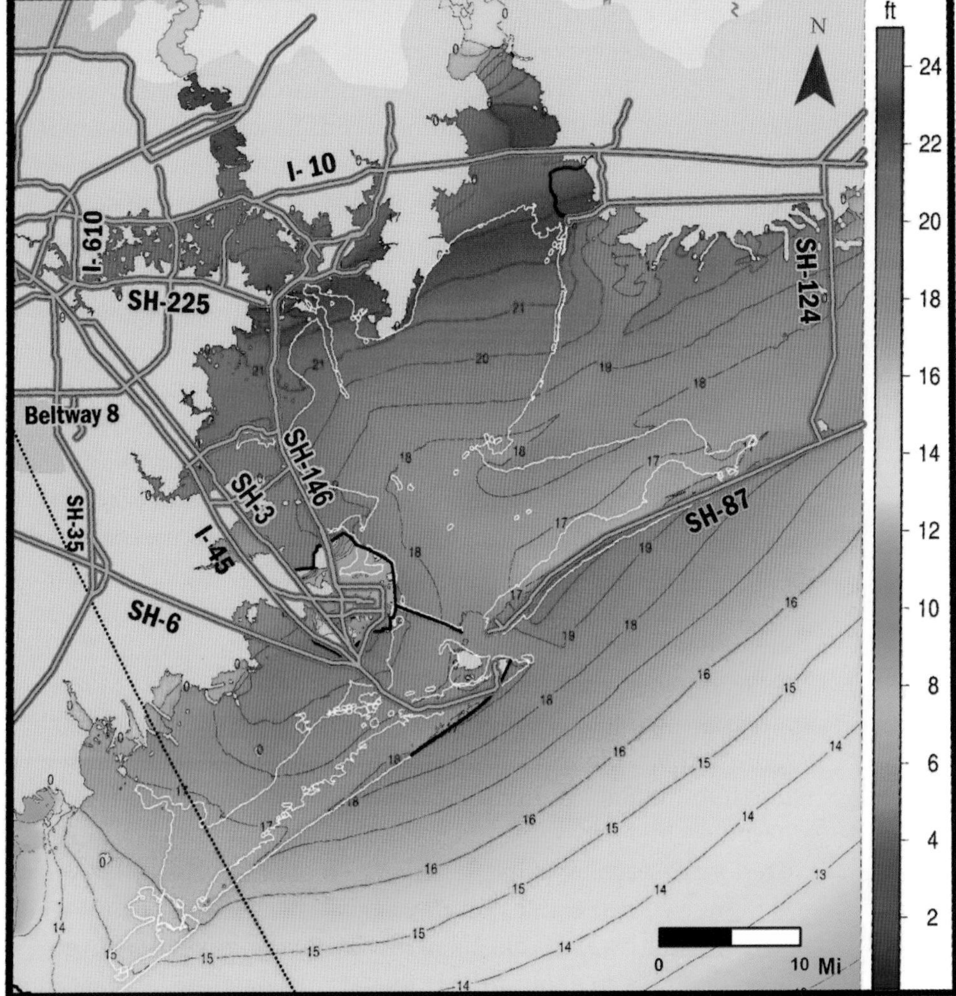

Figure 4.5. A reasonable worst-case hurricane striking the Houston area. This storm coming ashore on the dotted line path would generate a surge in the Houston Ship Channel of almost twenty-five feet, as shown in purple.

Assuming that they evacuated, over two hundred thousand people in southeastern Harris County and eastern Galveston County would return to homes damaged to various degrees by the flooding and winds. Most of these homes would not be suitable for occupancy without major repairs, and many would be destroyed beyond repair. Many people who did not evacuate would likely perish. The storm would rip up the first row of housing all along the bay shore and toss the debris against the homes behind it, creating a moving wall of destruction. If the evacuation rate were no better than it was during Ike, it is certainly conceivable that several thousand people could die.

The Houston-Galveston area is not the only area on the coast that is subject to these major storms. Storms have crisscrossed the Texas coast for centuries. They are part of the reality of the coast, as is the destruction they bring.

Indianola, a major port on Matagorda Bay, was abandoned after being destroyed by a hurricane in 1876 and another in 1886, a fate shared by the Port of Copano, a former key port facility near the current community of Bayside on Copano Bay that was abandoned by 1888 after being hit by several hurricanes. Galveston was struck a deadly blow by the great Hurricane of 1900 and by another in 1915, and while the city leaders built the seawall and filled much of Galveston behind it, the city lost its place as the premier Texas port and has never returned to its former glory. The paths of the hurricanes from the last hundred or so years are shown in figure 4.6.

As this figure shows, more hurricanes seem to hit from Matagorda Bay northward to the Sabine River than south of Matagorda Bay. This is important because the upper coast has a much larger outer continental shelf, which increases the size of the surge. Through the SSPEED Center, I met Hal Landrum, whose PhD dissertation at Louisiana State University on historic hurricanes hitting the Gulf Coast of the United States yielded some interesting results. All of the Gulf Coast is vulnerable to large storm surges, but some areas are much more vulnerable than others. The area from Matagorda Bay north to the Sabine River is very vulnerable to high surge based on historical records; Dr. Landrum found that a hundred-year storm approaches twenty feet at the coastline and is higher within Galveston Bay as well as within Lavaca Bay. Moving southward from Espiritu Santo, the expected surge level declines to about fifteen feet at the coastline, at least in part because of the smaller continental shelf encountered farther south along the Texas coast.

Based on Dr. Landrum's analysis, a map of the coastal high-risk zones can be prepared, using the twenty-foot contour from Matagorda Bay northward and the fifteen-foot contour from Espiritu Santo southward. Such a map is shown in figure 4.7. Together, these two areas encompass over 3.3 million high-risk acres, representing about 34 percent of our coastal zone.

The surge zones described above may or may not be incorporated into formal floodplain maps, which have been more focused on riverine flooding than hurricane surge flooding, at least until recently. Riverine flooding is quite different from surge flooding, which is really restricted to hurricanes. Most of the time, rivers are restricted to the cut bank and the bed, which were formed over geologic time by the constant flow of water. However, there is an area adjacent to the river that

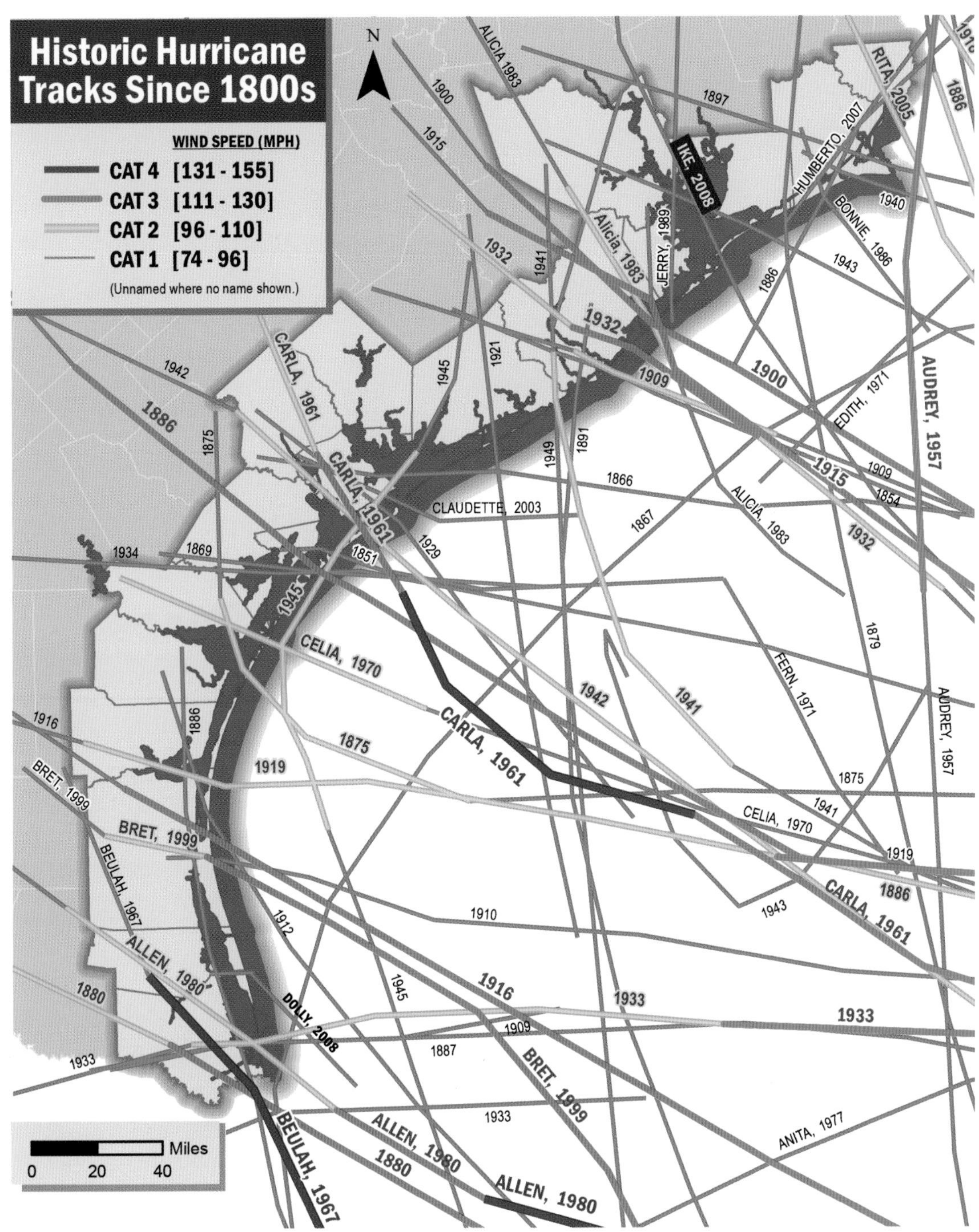

Figure 4.6. The Texas coast has been crisscrossed by many storms in the past, including the Hurricane of 1900, which destroyed Galveston; Hurricane Celia, which hammered the midcoast in 1961; and Hurricane Ike, which was "only" a category 2 storm at landfall and caused about $25 billion in damages, making it the fourth worst in US history. Note that the color of the storm path changes with the wind speed.

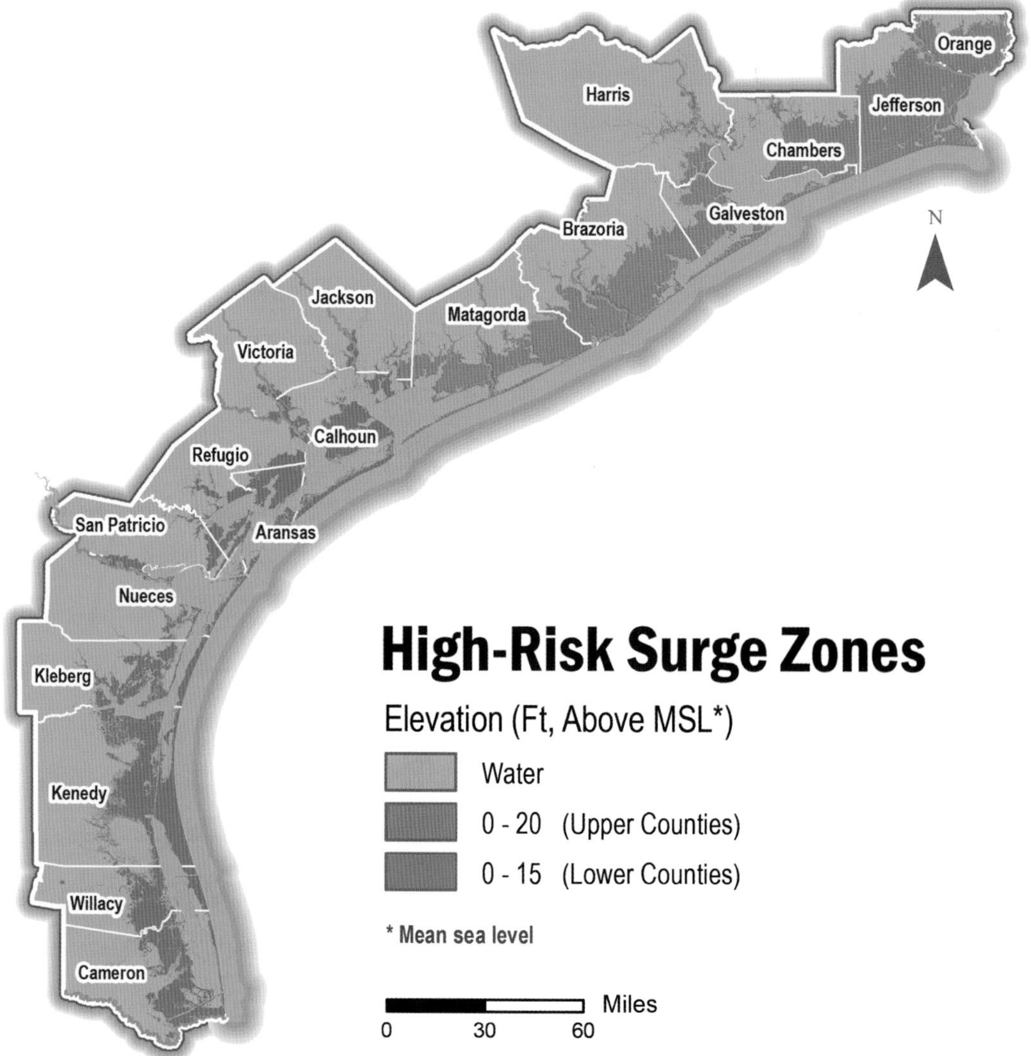

Figure 4.7. High-risk surge zones based on twenty-foot contours on the upper coast and fifteen-foot contours on the lower coast. The difference in risk is due to the difference in the outer continental shelf as well as differences in historical patterns, based on the work of Dr. Hal Landrum.

becomes occupied by water following one or a series of larger storm events. These so-called floodplains are often labeled by the recurrence interval of the storm generating the flood, such as fifty-year, hundred-year, and even five-hundred-year floodplains. And while human property law draws hard boundaries, nature does not. The river simply expands to take as much space as is needed for the amount of water flowing past a particular point.

When I first started researching flooding and floodplains on the Texas coast in 1975, there was almost no data available except for special reports prepared by the Corps of Engineers. However, in 1973, Congress had passed the federal

Flood Disaster Protection Act, which required flood insurance for all federally guaranteed loans, of which there were many. In order to qualify their residents to purchase flood insurance, local communities had to join the federal flood insurance program. As part of this program, local communities were required to pass certain regulations that were based on floodplain maps developed by the Federal Emergency Management Agency (FEMA), specifically maps based on the hundred-year floodplain.

Today, most counties, towns, and cities along the Texas coast participate in the subsidized federal flood insurance program because flooding is a major problem. Our citizens need access to this insurance program in order to protect their property because private policies are very expensive if they are available at all. However, it should be noted that residents are not automatically enrolled in the flood insurance program. Community eligibility means only that the citizens of that community may purchase flood insurance, not that they are automatically covered. If the community has joined the program, then today a comprehensive map of the hundred-year floodplain as set by FEMA exists. The hundred-year floodplain is the area that would be flooded by the runoff from a rain event having a recurrence interval of once every one hundred years. The size of this rainfall event varies from area to area and is established through statistical analyses of past rainfall patterns. Then, hydrologists use sophisticated computer models to predict what area would be inundated by the runoff from the hundred-year rain. A composite map of the FEMA hundred-year floodplains for the Texas coast is shown in figure 4.8.

Most Texas counties have substantial areas that would be inundated by the projected hundred-year flood. Together, these floodplains make up about 37 percent of the Texas coast, covering almost 5,800 square miles, or about 3.7 million acres. Research from the SSPEED Center indicates that there is likely a larger area subject to the hundred-year hurricane surge than is shown on these FEMA maps. Or stated another way, although there is overlap, figures 4.7 and 4.8 are not the same. When the floodplain is overlaid with the twenty- and fifteen-foot contour map, the total high-risk zone within the coastal counties rises to over 4.49 million acres, representing 45 percent of the land area of coastal counties, as shown in figure 4.9.

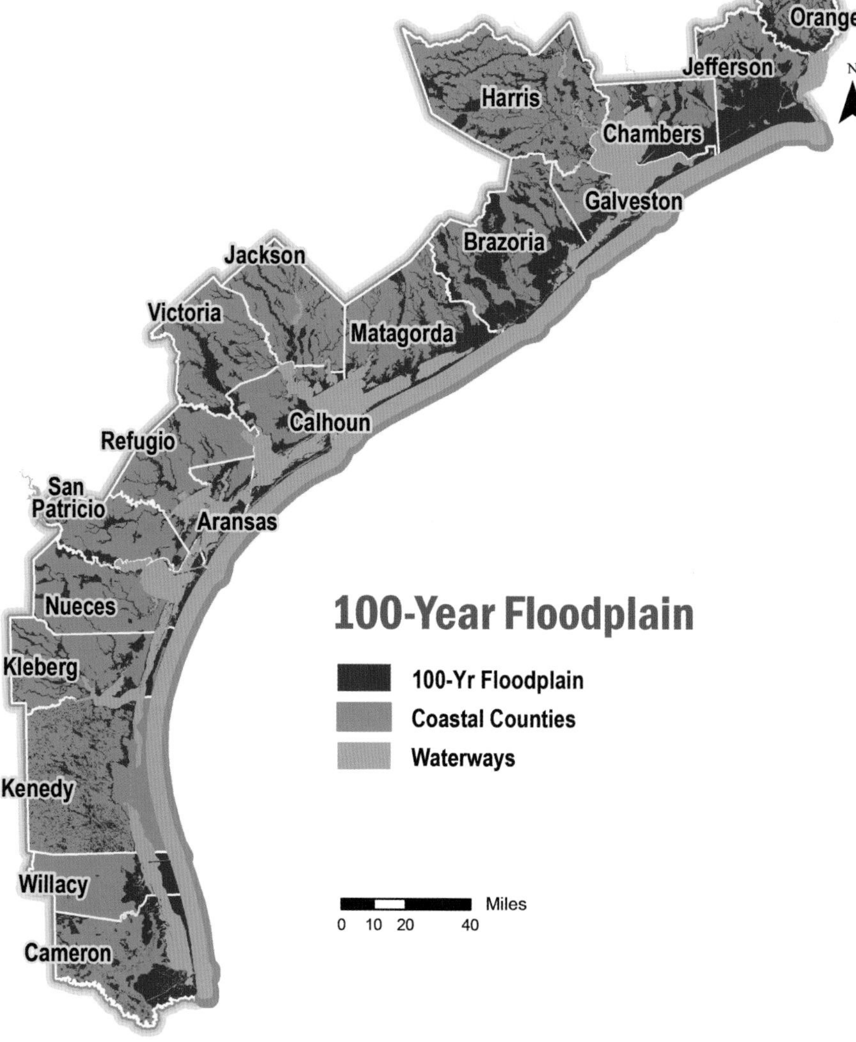

Figure 4.8. Official FEMA hundred-year floodplains show a significant portion of the Texas coast subject to riverine or coastal flooding.

There is no doubt that these FEMA floodplains represent high-risk areas for human habitation. Interestingly, these areas are also very important from an ecological standpoint. Most of these floodplains are populated by wet and dry riparian forests and various types of wetlands that offer a variety of trees and other vegetation as well as habitat and corridors for wildlife. They are both water and wildlife travel zones.

So, much like water, hurricane surge zones and floodplains represent both green and gray infrastructure. They are both corridors and drains. However, most of these areas are private property and could be developed assuming floodplain regulations were met where they apply. They might more appropriately be labeled as red or dangerous for infrastructure, a truth that we fail to tell often enough or even at all. Figure 4.9 shows hazard areas merged together with existing developed lands as well as the lands set aside for wildlife and/or recreation. Note the overlap between these wildlife lands and the floodplain/high risk lands. That is no accident. These set-asides are beneficial for fish and wildlife as well as for humans.

Protection Strategies

As an environmentalist, I have very mixed feelings about structural flood solutions. Many structural solutions have led to great structural disasters, such as the failure of the levee during Hurricane Katrina, which flooded much of New Orleans. People tend to think they are safe within a levee, only to find out they were wrong, and in a lot of trouble at that moment of realization. On the other hand, there are several hurricane protection levees along the Texas coast such as those at Port Arthur, Texas City, Freeport, and Matagorda, as

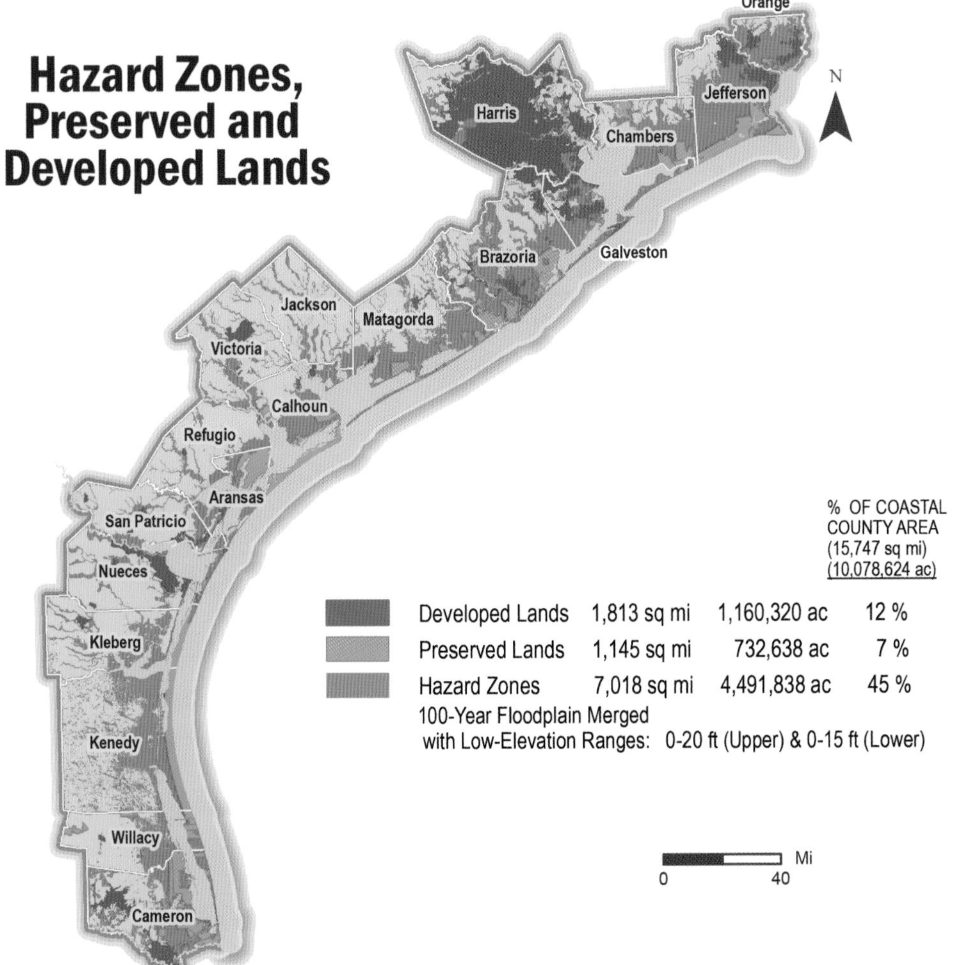

Figure 4.9. Many areas of the Texas coast are subject to a high risk of flooding, either from surge or riverine flooding. The lands that have been preserved by various entities are also shown, indicating the overlap of high-quality habitat with these flood-prone areas.

well as the seawall in Galveston. These systems have worked well so far, but they have never been challenged by a direct hit from a major hurricane.

I was not prepared, however, for what we have learned at the SSPEED Center from studying these storms. One revelation came from an evaluation of the impact of a projected hurricane such as Ike with 15 percent higher winds making landfall around San Luis Pass, as shown in figure 4.5. As mentioned, Dr. Padgett estimated that up to 90 million gallons of oil and hazardous substances could be released if some storage tanks along the Houston Ship Channel were lifted from their foundations or crushed by the surge. During Katrina, Murphy Oil had a similar situation arise when an oil storage tank was lifted off its foundation, releasing almost one million gallons of crude and causing significant damage to an adjacent neighborhood.

We all need to pause and seriously consider what a spill of this magnitude means. The Exxon Valdez spill was about ten to twelve million gallons of crude. The BP Deepwater Horizon spill was about two hundred million gallons. This projected Houston Ship Channel spill would fall squarely between these two events, but it would spill into the Galveston Bay system, not open water. Galveston Bay, one of the most productive estuaries in the United States, would be destroyed for decades. The ecological harm would be massive, as would the economic damage and the human toll on communities adjacent to the channel. In short, it would be a disaster that is almost impossible to imagine, yet this scenario is very real and may become even more likely as sea level rises and hurricanes become more severe due to climate change (see chapter 5). In fact, future scenarios in Galveston Bay that take into account sea level rise and stronger hurricanes due to higher ocean temperatures indicate that a surge of thirty to thirty-four feet is reasonably foreseeable fifty years from now, well within the lifetime of solutions being discussed today.

Because of this horrific future scenario, I have become willing to seriously consider the construction of massive storm surge barriers to protect the industries on the Houston Ship Channel, the Bayport industrial complex, and Texas City as well as the many people living around Galveston Bay. These developments are definitely in harm's way. The sooner we recognize this reality and develop a plan to address it, the better for all. I make this statement fully realizing that there would certainly be ecological consequences from constructing hurricane surge abatement structures in or adjacent to Galveston Bay. This is one of the few situations I have encountered in my career in which the environmental consequences of doing nothing are likely far greater than the impacts of constructing various alternatives.

Our work at the SSPEED Center involved not only understanding the risk of hurricane surge for the Galveston Bay region but also evaluating various ways to solve this problem. When we began, Dr. William Merrell at Texas A&M University–Galveston had already proposed the Ike Dike, an approximately eighty-mile-long levee and gate system that would run down the length of the Bolivar Peninsula and Galveston Island, cross Bolivar Roads (the pass separating Galveston Bay from the Gulf of Mexico), and potentially cross San Luis Pass at the southern end of Galveston Island. Initially, the SSPEED Center work was seen as an alternative to Dr. Merrell's Ike Dike, and potentially in conflict with it. However, Dr. Merrell's team and the SSPEED Center team agreed in 2014 to exchange information and try to work together.

Any hurricane protection structure placed within Galveston Bay will require a navigation gate that can close the Houston Ship Channel before the hurricane comes ashore. A similar gate—the Maeslant Barrier—exists at Rotterdam in the Netherlands, and it is a large and incredibly impressive engineering accomplishment. Our work has revealed three possible locations for such a barrier—at Bolivar Roads, at a midbay location between Smith Point and Eagle Point, and at Baytown near the Fred Hartman Bridge on SH 146. At Bolivar Roads, the navigation gate would need to be accompanied by an eleven-thousand-foot environmental gate to attempt to reduce environmental damage to Galveston Bay, and levees would need to be extended down the Bolivar Peninsula and Galveston Island. The midbay gate structure would require the construction of a levee system along the Houston Ship Channel, which could be used for the disposal of dredge material as well. The upper bay gate structure would also need levees to connect to the high ground adjacent to the channel. In all three cases, the city of Galveston would need to be protected by a back-side levee. The Maeslant Barrier and the Eastern Scheldt environmental gate, both in the Netherlands, are shown in figures 4.10 and 4.11.

These three alternative structures are very different in

terms of cost and benefits. The upper and midbay solutions have been estimated to cost about $3 billion, whereas the lower bay (Ike Dike) solution is estimated at about $8–10 billion. On the other hand, the upper bay gate does not protect the Bayport industrial complex or the residential areas between Texas City and the Houston Ship Channel. The midbay solution protects all of these areas, as does the lower bay, Ike Dike solution. Of the three, the upper bay alternative likely generates the least environmental impact, the midbay alternative has the next greater impact, and the lower bay solution potentially has the most serious impact. Figure 4.12 shows the location of the area protected by the midbay solution.

Although a $3 billion alternative such as the midbay alternative could be constructed with local bond funds, there is no doubt that a project such as the Ike Dike would likely require federal funding to cover the $8–10 billion projected cost unless the state of Texas became serious about building and funding it. The need for federal funding raises a dilemma for local authorities. Most of these coastal politicians are anti–big gov-

Figure 4.10. The Maeslant Barrier across the Port of Rotterdam navigation canal is shown here in the closed position. Most of the time, a barrier such as this would be open and pulled to the side. It is difficult to understand how large this structure is from this photograph because much of the gate is underwater, where it reaches down to the bottom of the navigation channel, about fifty feet.

Figure 4.11. The barrier across the Eastern Scheldt in the Netherlands—a so-called environmental gate—has openings to allow the tide to flow in and out of the estuary. If a gate is placed across Bolivar Roads in Galveston Bay, it will need to allow the tidal flow through the pass. The extent of the openings will determine the extent of the environmental impact of such a structure.

ernment and anti–federal government. However, with a problem as difficult to solve as surge flood damage, federal money may prove to be a necessary evil, at least to their minds. Along with federal money comes any number of federal requirements, including new criteria controlling project design that emphasize climate change and sea level rise, ecological services, and solutions for reducing nonstructural flood damage. Such solutions emphasize protection by strategies such as buy-outs, open-space reserves, building regulations, and other forms of intervention that do not involve constructing levees, gates, or other structures. Examples of nonstructural alternatives can be found in chapter 6 with the Texas Coastal Exchange and in chapter 7 with the Lone Star Coastal National Recreation Area. This promises to be an interesting next phase.

A more troubling issue is raised by industry's apparent nonchalance about this hurricane surge flooding problem. Throughout several years of spirited discussions, industry leaders have been very quiet. They are worried about being asked to pay for many of these improvements, although they certainly would benefit from them. On the other hand, per-

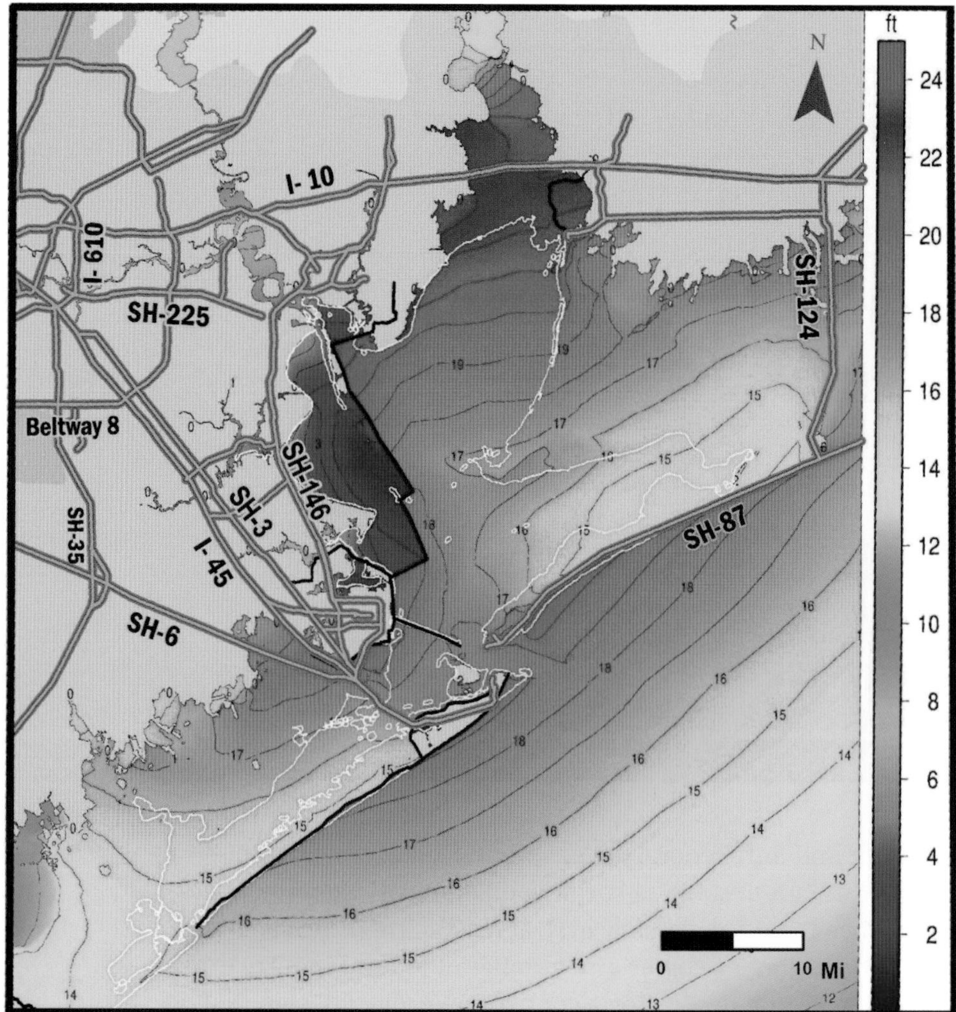

Figure 4.12. The area protected by the midbay solution developed by the SSPEED Center at Rice University, including the ring dike around Galveston, is shown with respect to a projected storm like Ike but with 15 percent greater wind speed coming ashore at the worst place for surge in the region near San Luis Pass.

haps not enough attention has been focused on the incredible liability that would result from multiple spills of oil and hazardous substances that would almost certainly kill Galveston Bay. BP found out that liability was more expensive than precaution. That unfortunate reality may be in the future of the Houston Ship Channel petrochemical industry, because a twenty-five-foot surge is reasonable and foreseeable, potentially eliminating a key defense to liability for negligence. And the industry attitude certainly seems cavalier if not negligent.

On the other hand, no one has ever seen a storm surge of the magnitude projected by the computer models. Computer modelers such as those at the SSPEED Center are projecting events based on near misses and larger storms that have occurred elsewhere along the Gulf Coast and that are reasonably foreseeable in our region over a period of time. Former mayor of Houston Annise Parker once said that the hardest thing one could ask a politician is to spend money on a project that would not be completed during their term in office. The same can be said for a plant manager, or a corporate executive. It is analogous to the so-called tragedy of the commons. We know the dangers we are facing, yet we can rationalize a course of action that ultimately destroys the commons, and in this case our industries, our homes, and our bay.

The problems on the remainder of the coast do not seem as bad as those in the Houston area in several respects. No other area has so many people living at low elevations. Industrial development at Port Arthur and Freeport is already protected by existing levee systems, leaving the upper Sabine-Neches Waterway (including Orange), the Port of Point Comfort, the Port of Corpus Christi, and the Port of Brownsville as well as development at Chocolate Bayou as the major exposed areas. And while these are substantial areas, they are relatively small geographically and can be protected with ring levees and dikes, if these are determined to be economically feasible.

Development on barrier islands such as South Padre, the North Padre Island part of the city of Corpus Christi, Port Aransas, and of course Galveston and the Bolivar Peninsula is vulnerable and very difficult to protect in an economically and ecologically sound manner. One positive is that these homes are required to meet minimum building elevation standards for FEMA flood insurance and have been covered at least to date (2016) by federally subsidized flood insurance. It is also worth noting that large stretches of barrier islands and beaches have been bought and set aside, such as Padre Island National Seashore and the Matagorda Island National Wildlife Refuge, and several other areas, such as Saint Joseph's Island and a portion of the Matagorda Peninsula, are privately owned and basically unreachable by the public.

A set of proposed structural improvements for the Texas coast is shown in figure 4.13. This includes the midbay solution on Galveston Bay, the back-side levee for Galveston, elevated roads on the west end of Galveston Island and Bolivar Peninsula, and a solution proposed by Jefferson and Orange Counties for extending the Port Arthur levee system across the Neches River and along the coastline to protect the Adams Bayou area. These structural projects combined are likely to cost more than $15 billion, and they would likely prevent more than $100 billion in damages.

None of these projects have been evaluated from an environmental impact standpoint. Until that occurs, they should be considered proposed but by no means automatically acceptable. In figure 4.12, the midbay solution is shown as phase 1 of a larger project that could include a gate across Bolivar Roads, and it is inexpensive enough that it could be funded with local bonds. The extension of the Port Arthur levee system has been proposed by the Gulf Coast Community Protection and Recovery District (GCCPRD), and it may not pass muster from either a cost or an environmental standpoint. A ring dike around the industries needing protection may end up being all that occurs east of the Neches River.

It is also important to note that various types of nonstructural alternatives can and should be developed to go with these structural alternatives. As a general proposition, nonstructural alternatives are often associated with land-use control concepts such as zoning. In my experience, additional land-use controls are not going to be acceptable on the Texas coast. However, two economic development concepts for the Texas coast that are set out in this book, the ecological service exchange discussed in chapter 6 and the ecotourism discussed in chapter 7, are compatible with surge flooding and Texas politics. A key concept for the future of the Texas coast is to reconsider what comprises a resilient economy and then to encourage these private-sector responses. As will be shown, these alternatives can and should be pursued.

Another nonstructural alternative worth serious consideration is the continuation of the subsidized federal flood insurance program. The Biggert-Waters Flood Insurance Reform Act of 2012 required that FEMA develop a plan for placing the National Flood Insurance Program on an actuarial basis. Overnight this caused insurance rates on the Texas coast to rise from about $900 a year to over $20,000 a year in some situations. Without flood insurance, home sales will likely drop substantially. It would seem that a continuation of the federal subsidy combined with a buy-out program might be worth considering, at least in the short term. I believe that these subsidies encourage further development in high-risk areas, but a lot of people already live around Galveston Bay in these high-risk zones, and they will need help when the next storm comes. However, everyone involved should clearly recognize that this flood insurance program is not a right but a "relief" program. The federal government is doing us all a favor here, yet we continue to bite the hand that feeds us. Not very smart.

Hurricanes and, to a lesser extent, flooding generally will

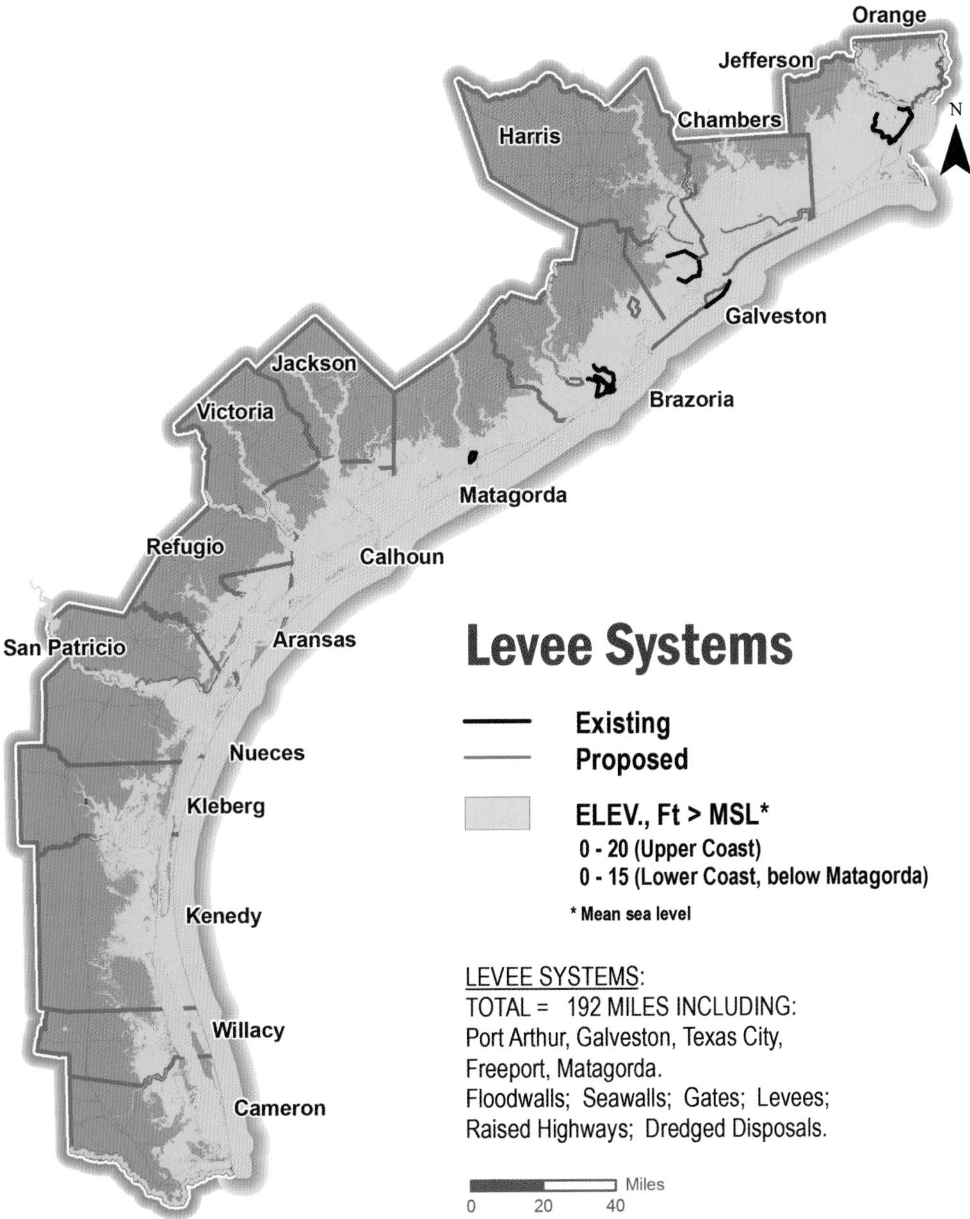

Figure 4.13. Hurricane Surge abatement structures proposed for Galveston Bay. Although I am generally opposed to structural interventions, the risk posed by surge damage to storage tanks and the spills that might result lead me to conclude that structural protection is necessary in the Galveston Bay area if not the Port Arthur–Beaumont–Orange area.

mold the future of the Texas coast. They have in the past and they will in the future. In the development of a conceptual plan for the Texas coast, it seems totally contrary to Texas values to suggest depending on the federal government to solve this problem, yet that seems to be the reality of the current political system. While the rhetoric and animosity fly against the federal government, our collective hands are out. This seems to have been the case for decades, tracing back to the development of our navigation channels and other flood-control projects, and is likely to continue, based on our experience in the

Houston-Galveston area. If a project with a price tag of about $10 billion or more is to be pursued, it will have to be built by the federal government. By contrast, the midbay alternative could be built by local and state bond money.

It is our practice on the Texas coast to use federal money for major infrastructure items, particularly ports, flood solutions, water supply, and road systems, to name four. However, it seems disingenuous to write a book about market systems and self-help and then ask the federal government to take care of us. In fact, the current thinking by some in the Houston-Galveston area is even more Machiavellian than simply asking the feds to bail us out. Many believe that we need to wait to undertake major hurricane protection until the next big storm hits and causes significant damage. At that point, the rest of the country will feel guilt over our horrific damage, and the federal money will come to bail us out in the form of the most expensive plans that are "on the shelf."

That thinking stinks, in my opinion. It reeks of laziness and the absence of leadership. We need to roll up our sleeves and figure out how to finance the midbay or other alternatives. This can be achieved by local or state financing that can be split between industry and the public that will benefit from these structures. It may be possible to use Port of Houston dredging money and/or Texas Department of Transportation road-building money. Those who underwrite bonds will benefit, as will one or more local law firms, as will the construction and engineering community. This is not a purely private-sector alternative, but it certainly includes elements of local entrepreneurship.

A similar option is potentially available to protect Orange County and possibly Jefferson County industry, except that these counties lack the population base to support major bond issues to build levee systems. It may be possible for the state of Texas to provide funding beyond the ability of the local industry to support these bonds. However, the financial challenges for this region are much greater than those in the Houston region, where the problem is absence of leadership.

As a general proposition, there is decent topography along the north shoreline and portions of the west shoreline of Corpus Christi Bay, so little to no levee work is required for these areas. Portions of the Corpus Christi Inner Harbor are a bit lower and may need protection, but these problems pale compared to those faced by the Houston Ship Channel and Bayport industrial areas. Those are the priorities.

Finally, we need to make sure people understand the risk they are accepting when they move into the coastal zone. The state, the community, and the federal government do a poor job of making hurricane and flood-related information available. Our FEMA flood insurance maps have done a poor job of incorporating realistic worst-case surge events into the hundred-year floodplain. If you are moving to the Texas coast from somewhere else (and most of us came from somewhere else), there is not a dependable clearinghouse for good information, particularly about the risk from hurricane surge and whether or not your home is in an evacuation zone. We are a state that believes in the market system rather than regulation, but the market system does not work if there is information of unequal quality between buyer and seller. Without good information, it is truly a buyer-beware system, one where the buyer can certainly wake up to a bad surprise here on the Texas coast.

If nothing else, there is a huge information gap. All regions should have hurricane evacuation zones and plans. All regions should place signs at key intersections indicating the flood level that would result from a category 3, 4, and 5 storm. Such a sign was placed in the Clear Lake area of southeast Harris County and was quickly removed due to complaints from real estate salespeople that the sign made it more difficult to sell property. Well, of course the sign made it more difficult. With good information, people make rational decisions more often than not.

We in Texas are unlikely to ever agree to any form of coastal zoning or strong land-use regulation, although there are certainly areas that should not be developed in the future. I hope that some of the tools mentioned in this book will assist in minimizing the extent of new problems in the future by encouraging flood-resilient economies. However, we do have a major issue in our legacy development. These vulnerable homes and industries need to be protected because it is no longer as simple as Indianola or Copano closing down and disappearing. Given the type of industry that we have on the Texas coast, the stain from a major surge event pounding the Houston Ship Channel, or Orange, or Corpus could easily become an indelible slash across the ecology, and livability, of the Texas coast.

CHAPTER 5

Climate Change

No issue is more contentious in Texas than climate change. It is a huge concern, one that threatens the resilience of coastal industrial and residential development as well as the future of the oil and gas industry. Make no mistake about it—this issue is real and is here to stay. Acknowledging and addressing this problem represents the essence of the transition from empty-world thinking to full-world thinking. It defines the future of humans on an Earth that is full of people and impacts; climate change will affect us all, and solutions to this problem will redefine the economy of the Texas coast.

Ron Sass is the former chair of the Ecology and Evolutionary Biology Department at Rice University and is one of the brightest and most intellectually open and honest people I know. He is a biogeochemist (which means he can speak on many scientific areas) and a bona fide authority on climate change. Over the last fifteen years or so, Ron has become both a professional colleague and a good friend.

Ron got interested in climate change long before most of us had heard of it. As chair of the Ecology Department at Rice, he had been conducting research involving biochemistry and clams and was looking for new challenges. After doing some research and discussing ideas with his peers, Ron decided to look into a relatively new topic called climate change with an emphasis on wetlands and methane emissions. Although carbon dioxide is the gas most often connected with climate change, methane is a very potent but less discussed greenhouse gas, a term that refers to gases that create effects in the Earth's atmosphere similar to those in greenhouses (also called hothouses) used for growing plants.

Over time, Ron reached out to Ralph Cicerone at the National Center for Atmospheric Research and Bob Harris at the National Aeronautics and Space Administration (NASA), who was head of the "Mission to Planet Earth." Through these connections, he became involved in researching methane emissions from wetlands and was also present when a special research group was formed that was associated with a new group called the Intergovernmental Panel on Climate Change (IPCC). As such, Ron became a member of the IPCC, which was formed in 1988 as an international panel of scientists and policy makers assembled by the United Nations Environmental Programme and the World Meteorological Organization.

The IPCC today is one of the most important scientific groups in the world. It is divided into working groups of various types that study and analyze the science and policy issues associated with climate change and publish documents assessing the current state of knowledge about it, including whether or not it is happening (it is) and whether or not we are causing it (we are). Among those who study these issues, there is no doubt and there is no debate except over what to do about it.

Ron has been involved with the IPCC from the outset. He has seen the arguments and counterarguments. He has been in the middle of the climate controversy, within the fray. He has observed his colleagues making mistakes in the manner in which they investigated and discussed this issue. He has seen the science being intentionally manipulated by the "deniers." He has watched with dismay as the media gave equal treatment to both sides of the debate even when the scientific community strongly agreed that the climate was changing and humans were causing it. He has watched the United States and the world struggle with this critical issue. And he remains steadfast in his belief that we should and, more importantly, can take action to address this current situation, one that easily ranks at the top of the world's crisis list for the twenty-first century, a world that includes Texas and the Texas coast.

Texas is a tough place to admit to climate change and to be an advocate for addressing it, particularly the role of humans and hydrocarbon combustion in creating this problem. Many of us rely on hydrocarbons for our livelihoods, particularly in Houston, which is wed to a hydrocarbon economy, and there is concern that to be an advocate for addressing climate change is to be against the oil and gas industry, which is simply not true. Yet within the center of Houston, Ron lives and thrives and even smiles now and then.

Ron is my mentor on climate change, an issue about which many of us know very little for any number of reasons. With Texans, concern about climate change has been growing as "weird weather" events have become more pronounced, particularly large flood events, although many state government officials deny it, at least as of 2016. And few will admit that carbon dioxide emissions or methane emissions or other human-generated pollutants are causing this change. Nonetheless, they are. So first, let's consider that the climate of the Texas coast is changing. What does this mean for those of us interested in the future of the coast?

On several occasions I have asked Ron to come to my class at Rice and discuss climate change. Over the years, his presentation has evolved as our knowledge of this tricky subject and our skill at discussing and presenting it have expanded. One of his presentations involves the bell curve, that famous statistical image of normal distribution. The middle of the bell curve represents the most common events, whether they be average rainfall or average temperature. These repeated events in the middle of the curve are very different from the events depicted by the two edges of the bell curve, which are the much rarer events.

The bell curve is a useful image for conceptualizing our changing climate. Climate change means that our past climate records are no longer reliable for predicting the future. The bell curve is a way of representing information, with the most frequent readings at the center of the bell (the highest point) and the least frequent occurrences at the edges of the curve. The important point is that the climate is changing, and this change is most dramatic at the edges.

According to Ron, the severe events that occur at the edges of the bell curve of weather—the less frequent events—are occurring more frequently as a consequence of climate change. Events that used to occur with a frequency of once every one hundred years are occurring more often than past statistics would suggest. Similarly, five-hundred-year events are also occurring more frequently. In keeping with this trend, events that used to occur once every one thousand or even ten thousand years will become more frequent, which is a very scary prospect. The "weird weather" of the recent past will be more frequent in the future. In other words, the entire bell curve is shifting in the direction of more severe weather events (both storms and droughts).

An excellent speaker once labeled the area at the edge of the bell curve with the letters "TBD." He asked the audience what that meant, and "to be determined" did not work. He then told the audience it meant "there be dragons." In his example, he was discussing data about stocks and bonds and extreme failure "at the edges." With climate, it means extremely serious storm (or drought) events, our climate dragons.

The implications of these changes for the future of the Texas coast are substantial. All projections of the climate future involve some estimation of the rate of carbon dioxide (or its equivalent) emissions. High-emission scenarios assume that emissions of carbon dioxide will continue worldwide without controls or limits, representing a "business as usual" scenario and a worst-case carbon dioxide future.

So, what does this "business as usual" future emission scenario hold for us? First, we will become hotter. According to some of the information Ron has discovered, with this high-emission future, we could be facing from 100 to 120 days a year with temperatures higher than 100 degrees Fahrenheit by the year 2100, compared to the current pattern of fewer than 30 days that exceed 100 degrees. As anyone who has lived through a summer on the Texas coast can attest, more than 100 summer days with heat exceeding 100 degrees would be seriously harsh, but it is only the beginning. And while the year 2100 is used for the projections, temperatures will rise throughout the time from today until then, and beyond.

Rainfall patterns will also change. When we have rain, it may come in larger, more intense (and flood-producing) storms. But perhaps more importantly, the overall trend in some areas of Texas may be a reduction in rainfall as we move forward into the twenty-first century and beyond. Rainfall under high-emission scenarios is projected to decline by as much as 30 percent, meaning that riverine flows during dry times would be substantially less than they are today. Given that the demand (as represented by issued permits for surface water withdrawals) exceeds the supply (as represented by dependable base flow during drier times) today, our riverine water-supply situation will worsen substantially. Stated another way, the dependable water supplied by our surface and possibly groundwater systems must be reconsidered in light of climate change, clearly leading to less water than is currently available and further complicating the water picture set out in chapter 3.

Reduced rainfall and reduced surface water will mean reduced freshwater inflow for our bays and estuaries. Demand for this water will increase and supply will decline. The bays and estuaries currently have few if any water rights. If that situation is not improved over the course of the next decade or so, our bays will be facing a much more dangerous situation in the future with climate change. And that still is not all.

As part of our work at the SSPEED Center at Rice, I asked Ron to take a look at the impact of climate change on hurricanes. It is a fact that hurricanes are fueled by the heat of the Atlantic Ocean, the Caribbean Sea, and the Gulf of Mexico. It is also a fact that the oceans of the world are getting warmer. So it should come as no surprise that Ron has advised us that the size of storms is likely to increase in the future, although he cautions that there is no evidence that the number of storms will increase. Our hurricane of the future will have more heat in the water to fuel the surge, the wind, and the rain, which are likely to exceed their levels in historical storms. That is not good news for residents of the coast. In fact, our storms of the future will become more and more deadly.

And then there is sea level rise. The sea level is rising and all students of the coast know this. It has risen to date, and it will rise more in the future. Current mainstream climate projections indicate that sea level will rise by about two to three feet by the year 2100, a number that has recently been raised to about six feet, a major change in forecasting. Figure 5.1 shows the area along the coast with elevations of three feet and lower in red and from three to six feet in orange. In a very simplistic manner, one can assume a three-foot rise would inundate a bit over 470,000 acres of the Texas coast and would substantially impact wetlands in Brazoria and Matagorda Counties that exist adjacent to the coast. Including the next three feet up to the six-foot elevation would inundate over one million additional acres. Such a rise means that the reach of storms in the year 2100 would extend at least three to six feet higher in elevation than was the case in the past, not counting the fact that hurricane surge might be larger in the future because of climate change, representing at least a two-pronged increase in risk.

On the other hand, another recent analysis, by James Hansen and sixteen coauthors, paints a much scarier future related to sea level rise. Hansen, who for decades was the climate change expert at NASA and who is a national figure known for being outspoken and even aggressive about his predictions, also enjoys a reputation for being right about our climate future. Hansen and his coauthors are concerned about

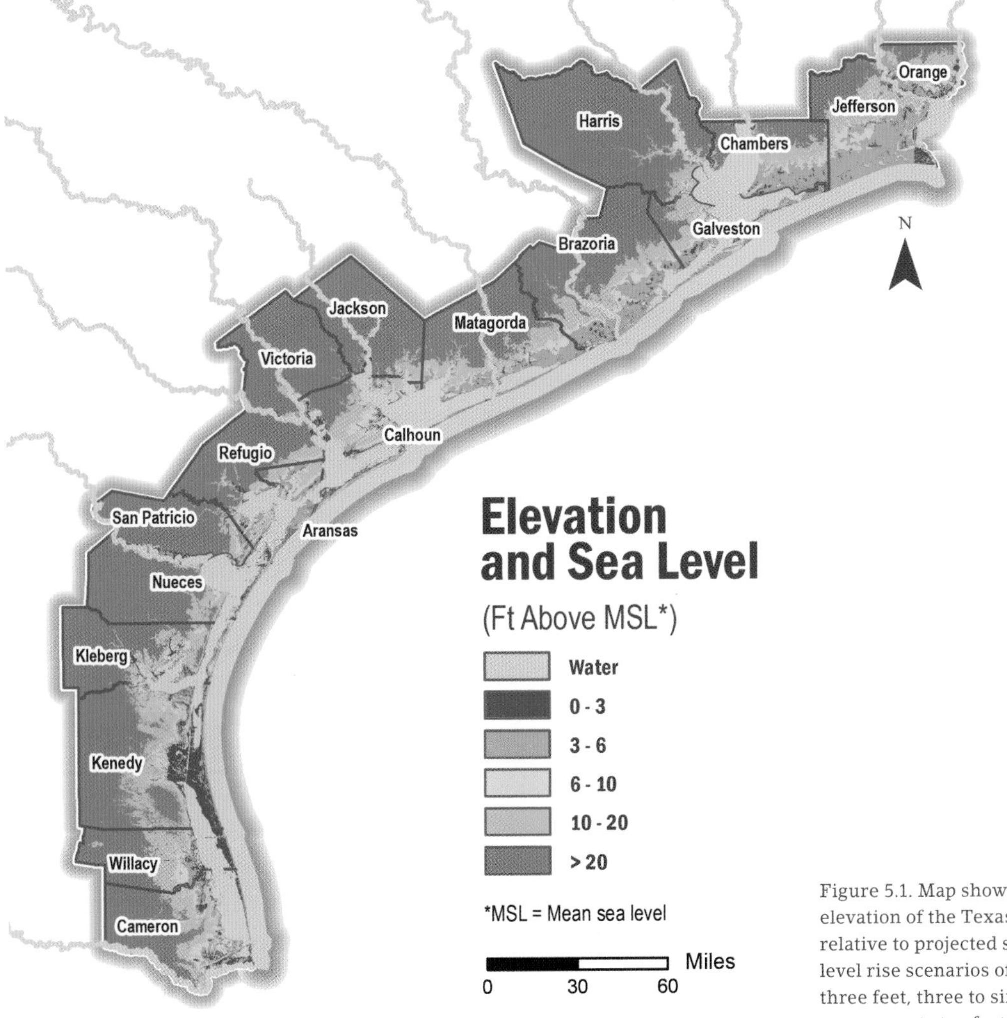

Figure 5.1. Map showing elevation of the Texas coast relative to projected sea level rise scenarios of one to three feet, three to six feet, or even up to ten feet.

the warming of the ocean and its influence on the bottom of the ice in Greenland and in the Antarctic. In both places, large amounts of ice sit atop a base of rocks. If the ice at the bottom of either of these two huge ice blocks were to melt due to the heat of the ocean acting through the rock, and if it were to create a liquid layer throughout the base, then a large ice block could slide into the water. If that were to happen, watch out. Sea level could rise by as much as ten feet very quickly, and Hansen and his coauthors believe that this may happen during this century. Increasing inundation by another four feet to reach the ten-foot elevation adds another 654,000 acres, leading to a cumulative total in excess of 2.1 million acres.

This warming mechanism is only now being understood and offers the prospect of major problems throughout the world as well as on the Texas coast. In figure 5.1, the potential impact of ten feet of sea level rise includes the yellow, orange, and red areas on the map. A rise of this amount would threaten all docks on the Texas coast. It would flood subdivisions adjacent to the coast. It would change the coast as we know it. It is serious, but it is only one of many vectors of change related to our future climate.

Climate change demands attention—attention that the United States and Texas have refused to pay so far. Climate change is like an overdue bill with interest growing every year. We are going to pay. The question is when and how much, but make no mistake about it—there is a cost of climate change to every one of us. Voluntary efforts to address climate change have been slow to materialize, although the attention paid to this issue on corporate websites and in corporate board meetings has been steadily increasing. These voluntary efforts are only now beginning to emerge, and they will become extremely important as we begin to address this issue. In fact, these efforts will form part of the response of the market system to protecting the Texas coast and the economy of the future, as described later in this chapter as well as in other chapters.

Climate change can be addressed. We can alter our cumulative carbon footprint through conservation, energy source substitution, and carbon storage in the soil. Over a decade ago, Stephen Pacala and Robert Socolow published a paper in the journal *Science* titled "Stabilization Wedges: Solving the Climate Problem for the Next 50 Years with Current Technology," in which they identified a pathway for reducing eight gigatons (eight billion tons) of future annual carbon emissions by breaking those emissions into eight smaller pieces of about a gigaton each called wedges. They then identified fifteen strategies that would lower future carbon emissions by a gigaton each in an attempt to stabilize emissions at or below eight gigatons of carbon per year (which is about a gigaton below the global amount of carbon dioxide emissions today).

By the way, in discussing these strategies, it is easy to confuse carbon emissions and carbon dioxide emissions. A ton of carbon equals about 3.67 tons of carbon dioxide. Sometimes emissions and emission reduction strategies are expressed as tons of carbon and sometimes as tons of carbon dioxide. It is easy to get these mixed up. The baseline used by Pacala and Socolow of eight gigatons of carbon is about twenty-eight tons of carbon dioxide emissions. A future emission scenario leading to sixteen gigatons of carbon means about fifty-six gigatons of carbon dioxide.

These so-called wedges offer a potpourri of strategies, varying from substitution of certain hydrocarbon fuels for coal, to offsetting or otherwise sequestering carbon dioxide, to bringing online new wind, solar, and nuclear projects.

There are two important points about the work of Pacala and Socolow. First, these two excellent thinkers demonstrated that the problem of reducing carbon dioxide emissions can be conceptualized in "bite-sized" portions. Second, their work set out a course of thinking about carbon and carbon dioxide emission reductions that can help shape public and private decisions about how to address climate change, flatten the growth of carbon emissions, bring ourselves more in line with the circular, sustainable carbon cycle of nature, and move us toward an economy that is circular, as opposed to our current linear growth model.

A logical conclusion from their work is that carbon sequestration by protected and restored ecological systems (as discussed in chapter 6 on ecological services) is a key part of the strategy for reducing carbon dioxide emissions for the future. At least two gigatons of carbon if not more could be sequestered by natural processes, and there is no reason why this sequestration could not and should not occur on the Texas coast as well as in Texas generally. Voluntary control programs by many industries and businesses are likely to emerge in the next several years. As these plans emerge, the Texas coast, and Texas generally, should be a major player in that sequestration future.

At this point, it is reasonable to ask, how realistic is it that voluntary or even regulatory programs will emerge to control carbon? After all, the US Congress has rejected virtually all concepts of carbon dioxide regulation, and it is unlikely that a carbon tax or a carbon cap and trade program will emerge until the 2020s if at all. Although the Obama administration has enacted numerous rules and issued several executive orders regarding climate and carbon, the likelihood of comprehensive regulation appears very low indeed. And in November 2016, Donald Trump was elected as the forty-fifth president of the United States, and he has publicly expressed doubts about climate change as a legitimate issue. So given this background, how would implementation of a concept such as the wedges occur?

Unbeknown to most, a quiet revolution has been occurring in the business world regarding social and environmental issues, climate included. This change traces back to the early environmental laws of the 1970s when industry was forced to meet certain minimum water, air, and hazardous waste standards. After a period of adjustment, compliance with these laws became the norm (of course with notable exceptions), but two books, *Beyond Compliance: A New Industry View of the Environment* and *Changing Course: A Global Business Perspective on Development and the Environment*, redefined the relationship of the business community with the environment as well as with society more generally. Interestingly, these two books coincided with the 1992 United Nations Conference on Environment and Development in Rio de Janeiro. This conference led to the first international treaty on climate change as well as the Rio Principles of sustainable development and the global biodiversity treaty, beginning a new international era in which the United States was no longer the acknowledged leader in environmental laws and regulations, or in environmental thinking.

Starting around the turn of the century, the corporate community became more and more involved in corporate social responsibility and corporate sustainability even though no law specifically required such action. Today, many will be surprised at the extent to which the concepts of social responsibility and sustainability, and more recently of climate change, have been written into corporate policy statements and websites. There are hundreds of examples, but consider these.

Coca-Cola is a leader in this emerging field of corporate sustainability. In 2016, it was selected by *Newsweek* as one of the most sustainable companies in the world. Coca-Cola has committed to achieve a number of goals by the year 2020. Among these are goals related to the health and well-being of its consumers, social goals related to the empowerment of women and the enforcement of human rights principles, and environmental goals related to the water, packaging, climate, and agricultural practices of those who supply goods used by Coca-Cola. The company discusses green, blue, and gray water, a sophisticated view that distinguishes water for direct use in products, water for indirect use in agriculture, and water for recycling and reuse. And among other goals, by 2020 Coca-Cola seeks to reduce its carbon footprint by 25 percent from 2010 levels.

A carbon footprint is a measure of the amount of carbon dioxide emissions for which a company is responsible. It includes direct emissions from combustion (scope 1), emissions from purchased electricity (scope 2), and indirect emissions associated with the corporation's value chain, including suppliers and delivery to consumers (scope 3). There are numerous websites that individuals can use to calculate their carbon footprint. However, calculating a corporate footprint is a very difficult task, and many corporations are now disclosing their carbon footprint, or at least their scope 1 and scope 2 emissions.

Another corporate leader is Nike, which *Newsweek* also selected as a 2016 best company relative to sustainability practices. Among the policies that gained Nike acclaim are (1) committing to 100 percent renewable energy, (2) involving workers in corporate decision making, (3) moving toward closed-loop (zero-waste) products, and (4) achieving a 25 percent reduction in carbon emissions by 2020.

Other business leaders either are currently carbon neutral or will become carbon neutral by early 2020. The excellent biomedical engineering company Biogen reached carbon neutrality in 2014, meaning that it calculated its sources of emissions and either reduced or mitigated them. Among the techniques used to achieve carbon neutrality are energy efficiency, substitution of renewable electrical energy for fossil sources, and purchase of carbon dioxide storage capacity in the soil for the remaining carbon emissions. This soil storage is an ecological service provided by natural ecosystems such as prairies, marshes, and forests, as discussed in chapter 6.

So, how would such a carbon-neutral future unfold on the Texas coast? To begin with, many entities on the coast have already committed to becoming carbon neutral. David Lebron, president of Rice University, and over six hundred other university presidents around the state and the country, including Houston Community College, have signed a pledge to become carbon neutral in the future. My staff at the Blackburn and Carter law firm developed a carbon footprint of the firm's activity during a period when we had ten employees in a four-thousand-square-foot converted house. We all drove to work except for Charles, who rode his bike every now and then, and we had several hybrid vehicles. We used electricity and natural gas at work. Sometimes we flew to meetings or to a trial. We used paper products. We created waste. We also had solar photovoltaics on our roof and energy-saving features in our building. Taking these activities into account, we calculated the firm's carbon footprint to be about fifty tons of carbon dioxide per year after taking credit for the electricity produced by our solar photovoltaic system. The distribution of our carbon footprint is shown in figure 5.2.

Then, we looked into finding a way to "zero out" our emissions. One way to do this was to purchase carbon sequestration rights in natural systems. As discussed in chapter 6 on ecological services, carbon can be sequestered by prairies, forests, and marshes. For our firm's offset, I chose to purchase carbon sequestration rights in a Galveston Bay marshland project. I arranged to pay the Galveston Bay Foundation for the rights to about fifteen acres of wetlands, thereby securing capacity to offset our emissions. I might add that Bob Stokes, the president of the foundation, was only too glad to sell me these rights since I was the only buyer he had encountered in the last ten years. In this way, our firm letterhead could say that we were a carbon-neutral law firm, a distinction that no one ever commented on over several years, but one that might be important for firms in the future. Regardless, I felt good about it.

If all businesses on the Texas coast committed to becoming carbon neutral and secured their carbon dioxide offsets locally, the result would be amazing. My firm had about ten employees at the time we undertook this experiment. Think about a law firm with about one hundred employees. It might need the rights to somewhere around 150–200 acres of wetlands (depending on the amount of air travel, the energy effi-

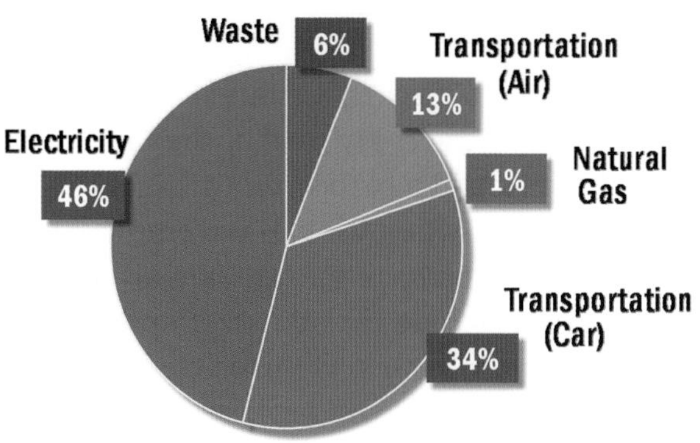

Figure 5.2. The calculated carbon footprint of the Blackburn and Carter law firm.

ciency of the building, the types of cars driven, etc.). If all law firms on the coast made that commitment, it would likely require thousands of acres of marsh or prairie or forest. And if CPA firms and educational institutions and medical facilities were to make the same pledge, well, you get the idea. It is doable.

But why should a law firm or an accounting firm become carbon neutral? Well, think back to the scope 3 emissions of a corporation. A law firm or an accounting firm used by that corporation is in that corporation's "value chain," meaning that its services are purchased by the corporation. If the corporation were trying to become carbon neutral, carbon neutrality in the accounting and law firms working for that company would be important in the future, if not today. It is a bit like drug testing in the workplace, which spread to contractors. So too will carbon neutrality concerns. An aggressive firm might want to get in front of what will ultimately become an industry standard, just as "Beyond Compliance" emerged in the early 1990s as an industry performance concept.

So, let's get real about the Texas coast. Currently, every major oil and gas company has extensive knowledge about climate change and its carbon footprint, although this may not be public information. Most of the majors have teams working to understand the implications of carbon on their business models, and there will be significant implications. There has been serious evaluation of carbon-neutral gasoline. Although consumer demand has not yet emerged, these companies are evaluating both when and how to offer carbon-neutral gasoline, meaning gasoline whose carbon footprint has been calculated and mitigated by purchasing carbon dioxide storage rights in the soil. So let's do some math and see what carbon-neutral gasoline might cost.

According to the Union of Concerned Scientists, from 2004 to 2008 the average Gulf Coast refinery emitted about 111 pounds of carbon dioxide per barrel of crude refined. By this metric, a 150,000-barrel-per-day refinery would emit about 8,300 tons of carbon dioxide per day, or about three million tons per year. Assuming a carbon storage (sequestration) rate of three tons of carbon dioxide per acre, about one million acres of restored prairie would be needed to offset these carbon emissions. It is a lot, but it is doable. At a projected price of $40 per ton of carbon dioxide, a refinery might put out $120 million per year for sequestration rights. And when those one billion gallons of produced gasoline are burned, another 10 million tons of carbon dioxide are released, necessitating another 3.3 million acres of sequestration. Again, it is a lot, but it is doable. At a projected price of $40 per ton of carbon dioxide, a refinery might put out $520 million per year for sequestration rights.

If one considers this in terms of gasoline, a bit less than 50 percent of the crude processed by a refinery can be converted into gasoline. So, a 150,000-barrel-per-day refinery would, at most, produce 75,000 barrels of gasoline. At 42 gallons per barrel, that represents 3.1 million gallons per day times 365, which is about 1.1 billion gallons of gasoline per year. If the cost of the sequestration (for the whole refinery) were borne by the price of gasoline, the price would rise by about 12 cents per gallon at $10 per ton of carbon and 50 cents per gallon at $40 per ton. Although upstream carbon emissions (those from exploration and transport) are not included in this example, the numbers are reasonable. This can be done.

Implicit in this example is the use of the natural system to store carbon dioxide emitted from the refinery and from cars. Carbon dioxide is a bit different from other pollutants in that it is a global rather than a local pollution problem, meaning that carbon dioxide can be taken out of the atmosphere anywhere in the world and be counted against an emission source. This natural removal is discussed further in chapter 6.

We know that various amounts of carbon dioxide can be sequestered by various systems. And we know that landowners are prepared to change their agricultural and ranching practices to provide solutions to this carbon sequestration problem. All that is needed is for the companies in Houston and on the Gulf Coast to start spending money in this manner.

Sequestration of carbon dioxide emissions through local farmers and ranchers on the Texas coast is an excellent alternative for those companies that are currently responsible for relatively large carbon footprints. Local offset of global emissions could and should be the strategy for carbon reduction by our local oil and gas and similar companies. The coast and Texas are responsible for a lot of carbon emissions. Harris County is the largest source of emissions in the United States when compared with all other counties in the country. We are heavily invested in carbon dioxide emissions. According to Purdue University, Harris County emits sixty-eight million tons of carbon dioxide per year, attesting to it being a center of oil and gas and plastics processing and manufacturing. If this carbon footprint were sequestered, it would take about fifteen million acres, or about 9 percent of the surface area of Texas. Investing in the sequestration might be the smartest move that the Houston region could make for long-term economic sustainability. There is only so much land for sequestration, and the opportunities that exist today will be gone in the future.

We should similarly be the source of significant carbon sequestration services rendered locally in exchange for money. As will be explored in chapter 6, this potential market will transform the agricultural community as well as the oil and gas and plastics industries. If we run out of sequestration opportunities on the coast and in Texas, we have the rest of the United States to work with.

Interestingly, various certification programs such as the LEED green building seal, SITES landscaping, the Envision ISI program for engineering projects, and the Living Building Challenge (see chapter 11) are moving from minimizing harm to making projects affirm, restore, and regenerate the ecological system. More and more, these programs are incorporating concepts of natural system regeneration and ecological offsets such as carbon sequestration and habitat replacement into their protocols. Many universities have signed the carbon neutrality pledge. Many individuals and corporations are beginning to be concerned about carbon. The reality is that counting carbon emissions will be in all of our futures. And we are going to live with it and thrive. This will not be a future of doing without, but rather one of careful spending and full appreciation of the carbon that we do choose to burn.

All of this implies change, and Dr. Henk Mooiweer, a former leader of the GameChanger program at Shell Oil (see chapter 6), tells an interesting story about revolutionary change in a corporate context. Henk thinks of corporations as organisms, with "white blood cells" in the corporate structure whose job is to protect the corporate institution, to attack and remove "risk" to ongoing operations. On the other hand, Henk describes himself as a "virus" within the corporate structure, generating new ideas for business propositions and feeling the full pressure of the "white blood cells." At issue is nothing less than the future of the organism, otherwise known as change. If the idea survives the attack of the white blood cells, then it might have a future within the organization. If it doesn't, then it is time to find another idea.

I like Henk's imagery of the process of change. In many ways, his mindset is that of the old oil wildcatter. We need a wildcatter mentality regarding the carbon future. There is as much opportunity in the future with carbon emission concerns as there is today, if not more. The oil and gas industry has been slow to move in this direction. It needs to embrace this change and ride with it, not against it.

The wildcatter future of the oil and gas industry will involve the sequestering of carbon, and terrestrial sequestration is the easy answer, the no-brainer in that it is proven. I have been working with Henk on what he calls the million-ton challenge, a way for the oil and gas industry to begin on a new path in a difficult time. The challenge is easy—the oil and gas industry, or some subset of the industry, commits to make a good-faith down payment on its carbon emissions by committing to sequester one million tons of carbon dioxide as soon as possible, to be followed by one hundred million tons in the next ten years. It is not impossible. It is very doable, potentially within the United States, but the key will be to maximize sequestration in each ecosystem type.

Others could join this million-ton challenge as well. There is no reason why individuals, other corporations, religious and scholastic institutions, and the government could not join in this effort. The federal government once launched a strategic petroleum reserve. Why not initiate a strategic carbon reserve and use some of the $20 billion in yearly agricultural subsidies to jump-start carbon sequestration and carbon farming? All of us need to be conscious of and reduce our carbon footprint. And it will be so much easier if we do it together. We just have to take this challenge on and move forward. The future belongs to the bold. Along the way, we may eventually restore several hundred million acres back to native prairie, hardwood forest, and salt marsh. That to me is a good future.

Our future climate will be an agent of change in many ways. It will change our physical reality, our Earth, and its systems. Sea level will rise, storms will become more severe, and droughts will worsen. But at the same time, opportunities will emerge, and those who take advantage of these opportunities will be the survivors, the beacons. If the people of the Texas coast want to retain jobs and income from oil and gas refineries, they will have to learn to think in terms of living with climate change and the realities it brings.

My business mentor, Jake Hershey of Houston, once told me

about how quick business was to change and how ruthless that force was. He asked me about the buggy manufacturers of the past and where they were today. I looked at him, perplexed, and he said they were gone because they did not adapt to the automobile. They became obsolete.

There is a path forward for the oil and gas industry. Economic resilience can be found, and terrestrial sequestration is the key. As I will discuss in the next chapter, sequestration capacity is limited. Pacala and Socolow estimated that there is capacity to store about two billion tons of carbon. We need about six to seven billion tons of capacity. On its face, there is a several-billion-ton shortfall in soil storage capacity. Do you have yours?

PART 3

Solutions for the Texas Coast

CHAPTER 6

Ecosystem Services and Ranching

As a researcher, I have read about scientists in the laboratory having moments of startling realization when they understand the implications of an experiment they have completed. Sharon Roan writes in *Ozone Crisis* about such a moment with Dr. Sherry Rowland and Dr. Mario Molina when they realized that the chemistry of the chlorofluorocarbons they were researching might provide a critical understanding of the danger these chemicals pose to stratospheric ozone. These two men went on to win the Nobel Prize in chemistry for this work.

I have had a similar moment of clarity regarding climate change. I now understand that one key piece to solving climate change problems as well as increasing water supply and reducing flooding is rooted in understanding ecosystems as well as farming and ranching. I would not have believed that simple statement five years ago, but I absolutely believe it today. And it has the potential to transform not only the Texas coast but the United States and the world.

Nothing could be more timely than a large-scale opportunity for Texas coastal farmers and ranchers. One of the biggest threats to the long-term future of the Texas coast (and perhaps Texas generally) is the potential breakup of large landholdings. The continued presence of these large tracts devoted to cattle ranching and wildlife is a centerpiece of the charm and ecological abundance and variety of the Texas coast. These ranches create the landscape of much of the coast that I find so enjoyable as I drive from Houston to the Valley or east to Port Arthur. They provide fabulous wildlife habitat, holding ducks and geese on the ponds and short grass and deer in the woodlands. And they can be flooded without great economic damage. So, finding creative ways to improve cash flow for these large landowners is a key aspect of the future of the Texas coast. If we could increase the ecological value of these lands at the same time, that would be a fantastic result. And we can.

This concept goes back to a board retreat for a nonprofit called Houston Wilderness where something special happened. A round-table discussion led to the proposal to create a "green think tank" to develop innovative ideas about combining the business world and the ecological one. Elizabeth Winston Jones, a board member and Houston native, and I volunteered to cochair this committee, and we have worked as partners on these creative green think tank ideas ever since that retreat. One of the key ideas we developed early on was to incorporate the concept of buying and selling ecosystem services (also called ecological services) into the ways we understand and protect the natural systems around Houston.

Ecological services are "goods" provided by a functioning natural ecosystem—goods that have value, although this value is not always reflected in dollar terms, as discussed in chapter 3 regarding water pricing. Some natural systems provide wood to burn for heat or to build houses and other things; other ecosystems provide oysters, fish, and shellfish to eat. These goods typically have dollar value for the harvester if not the landowner in all cases. Some ecosystems provide habitat and nourishment for bees that pollinate both wild and cultivated crops and make honey. Trees and other plants take carbon dioxide out of the atmosphere through photosynthesis and take nitrogen and phosphorus out of the water and sequester it in their tissues. These latter items have seldom been valued in a dollar sense. Some ecosystems provide cultural benefits like hunting and fishing and bird-watching, some with dollar values, some without. Our native ecosystems near the coast store lots of water when surge flooding occurs, and our floodplain forests store the river when it decides to occupy larger areas after heavy rains, a concept not generally valued in a dollar sense. The extent to which ecosystems produce more water for streams or springs has also never been valued monetarily.

This concept of ecological service value was embraced by the SSPEED Center at Rice after we received a grant from the Houston Endowment to study the effects of Hurricane Ike, which pounded Bolivar and Galveston in 2008. Our team of researchers and planners was impressed by how much water came ashore in Chambers and Jefferson Counties, yet the surge in this area did relatively little economic damage to the farms and ranches there over the longer term. Much of this land was used for cattle grazing, and the vegetation in this area is resilient to inundation because it is native there and has evolved over the centuries to withstand saltwater inundation for short periods. These low-lying lands absorbed the billions of gallons of water that flowed off these lands for many days after Ike came ashore (see figure 6.1), yet the marsh and prairie grasses looked healthy several months after inundation, which could not be said of the human ecosystem of the Bolivar Peninsula.

It was clear to our research team that in much of our study area, we did not need to build a resilient system; rather, we had to maintain or perhaps restore that resilient system. This has evolved into one of the most exciting concepts I have encountered, both for its potential on the Texas coast and for its potential to transform conservation thinking nationwide—thinking that was set in place in the early 1900s and is prime for advancement.

The concept behind utilization of ecological services for the future of the Texas coast is quite straightforward. Much of the area overrun by Hurricane Ike was and is owned by private landowners. If there were a way to generate income for these landowners that would allow them to maintain or restore their native landscape and continue to use it for grazing purposes, then that land could be flooded every so often when a major hurricane hit without the owners suffering substantial economic harm. From what landowners have told us about the economics of ranching, most ranchers are having a

Figure 6.1. Runoff flowing from marshlands and prairie is shown below in a photo taken about four days after Hurricane Ike came ashore. The water is flowing back into the Gulf from flooded marshes and ranchland over the clay chenier that separates the low-lying coastal lands from the Gulf of Mexico. Photo by Bryan Carlile.

hard time breaking even (unless they have oil and gas income) and are generally searching for methods to increase income. If a method of increasing cash flow could be found that could be added to existing ranching income, then the landowners would be paid for restoring and maintaining native landscapes that will occasionally flood. At the same time, the coast would receive fish and wildlife benefits.

Figure 6.2 shows the transactional concept we developed at the SSPEED Center, called the Texas Coastal Exchange (TCX). Our basic idea was to assist in the development of a market for buying and selling ecological services by putting buyers and sellers together and by developing various tools to facilitate these transactions. Such tools include identifying those services for which a market may exist or will exist, developing a geographic information system to help landowners understand the potential of their land, establishing standards for these transactions, and developing measurement and verification tools. But before we get into the details of this voluntary market, I want to take you back and help you see this potential as we discovered it.

In researching the potential dollar value of these ecosystem services, Elizabeth and I contacted Adam Davis of Ecosystem Investment Partners. Adam is a California guy with a sly smile and an eye for the economic potential of natural systems. His company raises and uses capital to invest in natural systems, not for philanthropic reasons but to make money and perhaps do some good along the way. Adam introduced us to a community of researchers who have been creating systems for buying and selling ecological services in various areas of the United States. However, the market they were exploiting was created by federal, state, and even local environmental regulations around the United States. Adam was quick to advise us that the "regulated market" and the "voluntary market" for ecological services were quite different, and that the voluntary market had a huge upside, but it was not as dependable or predictable as the regulated market.

As an environmental lawyer, I was familiar with the statutory basis for most of the regulated markets. Through my work on the coast and my teaching for the US Army Corps of Engineers in the 1980s, I knew about "wetland mitigation banks," created by the regulatory program of the Corps of Engineers under Section 404 of the federal Clean Water Act. As set out by President George H. W. Bush, there was to be "no net loss" of

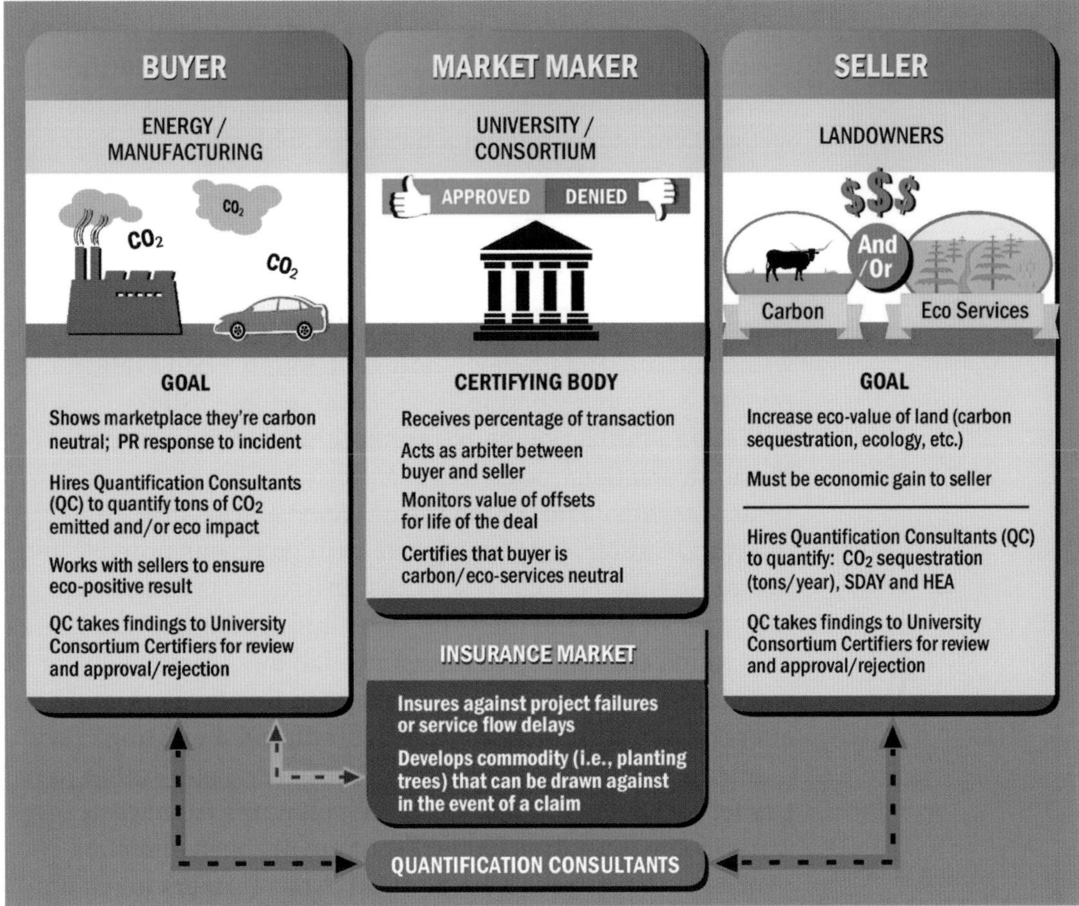

Figure 6.2. This diagram presents a conceptual model of the market that the Texas Coastal Exchange is attempting to facilitate or establish. Here, a potential buyer is put together with a potential seller by an entity—the market maker—that expedites and certifies the transaction. Adapted from diagram prepared by Pillsbury, Winthrop, Shaw, Winston Law Firm, © Pillsbury, 2016.

wetlands under the 404 program. Someone requesting a permit to fill wetlands is required to create an equal or greater amount of wetlands to compensate, or mitigate, the ecological harm caused by filling the wetlands. To meet the demand for these compensatory lands, wetland mitigation banks sprang up around the country, and Adam's company completed a five-hundred-acre wetland mitigation bank east of New Orleans at Chef Menteur Pass at the end of 2014.

One cold day in January, I flew to New Orleans to view Adam's bank at Chef Menteur, and I was blown away. The dredges had "mined" sediment from Lake Borgne and pumped it into an area where wetlands had once thrived but had been lost, eroded away like much of coastal Louisiana. Here, Adam's team had pumped this mined sediment into leveed areas and had leveled them off precisely to allow tidal waters to come into the parcel. The team expected that there would be sufficient seed stock in the sediment to grow marsh grass, but if not, they were prepared to seed this area. However, their previous venture here, a hundred-acre site that was beautiful on this crisp cold day, had required no seeding, and all of the wetland credits in that bank had been sold.

Adam's Chef Menteur project is most aptly described as industrial-scale ecological restoration. This five-hundred-acre project was built by two barges dredging sediment from Lake Borgne, supported by as many as fifteen floating backhoes and a fleet of airboats. This was a restoration project that was about making money. And I have found when I talk about ecology and money on the Texas coast, people listen.

Wetland mitigation banks are not the only regulatory system in which these ecosystem service transactions occur. Under Section 303(d) of the Clean Water Act, several types of innovative water-quality improvement programs propose buying and selling ecological services. In programs established on Chesapeake Bay and the Ohio River, nitrogen and phosphorus (which are water pollutants) needed to be removed from waterways, and researchers determined that farmers could alter their cultivation practices and reduce the existing runoff of nitrogen and phosphorus from fertilizer usage. Rather than pay for technology to remove these pollutants from wastewater, companies wanting to discharge nitrogen and phosphorus in these areas were allowed to pay farmers to restore native vegetation. Such plants do not require fertilization and can remove nitrogen and phosphorus from runoff that would otherwise add these elements to the water.

Under another water-quality program, in Oregon, the Willamette River was considered to be too hot for salmon because of thermal pollution. Here, rather than install very expensive heat-removal technology, power companies were allowed to pay farmers to plant trees along tributaries of the Willamette to produce shading that would lower the heat (BTU) content of the water. This would allow the power companies to avoid paying for the design and construction of major cooling facilities, saving them money and also making money for the farmers.

In both cases, payments were being made to landowners for undertaking actions that restored native ecosystems that do important work for us, work that we call ecological services. These methods are similar to classic environmental engineering methods in which we use microorganisms to remove pollution in wastewater treatment systems, except that in the case of nitrogen and phosphorus and heat, ecosystems or natural elements are being used to remove the pollutants rather than constructed basins and technology.

There are also numerous ecological service transaction programs being developed under the Endangered Species Act to allow purchase of habitat credits in exchange for permits to go forward with various activities such as oil and gas drilling in areas where "harm" might occur to these listed species. These credits are created by developing or enhancing habitat, as is being proposed by the Wyoming Conservation Exchange and the Environmental Defense Fund along the Green River in Wyoming. Here, the created or enhanced habitat units are sold by the landowner to the business needing to offset habitat that it will be impacting. In these situations, the issue is protection and upgrading of habitat for species as diverse as sage grouse and desert lizards. And these programs are expanding around the United States.

In developing a potential market on the upper Texas coast, our review indicated few regulatory-related opportunities other than wetland mitigation banks, for which there was a limited need. Our goal for the SSPEED Center was to provide natural resiliency across more than two million low-lying acres in Chambers, Galveston, Brazoria, and Matagorda Counties. And we knew there was no chance of local or state governments creating a regulatory system for the Texas coast. That was simply a nonstarter of an idea. In keeping with this philosophy and reality, our SSPEED Center team, with help from Adam Davis, developed the concept of a voluntary ecosystem services market, one where willing buyers for these sources contracted with willing sellers to establish these transactions.

In our research and thinking about creating a longer-term commitment to resiliency for these low-lying lands, we evaluated the possibility of willing-buyer transactions where the federal or state government would secure ecological resources, either by fee simple purchase or through a conservation easement transaction whereby landowners restrict their property from development. However, we eliminated this idea from the outset because many of our coastal landowners have been approached by either federal or state governmental entities or nongovernmental organizations interested in buying their property, and most of the remaining landowners are simply not interested in losing long-term control of their land. And if the sellers are not willing to sell, the system will fail.

On the other hand, most if not all of these landowners were willing to talk about long-term commodity contracts associated with the development and selling of ecological services. In many respects, this would be the breakthrough market. When it emerges, the market for ecological services will transform ranching on the Texas coast as well as conservation thinking across the United States. The voluntary market for ecological services is a bit like the Holy Grail—something imagined, something talked about, something that many will argue does not and will not exist. Or will it?

Dr. Henk Mooiweer was with Shell Oil when I first met him, and his job with the GameChanger program was to bring revolutionary change to the thinking and business propositions of Shell Oil, as discussed in chapter 5. Our first meeting was at the faculty club at Rice and to this day this conversation sticks with me.

Henk and the unique "Project Meadowlark" team, led by Professor Peter Byck, a movie maker from Arizona State University, were developing a GameChanger proposal concerning carbon dioxide emissions from the oil and gas industry and a possible approach to addressing them. Although the relationship between climate change and the oil and gas industry was banned from polite discussion in Houston until recently (maybe), the majors such as Shell have been studying this

Figure 6.3. Cattle (shown here on the King Ranch) and restored native prairies may be key elements of the concept of removing carbon dioxide from the atmosphere and storing it as carbon in the soil. Photograph by Geoff Winningham.

problem for many years, seeking to find economically viable ways to remove carbon dioxide from the atmosphere. They have not been standing idly, ignoring this issue. They have been quite busy.

The Project Meadowlark team proposed restoring native prairies and using this natural system to store large volumes of carbon dioxide as well as water in the soil. The specific proposal used adaptive multipaddock (AMP) cattle grazing to replicate the function and impact of buffalo herds grazing the Great Plains of the United States. The Great Plains once hosted a massive native prairie grassland ecosystem. Buffalo would come through and graze an area extensively, defecate and urinate, and then leave, perhaps not returning for months or even years. These native prairie plants evolved extremely deep root systems that allowed them to be denuded above the surface, only to grow green shoots again after being fertilized and watered. The power of this prairie ecosystem was the relationship between these deep roots, the organic soils, and the microbial community that received carbon from this root system and stored it in the soil. These soils became extremely fertile, holding tremendous volumes of organic carbon and also near-surface water, in essence becoming a type of shallow underground reservoir.

Given the impracticality of restoring free-roaming herds of

buffalo, AMP grazing was proposed, which involves restricting a herd within a relatively small area (the paddock) where they eat much of the grass in a form of competitive grazing, replicating the action of the buffalo. When that grass is consumed, the herd is released into the next paddock, which has not been grazed for many months, to once again competitively graze. The GameChanger proposal was to use this paddock grazing process to bring back the native prairie (with its fifteen-foot-deep root system) and allow it to send carbon dioxide from the atmosphere into the soil as a means for Shell Oil to offset its carbon footprint, which is substantial, as are the footprints of most of the other major oil companies.

This GameChanger proposal was developed assuming that there was no carbon dioxide regulatory process. The challenge was to discover various ways for Shell to realize value from this sequestration venture. In addition, this creative group came up with several business pathways to stimulate the paddock grazing opportunity. One way was to grow and sell grass-fed cattle, a preferable alternative to corn-fed beef from the carbon life-cycle standpoint. Another money-making concept was to market carbon-neutral gasoline, for which the carbon dioxide footprint of its manufacture and use was offset by Shell using credits for sequestration through this paddock grazing. Another potential money-making concept was to sell or otherwise realize income from the additional water that would be stored in the soil and liberated months after the rain in the form of seeps and springs. Still another concept involved several ways to support ranchers and farmers when they migrate their practices to AMP grazing, and yet another involved setting up a consulting firm to monitor the carbon placement in the soil and developing ways to do this more efficiently. In addition, seeds could be marketed and consulting help could be provided in establishing native prairies. In the long term, it was not necessarily anticipated that Shell would undertake all of these business ventures, but it or someone else could. However, Shell would benefit if the net result was to reduce the overall cost of the carbon dioxide removal.

As we talked, Henk and his GameChanger partner Russ Conser mentioned that a back-of-the-envelope calculation the team had made of the footprint for all of Shell's global operations revealed that about two-thirds of the state of Texas would need to be converted back to native prairie in order to sequester its footprint. Then one of them said, "It's doable."

What a gift that statement was and remains. Here was a message from inside a major oil company saying that not only was it considering pursuing ecological service credits for carbon dioxide offset, but it was also operating at a mind-blowing scale, well beyond our two million acres of low-lying land near Houston that we had initially focused on at the SSPEED Center. Of course, in order for Shell or any other oil company to claim credit for the sequestration, it would have to arrange a transaction with a landowner whereby the landowner would be paid for the "crop" of carbon sequestration. That is why Henk's message was so powerful—we might have a serious voluntary buyer in the next few years.

The amount of land in private hands on the coast is stunning. As shown in figure I.3, 80 percent of the Texas coast is in private hands and is relatively undeveloped. Much of this undeveloped land is in larger landholdings, with many of the individual tracts larger than five thousand acres and a few in excess of one hundred thousand acres. Yet these properties share one thing in common—it is hard to realize consistent income if there is no oil and gas production.

We had known for some time that there was a potential private market for these services. We had become students of corporate websites, which, if nothing else, demonstrate the way that corporations would like to be perceived and what issues they believe to be important. One thing we discovered is that most corporations are keeping metrics about their carbon footprint, about the amount of carbon dioxide they emit directly and indirectly. If corporations keep and publish metrics about various issues, they are likely to do something about those issues in the future. But with the GameChanger meeting, it became clear that the level of consideration of these issues within the big oil companies was substantial and was happening now.

Project Meadowlark involved exploring and preparing for the sale of the ecological service of carbon dioxide removal consistent with the natural carbon cycle. But carbon dioxide removal is not the only ecological service that is capable of being bought and sold on the Texas coast. Indeed, the potential exists for many different types of transactions in at least four distinct ecosystem typologies—estuarine wetlands, timberlands, prairies, and oyster reefs that exist throughout the coast, as shown in figure 6.4, as well as in figures 1.8 and 1.10. It should be noted that cropland is called out because it is capable of being converted back to native ecosystems with the greatest "uplift," which is the difference between the "before" and "after" services delivered by a particular piece of property, an important issue in this business. Dryland agricultural fields might have the greatest potential for conversion back to native prairies, although the conversion of active rice-growing areas back to native prairies will offer the additional benefit of eliminating the methane emissions from rice farming.

The ecosystem service value of coastal saline and brackish wetlands has long been known. Back in the 1970s, I remember reading a study from Louisiana State University, the first I ever saw regarding ecosystem services, asserting that the value of coastal wetlands was at least $50,000 per acre. More recently, an economist named Robert Costanza set the value of coastal wetlands at about $5,500 per acre per year. However, those values are more theoretical than real. To determine "real" value, one has to identify the individual services being

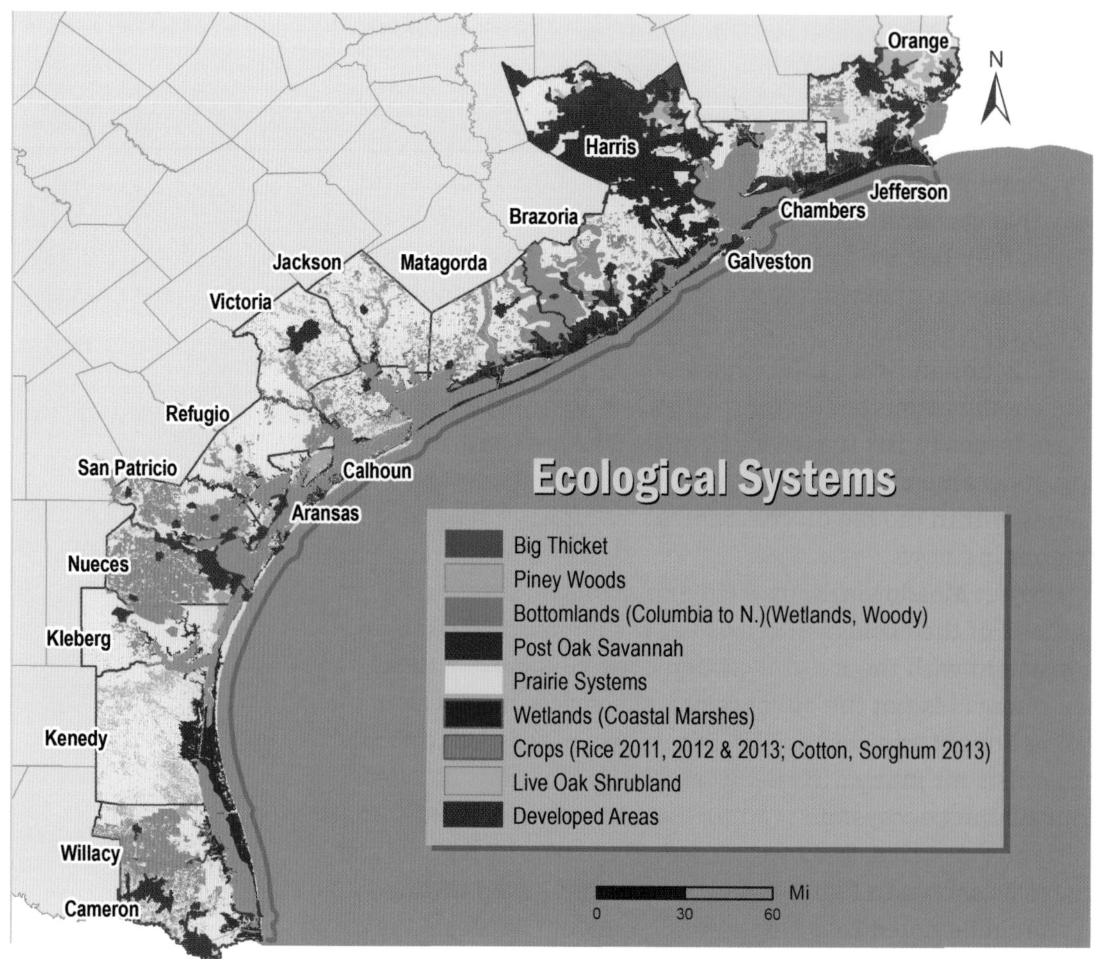

Figure 6.4. Generalized ecological systems of the Texas coast demonstrating the large acreage of prairie lands, wetlands, and timberlands as well as croplands that may be suitable for ecosytem service transactions.

provided and determine whether there is a willingness to pay on the part of some buyer.

Marshes are great at storing carbon. A marsh in California was found to be sequestering as much as twenty-five tons of carbon dioxide per acre per year. California has developed a regulatory market for carbon dioxide, and a ton sold for about eleven dollars in 2016, although internal oil company projections establish the value at closer to forty dollars per ton in the future. Texas coastal marshes pump less carbon into the soil than these California marshes, representing somewhere in the range of four to eight tons of carbon dioxide per acre per year. As sea level rises, salt marshes will expand (or will need to be expanded) back into brackish high marsh, which in turn may expand into low-lying adjacent prairie. Landowners with coastal marsh may be in a position to gain from this sea level rise with a bit of forethought.

Marshes, however, do much more than store carbon. An acre of estuarine marsh is a nursery, providing day and night care for about 7,800 brown shrimp, 7,000 white shrimp, 6,800 blue crab, and about the same number of flounder per acre. The presence of a healthy estuarine marsh is one key to a successful fishery. These marshes are also home to fish-eating birds, and studies have linked the abundance of various species of these birds along the coast to marsh acreage. Most coastal duck hunters are very familiar with the relationship between a quiet marsh pond and waterfowl. A well-established marsh fringe can significantly reduce shoreline erosion, a very real benefit to coastal landowners, and a fringing marsh can also reduce wave heights and damage. Further, marshes remove nutrients such as nitrogen and phosphorus from storm water.

Freshwater wetlands occur in many areas of the Texas coast and also provide excellent ecological service benefits. They are extremely important for wintering waterfowl, and they also collect rainfall, providing benefits both by storing excess runoff that might otherwise worsen flooding and by recharging freshwater systems in certain areas. However, unlike saline and brackish wetlands, freshwater wetlands do not contribute much (if at all) to a net reduction in greenhouse gas levels in the atmosphere because these wetlands also emit methane, another greenhouse gas, such that there will likely be no net reduction in climate-changing compounds in the atmosphere.

On the uplands adjacent to coastal marshes are coastal prairies, the most extensive of the ecological systems on the Texas coast, and the ecosystem of focus in the paddock grazing concept of Project Meadowlark. Prairies sequester carbon, with estimates as high as two or three tons of carbon dioxide per acre without paddock grazing and substantially higher with paddock grazing. Prairies also provide habitat for bees and birds and other wildlife, remove nitrogen and phosphorus, and provide food for cattle. These prairies are home to both wintering waterfowl and wildlife such as deer, turkey, and quail, providing excellent hunting and wildlife viewing. And, of most interest to Texas water users and providers, a restored prairie is a near-subsurface reservoir that is recharged with each rain and that slowly releases water through subsurface lateral movement into stock tanks as well as seeps and springs. If it can be proven that restored prairies contribute to the base flow of streams and rivers during times of drought, there will be a solid rationale for water interests to pay landowners to restore these prairies, potentially creating a huge additional market for restored prairie ecological services.

Coastal bottomland forests also provide significant ecological services. Forests such as the Columbia Bottomlands of Brazoria and Matagorda Counties sequester carbon dioxide

Figure 6.5. A prairie ecosystem such as this, if restored, can take 2–3 tons of carbon dioxide into the soil per acre restored. Photo by Kathy Adams Clark.

Figure 6.6. The Columbia Bottomlands shown here adjacent to the Brazos River sequester carbon in the wood of the trees and in the soil and can supplement the riverine base flow in areas that are restored. Photo by Kathy Adams Clark.

in the soil as well as through tree growth, sequestration that can continue even if trees are harvested for wood (depending on the end use of the timber and the efficiency of lumber production). Texas coastal forests are essential in the life cycle of neotropical migratory songbirds, providing food, shelter, and water for these migrants as well as nesting habitat for native species. These coastal forests generally occur within the floodplains of rivers and creeks, where they perform an essential function of flood storage as well as water-quality services by removing nitrogen and phosphorus.

Oyster reefs are the fourth ecosystem of particular interest, and they also provide significant ecological services. Almost all coastal fishermen can attest to the fishery production value of oyster reefs, as they are among the favorite fishing spots because of their ability to concentrate predators such as speckled trout and red and black drum, among other species. Oysters are filter feeders and provide excellent water-quality enhancement, and of course oysters are great to eat. We are researching the chemistry associated with the growth of oyster shells to determine the amount of carbon dioxide that can be sequestered through the formation of calcium carbonate shell, although folks who know about these things advise me that there might not be any net gain here. Regardless, an oyster reef has great value near the shoreline as a buffer against wind-generated waves that cause extensive shoreline erosion, to the point that coastal landowners might be willing to finance a reef just to protect their shoreline.

In addition to these specific ecosystems, which offer marketable value when restored, there are also certain unique opportunities. For example, if a landowner owns property between fifteen and twenty feet in elevation on the upper coast (the edge of the hurricane-surge risk zone), there may be a market for flood storage. In sites with marshes backing up to low-lying prairies, there may be an opportunity for marsh expansion as sea levels rise. For those owning higher-elevation land immediately proximate to the shoreline or marshes, there is an opportunity to plant coastal woodlots that are important to neotropical migratory birds. And there are likely several more opportunities we have not thought of yet.

Most landowners Elizabeth Jones and I approached are willing to seriously discuss commodity contracts for the sale of these ecological services if a market approach that protects private property rights is inherent in the process. Many landowners along the Texas coast are hard pressed today to make ends meet. Many of the rice farmers of the middle coast were placed at the bottom of the water-rights priority system and denied surface water during several years of drought starting in about 2010–2011. These farmers are looking for new opportunities. Many of these landowners would consider an alternative that would generate income greater than what they are currently making. And while it is difficult to get a farmer or rancher to give you a number, an annual income greater than $100 per acre per year would get most everyone's attention, and more than $200 per acre would generate significant interest.

Certain aspects of such transactions will be deal killers from a landowner perspective. First, most landowners along the coast have had ample opportunity to sell their land or sell conservation easements and have chosen not to do that. For this reason, these ecosystem service transactions will need to be long-term commodity contracts rather than easements. This will require landowners and buyers to agree on the length of the contract in order for the buyer to receive the type of benefits being purchased. Carbon sequestration for one year is of no value. Carbon sequestration for twenty, thirty, or fifty years is of great value. Timing of restoration will be an issue—does the landowner restore an ecosystem without a long-term contract in place or does he or she wait until there is a contract in hand? Most advisers knowledgeable about these transactions recommend waiting until a contract is in hand to undertake restoration, although the SSPEED Center is currently researching the feasibility of creating a bank to hold these credits pending market development. The concept of the carbon bank currently being investigated by the SSPEED Center is shown in figure 6.7.

These are important yet difficult issues. As work progresses on the development of this concept, it will be important for buyers and sellers to meet and begin to agree on how this system will be organized and operated. The Texas Coastal Exchange at the SSPEED Center (see figure 6.2) is developing proposals to create and act on this potential market, including how to proceed in the absence of firm details, such as exactly how much carbon dioxide sequestration should be contracted for each acre of prairie, marsh, or timber restored. Estimates exist for each of these ecosystems, but the data is seldom from the specific region of the Texas coast where the project is located, and variations in rainfall, climate, and soils will affect sequestration rates. Therefore, buyers and sellers will need to work together to sort out issues of sequestration of carbon per

A Voluntary Carbon/Eco Services Market

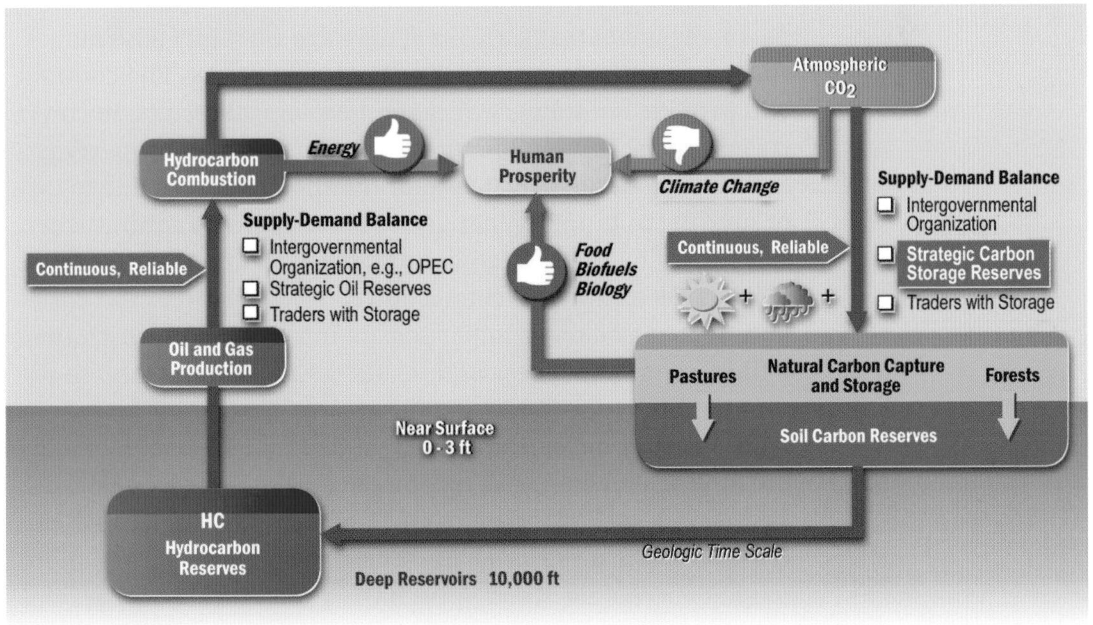

Figure 6.7. The concept of a carbon dioxide bank is set out in this drawing. The bank holds credits created by natural carbon capture and storage and uses these to offset the combustion of hydrocarbon reserves, allowing energy to be used, ecology to be restored, and climate change to be addressed. Figure prepared by Dr. Henk Mooirweer, Innovenate, for the SSPEED Center.

acre restored, or of gallons of water generated, or of numbers of fish and wildlife supported.

It is important to note that this voluntary system is being developed outside of any regulatory process. If buyers and sellers can agree on how they wish the system to be structured, then the system may be designed to meet those specifications. Transparency is the most important requirement of any system, including specification of the terms and conditions of the transactions and reliable verification and validation procedures. To the extent that any participant would wish to use these transactions to reduce exposure under other laws (such as a future carbon tax), then such compatibility would need to be integral to the design of the voluntary system. Regarding buyers, the issue is how and when a voluntary market will emerge. This voluntary market is difficult to pin down, but certain trends and programs are likely to arise. Our analysis to date has identified five potential types of buyers within this voluntary system: (1) philanthropic, (2) corporate strategic, (3) institutional, (4) governmental, and (5) gift.

The philanthropic market is traditional, well known to nongovernmental entities, and comes in several forms. There are foundations that make grants to buy and set aside property. There are corporations that make similar grants. However, in virtually all cases, philanthropy has been focused on buying either fee simple or easement rights in property. However, the hope is that the philanthropic market will be open to considering ecological service contracts rather than fee simple or easement transactions. There are certainly advantages that come with a contract for ecological services. The contract will provide for delivery of certain ecological results, in contrast to the relatively common situation in which property is removed from the private sector but then degrades due to lack of funding to properly manage it. Management requirements can simply be written into a commodity contract. With proper safeguards and well-written contracts, foundations and corporations may choose to participate in a system in which their philanthropy produces solid results while keeping land in private hands.

The philanthropic market might be flexible enough to allow the buying and selling of existing ecological services as well as created ecological services. If there are existing ecological resources whose services are considered extraordinary, there might be a role for simply purchasing those ecological services for a period of years. For example, some of the prime marshlands within the study area are owned by individuals not interested in selling the land in either fee or easement transactions. They might, however, be willing to contract to manage these wetlands in ways that address the impacts of sea level rise. This could include securing the wetland land base by various forms of protection or perhaps allowing expansion of the wetlands as water levels rise. In either event, a commodities contract will be much more inviting to such landowners than any land-sale arrangement.

A major philanthropic opportunity exists in the form of significant ecological resources adjacent to existing preserved lands. Corridors are important for wildlife, particularly corridors that connect protected areas, because they allow movement from one reserve to another and facilitate gene pool exchange. In this manner, conservation of lands adjacent to conserved land areas can provide linkages and expansion of preserves, providing greater conservation benefits than obtaining green spaces where conservation is not well established. Figure 6.8 shows all land areas within one mile of the boundary of an existing preserved land area. These are the high-value philanthropic areas. Money spent for ecological services here will be well spent.

The corporate strategic market (as opposed to the philanthropic market) for the purchase of ecological services is defined by the existence of sales advantages (e.g., strategic advantages) within various industry sectors arising from the comparative carbon, water, and ecological footprints of various products and the ability to make representations about these lowered footprints. Every product made by corporations or individuals comes with an investment of energy, carbon emissions, water inputs, pollution outputs, and ecological impacts. This is true not only for creating and marketing a product, but also for providing necessary ingredients for production within the corporate supply chain (e.g., the purchased materials that support the corporation's product). These resources and impacts dedicated to a particular product are included in the product's footprint. Traditionally, corporations have considered these issues from both cost and regulatory standpoints. However, trends on corporate websites indicate that competitive advantage may exist in being able to "brand" a product as carbon neutral or even net ecologically positive, much like the GameChanger concept of proposing carbon-neutral gasoline.

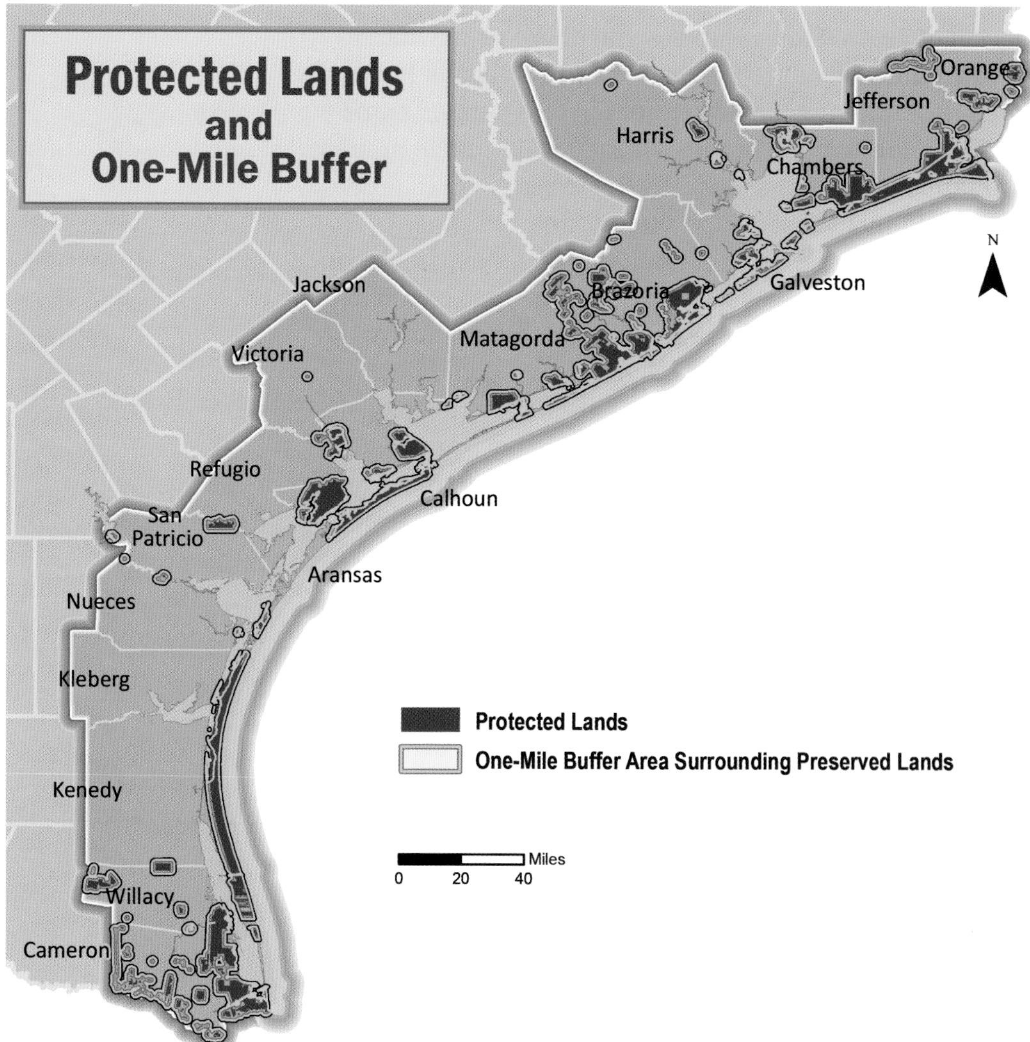

Figure 6.8. Lands adjacent to existing protected lands are considered to have greater conservation value for wildlife purposes than more detached tracts in that the adjacent lands have the inherent ability to establish corridors and other connections.

To the extent that consumers demand a lower or zero footprint for the products they purchase, corporations will respond.

Footprinting metrics can be found on virtually every corporate website, and some corporations are going beyond metrics and making commitments to reduce or eliminate certain footprints. For example, Google is including information about offsetting the carbon footprint from its data centers, and Coca-Cola has information explaining water use for Coca-Cola products, including the amount of blue (consumption-based water supply sources), green (rainwater used in crops providing product), and gray (wastewater) water that it uses. At least in part, this interest in the water content of Coca-Cola products comes from a major controversy over groundwater usage in India. Of course, one should be cautious about website examples because there is quite a distance—and difference—between a statement on a website and the actual expenditure of money.

Nonetheless, the expectation is that corporations will emerge in the voluntary market in the not-too-distant future. One can envision having a choice to purchase from a gasoline dealer that provides carbon-neutral gasoline at a slightly higher price than non-carbon-neutral gasoline. If even a relatively small proportion of the consuming public would respond to such a product, it could create a significant carbon market literally overnight. For more information on becoming carbon neutral and the possible markets associated with carbon neutrality, see chapter 5.

The third potential buyer is various institutions, such as universities. Six hundred seventy-seven university presidents, including David Lebron of Rice, have signed the American College and University Presidents' Climate Commitment. This commitment includes both a statement and a pledge. The statement considers the current knowledge about climate change and states that our climate is changing and that humans are causing it. The pledge involves understanding the carbon footprint of the university and taking steps to reduce that footprint. At Rice, a comprehensive Climate Action Plan has been identified that initially focuses on energy conservation, purchased electrical sources, and the calculation of the benefits (offset) provided by the Rice Endowment's ownership of substantial timber acreage in Louisiana. Over time, the plan is to compile the full carbon footprint, including the scope 3 emissions, which include purchased supplies, food, and other goods used by Rice, and then to neutralize these emissions. Of course, one potential offset is the purchase of carbon dioxide credits.

The fourth potential buyer is one of three types of governmental entity. First, consider a buyer with a specific mission such as flood control. The Texas Coastal Exchange (TCX) is being developed in an attempt to minimize hurricane surge damage. The TCX is focused on lands twenty feet in elevation or lower. One product that could be sold is flood storage capacity. Such a purchase may be a value investment for an agency such as FEMA, which could take proactive steps by purchasing flood storage easements or contracts for lower-lying properties that are most likely to be subject to development pressure, such as those adjacent to urban boundaries. Similarly, to the extent that the Corps of Engineers develops a flood damage reduction plan for congressional authorization, it is likely that a nonstructural component would be required. In addition to the TCX itself as a nonstructural alternative, the purchase of flood storage easements might also be part of such a package.

A governmental entity focused on fish and wildlife protection and conservation might also potentially consider a long-term commodity contract for a landowner to deliver ecological services such as prairie, marsh, or forest restoration. In such a case, these fish and wildlife payments could be layered with carbon and perhaps water payments to yield a positive result for the landowner and the various buyers. And, as mentioned in chapter 5, the current agricultural subsidy program could be redirected to fund a strategic carbon reserve with some or all of the $20 billion the federal government currently spends on various forms of agricultural subsidies.

The fifth and most creative potential market is the gift market. It is conceivable that in some relationships, the "gift" of a carbon footprint offset, or the gift of neotropical migratory bird habitat, might be warmly received. Of course, for some, that might end the relationship. But seriously, think about how many worthless gifts you have received and then consider the gift of your carbon footprint being offset. Or as a fisherman or bird-watcher, think about a gift of enhanced habitat for fish or birds. The point is that ecological service gifts will emerge as an element of a future voluntary market. It may not constitute a huge part, but nonetheless there is a potential. Here, the availability of an online ecosystem service exchange, available to consumers throughout the state, the United States, and the world through the Internet, will be very important.

The bottom line is that voluntary markets for ecological services are emerging and will become more and more prevalent. In this way, ecological restoration will become a defining economic development tool of the future. And therein lies hope for many of the ranchers on the Texas coast who might otherwise face difficulties in the future as they try to maintain cash flow.

Now, all of this is not to suggest that this carbon market, or water market, or bird and fishery market will magically come into existence one day or that it will be easy to meet and maintain the necessary conditions. Commodity contracts will have to be developed that spell out buyer expectations and seller duties. At the least, buyers and sellers must agree on some baseline metrics. Buyers will be paying for carbon, water, or fish and wildlife. How much will sellers represent that they can produce? And at what cost? How is the provision of the ecological service to be verified? Through monitoring? By whom?

One difficult issue has yet to be fully resolved. The easy market for ecological services is for the creation of these services—for the uplift. Existing markets do not seem to reward prior stewardship efforts. If a ranch is in excellent condition, it might not be able to sell the carbon that will be added in the coming years because that is "existing" carbon stock. I think this is false reasoning to the extent that private property can be transformed at any time. It seems crazy that one would have to destroy good habitat in order to get credit for creating it, but that is at least one serious issue at this time.

To my mind, if I have a contract with a landowner to buy the right to sequester carbon on his or her land, I have the legal right to claim that carbon in my calculations of carbon footprint and offset. While this might not meet the rules of all carbon exchanges, it will meet the requirement for transparency, and it will provide income to keep landowners doing the right thing. To eliminate someone from the carbon market because of good stewardship practices seems the ultimate in wrongheaded practices. If nothing else, I think concepts of property rights will eventually determine that landowners own, and have a right to sell, the amount of carbon placed into soil storage on their property, regardless of uplift.

The buying and selling of ecological services promises to transform conservation thinking throughout the United States. By emphasizing and funding the role of private property in a long-term conservation strategy, ecosystem service transactions appear to have an unlimited upside potential. If this potential is realized, many of the larger ranches will be better able to be preserved, and they will be preserved with higher-quality habitat, a total win-win for the future of the Texas coast.

CHAPTER 7

Birds and Ecoplay

In addition to ecosystem service transactions, another concept that might be important to the future of ranching along the Texas coast is bird-watching and ecology-based recreation, or ecoplay. The Texas coast is the birding capital of the United States, with diversity ranging from the tropical species of the Rio Grande Valley to the neotropical migrants that move through the coast in their beautiful spring plumage to the fish-eating birds that call the coast home. The habitat of the Texas coast is varied, and the coastline funnels migrants to and from the continental United States, Mexico, and Central and South America. Texas is where eastern and western birds meet, and both are found at times along the coast. Our coastal area is full of unique opportunities that are not well known or appreciated and are waiting to be discovered.

I am fond of saying that birding on the Texas coast may be better known in Germany or England than in Houston, and I think it may actually be true. Many of us living on the coast don't recognize the bounty that is literally in our backyards. This bounty could be translated into dollars in many ways, with opportunities ranging from ecotourism to increased convention business to better employee recruitment in competitive employment markets. But at least for now, we are not focused on these opportunities, a situation I hope will change.

One way to discover bird-watching opportunities on the coast is to get out of your comfort zone a bit and participate in organized birding outings. Each winter, various chapters of the Audubon Society conduct Christmas Bird Counts at multiple locations throughout the Texas coast as well as throughout the United States. These counts are a tradition dating back over a hundred years. Each count occurs within a fifteen-mile-diameter circle, and one or more people (compilers) are responsible for conducting the count within that area. New bird-watchers are invited to join a group and learn to recognize birds and help with the spotting and counting.

The Freeport Bird Count was where I learned to bird. The

late Dr. David Marrack was responsible for a section of the Freeport count geographic area that included Jones Creek and what is now the Justin Hurst Wildlife Management Area, then known as the Stringfellow Ranch. I can still remember flushing a pair of beautiful barn owls from an old disheveled barn as well as encountering a catbird deep in the thickets of the Columbia Bottomlands, a gray bird with a dark cap and an eye that looked straight into my soul, connecting me with another living thing in a way I still feel today.

I came to appreciate the camaraderie and competitive spirit of these counts, which are reported nationwide. The competition is to determine which count areas have the greatest number of different species, and Freeport usually ranks very high nationwide by this metric. I can remember going to the meeting at the cafeteria at Dow Chemical in Freeport to tally the results—watching experienced birders taking evidence about alleged sightings, asking for details regarding the appearance, habitat, and habits of the bird that was allegedly seen, trying to ensure that the bird in question was really what the viewer thought it was. It is a rigorous and honest process of trying to understand bird diversity and individual species numbers over the years, a wonderful citizen science effort that is true recreation and a lot of fun. And the neatest thing about it is that beginners are always welcome.

On December 14, 2015, I met Dr. Jorge Brenner, a marine biologist with the Texas Nature Conservancy, well before daylight at the Conservancy's offices in Houston, where we joined up with two other Nature Conservancy staffers, Meagan and Adrienne, for the trip down to Mad Island, the promised land of bird counts. Mad Island is a Nature Conservancy Preserve on the north shore of Matagorda Bay gifted by Clive Runnells and his family, who were excellent stewards of a portion of the land amassed by Shanghai Pierce, one of the major Texas coastal cattlemen from the mid to late 1800s. The preserve is bordered by the Texas Parks and Wildlife Mad Island Wildlife Management Area, and the habitat within the Mad Island Christmas Count circle is quite varied, including farmlands, pastures, prairies, scrublands, forests, freshwater marshes, brackish and salt marshes, a power-plant cooling pond, riparian corridors, beaches, bays, and Gulf waters. An aerial image of the Mad Island Christmas Count area is shown in figure 7.1.

Our small group's count area was the habitat adjacent to the Conservancy's lodge on Mad Island Lake at the far western

Figure 7.1. Christmas Bird Counts are conducted within fifteen-mile-diameter circles, such as this one for the Mad Island Count in Matagorda County.

edge of the count circle, a large brackish water body surrounded by marsh and salt grass prairie. From the pagoda on the lake, we saw many duck species, including redhead, scaup, green- and blue-winged teal, pintail, and shoveler, as well as coots, pied-billed grebes, and common loons, along with a possible but unconfirmed western grebe, which would have been a great bird for the count, as it had been seen only a few times over the years of the count. However, when we tried to confirm it later, it was nowhere to be seen, falling into the category of an alleged western grebe, and not counted. Perhaps the best sighting of the day, although not rare, was an osprey crashing into the water and coming up with a fish so large that this predatory bird with a six-foot wingspan could rise only about ten feet above the water as it flew to a fencepost to eat its meal. Really nice.

Figure 7.2. This meadowlark was a welcome sight to birders trying to identify difficult sparrows on the Mad Island Christmas Bird Count. Photo by Kathy Adams Clark.

On that day the tide was high, covering the shoreline, pushing wading birds into other areas and leaving us to search for sparrows in the bunchgrass and shrubs on the higher elevations (think inches higher rather than feet higher). We saw savannah sparrows and Nelson's sharp-tailed sparrows along with a loggerhead shrike and a mockingbird, when suddenly a larger bird with a beautiful yellow breast and black bib flew to the top of a shrub and stared straight at us. It was an eastern meadowlark, which all in the group could clearly identify, a welcome relief from trying to identify the small brown sparrows darting here and there, all looking very similar yet potentially different.

Later, the number of birds our group saw increased when we moved north and east into higher elevations, where we found a flooded pasture loaded with waders of all types, including willets and egrets, as well as an alligator sunning on the bank of a small stream. A belted kingfisher followed us down the road, coming by now and then to fuss at us for violating his space, and we increased our species count with white pelicans, sandhill cranes, black vultures, kestrels, and harrier hawks. Collectively, our small group, led by Jacqueline Ferrato of the Conservancy, identified about fifty or so birds,

Figure 7.3. A vermilion flycatcher with its gorgeous red and black plumage will bring a smile to the most jaded birder. Photo by Kathy Adams Clark.

and these spottings were added to the other teams' totals when we met for lunch over picnic tables under the Conservancy's awning.

At this lunch meeting, the various teams working in and around the Mad Island Preserve came together to tally the results from our portion of the fifteen-mile-diameter circle. This tally effort was led by Dr. Rich Kostecke of the Conservancy, who called off species and asked for a show of hands for sightings of each bird. The total was 142 species, a tally that Rich took to the final gathering of counters at Wadsworth, Texas, late that afternoon, where it was determined that a final count of 239 species had been seen within the full fifteen-mile circle, the highest number ever reported for the count, and the highest in the United States in 2015. The Guadalupe River Delta–McFaddin Ranches came in at 223 species, number two in the United States, and Freeport came in at 211 species, which was fifth in the United States.

The day ended beautifully. We decided to quit shortly after lunch and drove to the parking area to pick up our cars. As we stepped out, we all marveled at a beautiful red bird with black wings—a lovely vermilion flycatcher—that sat on a telephone line, watching as we weary birders loaded up. On the trip

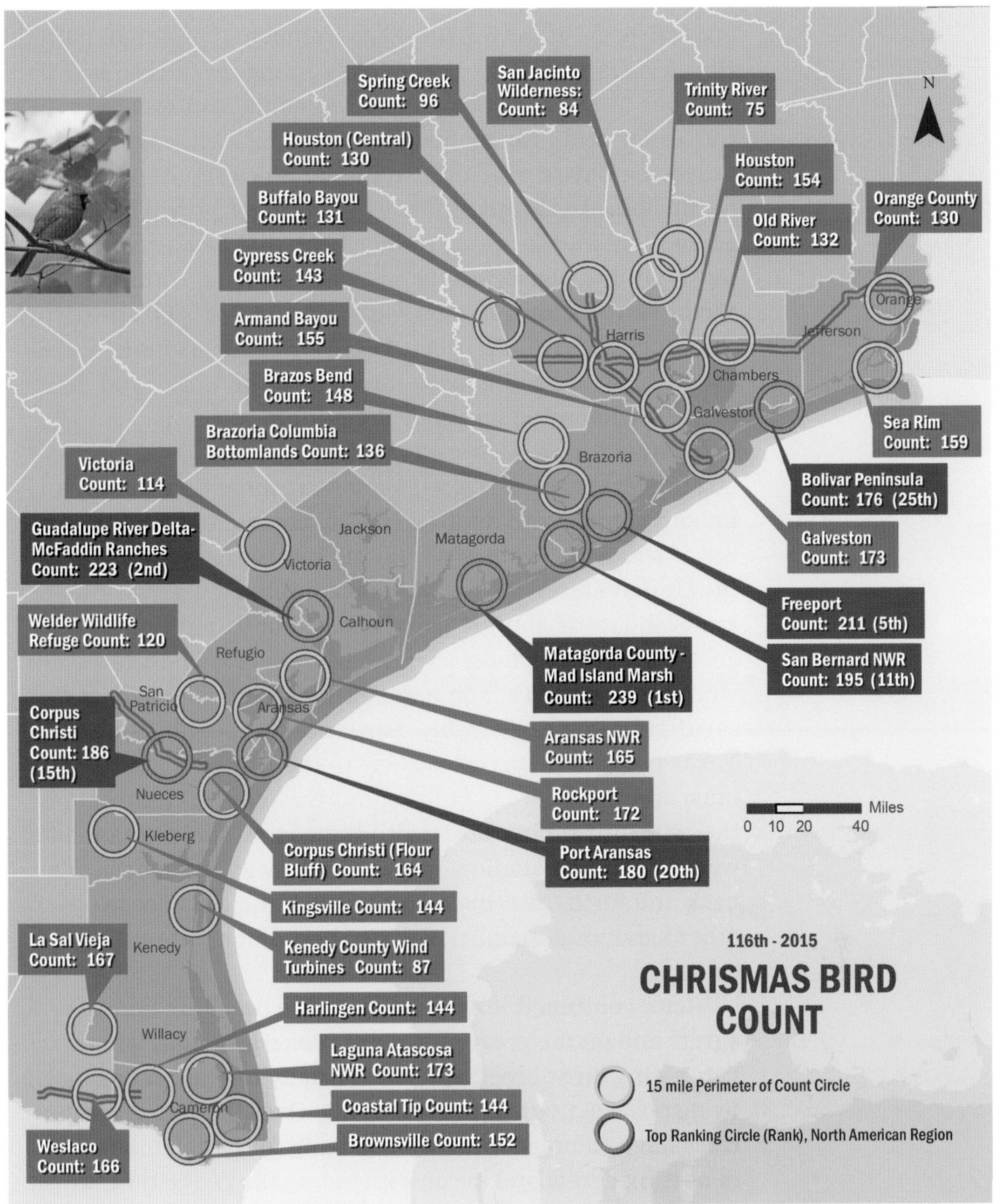

Figure 7.4. Christmas Bird Counts are a great path to learning bird-watching, and they offer great birding at excellent locations. Among the counts shown here are the Freeport, Mad Island, and Guadalupe Delta, which are generally in the top ten if not the top five counts in the United States in terms of number of species counted. Bird photo © Charles Brutlag | Dreamstime.com

back, several large formations of snow geese and blue geese flew over, seemingly bidding us good-bye. The location and results of the various Texas coastal bird counts for the previous year, 2014, are shown in figure 7.4.

I think the birding on the Texas coast is great, but just how good is it? To get an answer to that, I called up Victor Emanuel, one of the leading bird-watchers in the world. Victor and I go back to when we were both young, when he was the executive director of the Citizens' Environmental Coalition (of the Houston-Galveston area) and I was an inexperienced board member. We once put on an environmental conference in Galveston, and I remember Victor leading a birding trip into Galveston Bay in which the highlight was a report of an oystercatcher, a beautiful bird with a chocolate-brown head, white body, and shocking orange beak that reaches into oyster shells and plucks out the tasty morsel from within. Today, Victor runs Victor Emanuel Nature Tours (VENT), one of the most successful and respected ecotourism firms in the world, specializing in birding trips throughout the world, and more recently combining birding with cultural interests.

My question to Victor was simple. Just how good is the birding on the Texas coast? Victor's response surprised me, in both content and depth. First, he commented on the variety of wintering waterfowl, saying it was among the best in the United States. Those who have hunted the Texas coast know about the abundance of ducks, but this abundance goes further to include all types of waders such as red knots, whimbrels, curlews, and many others. Then he went on to say that there are probably more roseate spoonbills on the Texas coast than anywhere else in the United States, and I must add that there is nothing more wonderful than seeing these beautiful pink birds with their large spoon-shaped bills wading across a shallow marsh pond, swaying their heads back and forth, filtering water to catch the crustaceans and other small organisms that form their diet and provide their color.

Victor continued, commenting on the breeding herons and egrets and on the great number of rookeries, areas where fish-eating birds breed and nest, usually on the islands formed by disposal activities from dredging. Over the years, scrub trees have emerged, providing lodging for large numbers of nesting egrets and herons, including the reddish egret, a threatened species Victor noted as being present on the Texas coast in perhaps greater numbers than in any other place in the United States. A map of the rookery breeding areas on the Texas coast is shown in figure 7.6.

But Victor was by no means through. In addition to waterfowl and fish-eating birds, the Texas coast is among the best places in the United States to see migrating neotropical songbirds. These birds nest north of the Texas coast, often in the northern United States and southern Canada, and migrate in

Figure 7.5. A great egret in breeding plumage (note green eye patch) encountering a roseate spoonbill seemingly protecting turf within the tangle of limbs that houses the rookery where these fish-eating birds pack into tight quarters, build nests, lay eggs, and raise young. Photo by Kathy Adams Clark.

the winter through the Texas coast to either stay here or move farther south to Mexico and Central or South America.

These birds can be rather drab in color when they migrate through in the fall, but in the spring, the birds blossom with breeding plumage of every hue in the rainbow. There are the blues (indigo buntings, blue grosbeaks), the reds (scarlet and summer tanagers), the oranges (Baltimore and orchard orioles), and the greens (female tanagers, vireos). The red-breasted grosbeak, with its beautiful pink bib and black head, is often found eating mulberries, a delicacy enjoyed by tanagers and orioles as well.

And then there are the warblers, with variations of yellow and black stripes, dots, and dashes. There is the black-and-white warbler that clings to limbs, moving along the trunk, chasing insects. There is the brown-sided Cape May and the prodigious yellow-rumped, the Wilson's with its black cap and yellow head, and my personal favorite, the orange-and-black Blackburnian, not named for but claimed by me, a lovely bird

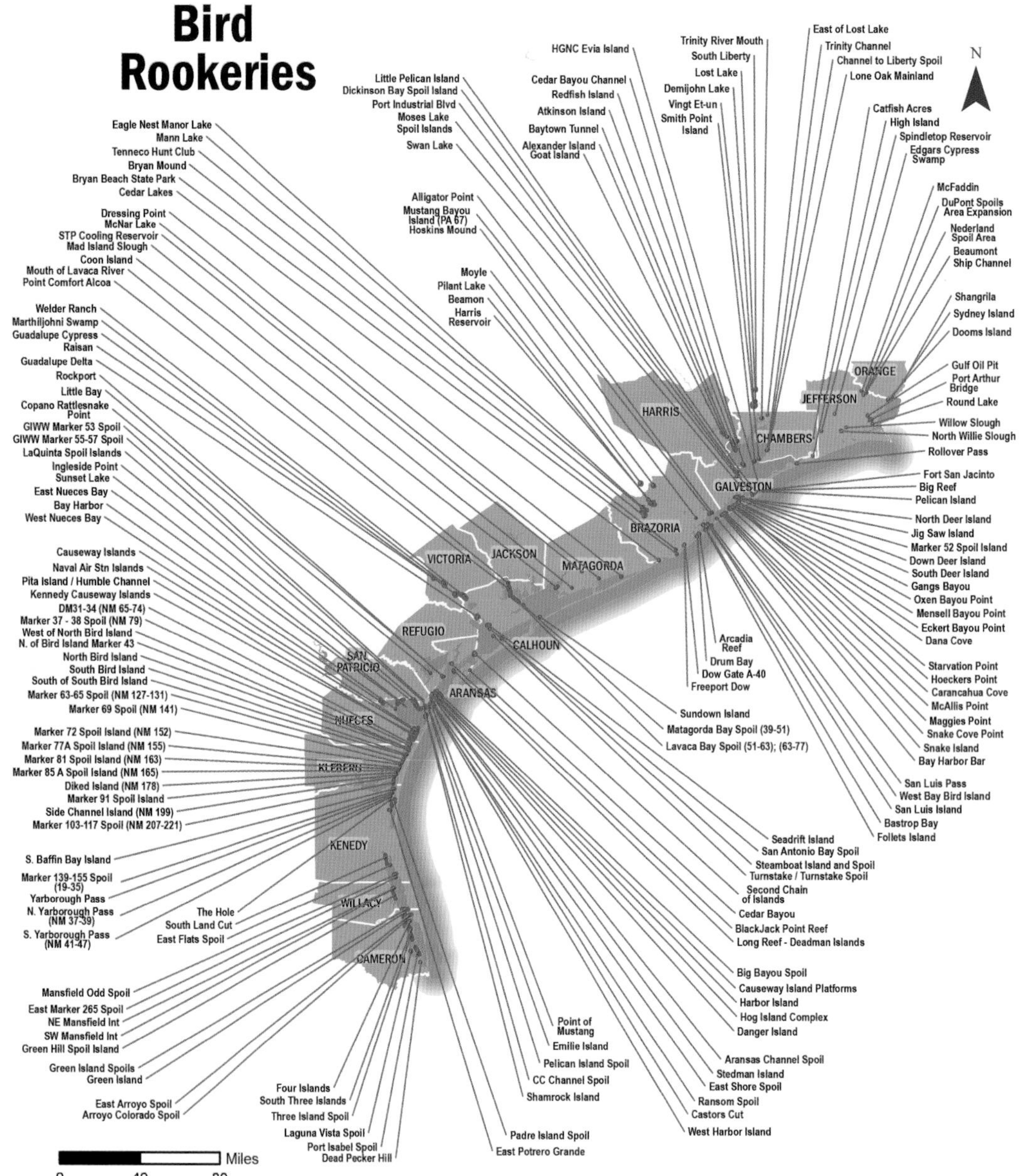

Figure 7.6. Fish-eating birds roost and breed in colonies called rookeries, many of which are distributed throughout the Texas coast.

to watch as it moves from limb to limb, chasing the insect hatch that seems to be timed to meet the migrating warblers, fueling them for the next stop along the way. The numbers can be impressive, with over twenty-four million birds passing through the Columbia Bottomlands of Brazoria and Matagorda Counties, migrating in flocks large enough to be followed on radar.

Again according to Victor, the Texas coast is one of the best two or three places in the United States to see this spring migration. Stories are legion about migrating flocks leaving the Yucatán Peninsula for Texas and getting caught on the treacherous trip across the Gulf of Mexico, where they become victims of spring fronts and their violent thunderstorms. When they reach the Texas coast, these birds literally "fall out" on the beaches, covering the sand just beyond the high water line with blues and reds and yellows, a virtual carpet of birds, both living and dying.

I'll never forget one spring day in Rockport when I was searching for migrants and found a pretty little wetland beneath a stand of hackberry trees, a small water body with a palmetto frond spreading above it. Much to my surprise, there on the green frond was an exhausted scarlet tanager, literally lying on its side so that I could see sand stuck to its breast from where it had rested on the beach. Luckily, the wetland was there for both the tanager and me. That image has stayed with me over the years as I have gone into court trying to protect coastal wetlands, lance and shield in hand, fighting for that tanager's right to life-giving water and shelter.

Victor started VENT on the Texas coast, operating for a year or two out of Rockport, an excellent birding venue with the spring migration, hummingbirds, and whooping cranes.

Figure 7.7. A personal favorite of the author, the Blackburnian warbler, in spring colors. Photo by Kathy Adams Clark.

Victor started with a Mercedes bus and has now expanded VENT into an ecotourism company spanning the globe with over 150 tours per year, taking 1,300–1,400 people on expeditions in Africa, Australia, Europe, South America, North America, Central America, and other parts of the world.

When asked about the market for ecotourism on the Texas coast, Victor is cautious. He says we have the birds to support a major birding-oriented tourist influx during certain times of the year, but it would be difficult to build and support a full-time lodge devoted just to birding. Several birding guides operate out of their homes throughout the coast, and with a little effort, these guides can be found. There is likely a combination of birding, kayaking, fishing, and hunting that would support a lodge or perhaps better accommodations for bird-watchers with money to spend, but they have been slow to develop and could be said to be in short supply today, an opportunity waiting for the right entrepreneur.

There is no question that a strong economic engine is represented by outdoor recreation. According to the Outdoor Industry Association, outdoor recreation is a hidden giant from an economic standpoint, generating $646 billion in direct and indirect economic activity along with 6.1 million jobs. According to a study by the US Fish and Wildlife Service, there were about forty-seven million birders in the United States in 2011, a huge number. This same study stated that birds accounted for about $40 billion in economic activity, including about $14 billion in trip-related expenditures, and they generated 660,000 jobs with about $31 billion in income. A Texas study by the US Fish and Wildlife Service indicated that 4.3 million birders annually birded in Texas. For those seeking a coastal birding adventure, a pathway has been created called the Great Texas Coastal Birding Trail, a concept funded by the Texas Parks and Wildlife Department and developed by Ted Eubanks and Madge Lindsay, true visionaries when it comes to bringing birding-based recreation to the public. The primary trail is shown in figure 7.8 as it extends from Louisiana to Mexico along the coast.

The Great Texas Coastal Birding Trail is a great idea. As I have studied this trail, I have become more interested in the thoughts and people behind this venture. I have known Ted Eubanks for decades, going back to my first contacts in Houston when I was asked to join the board of directors of the Houston Audubon Society by Terry Hershey, the mother of

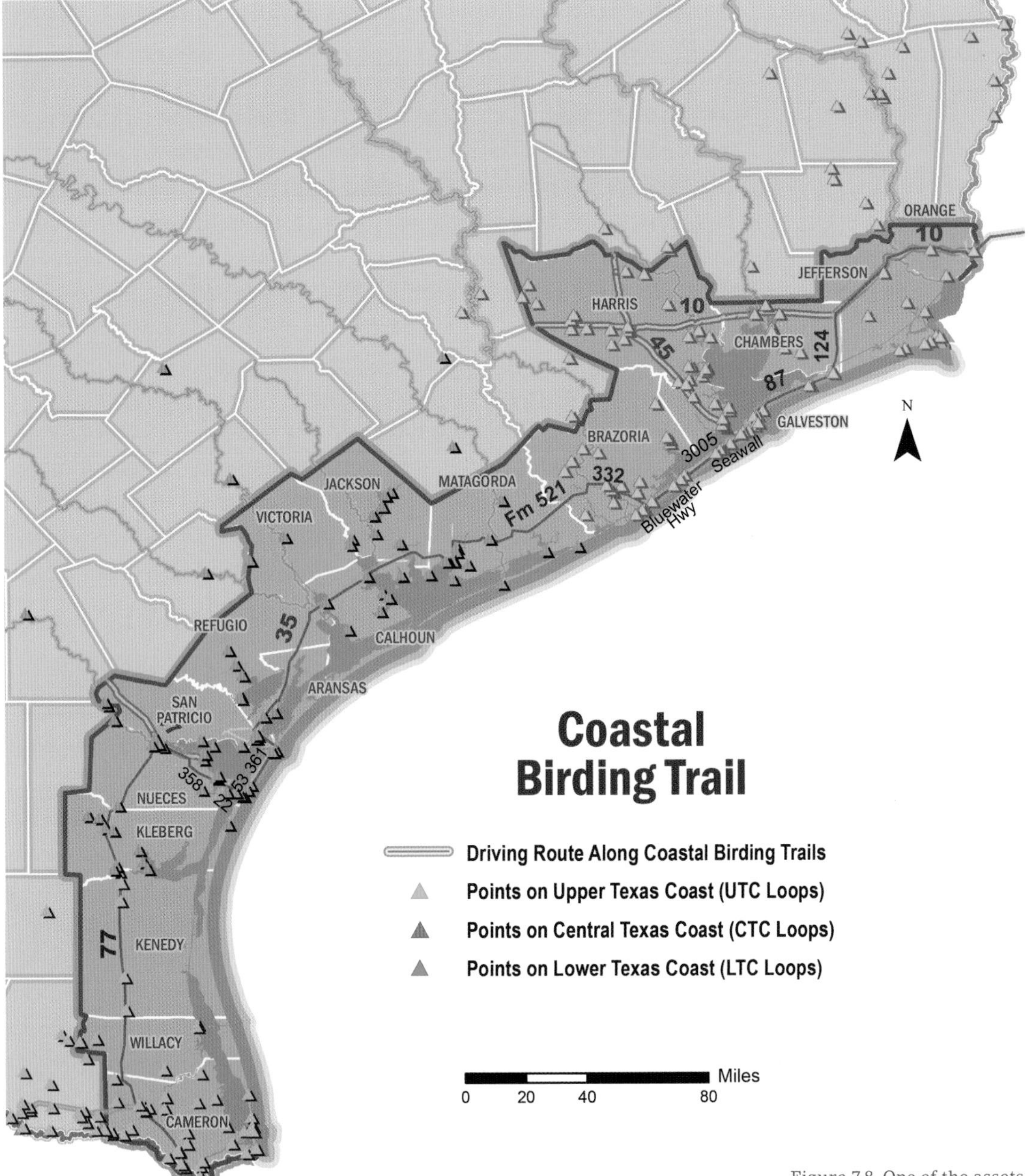

Figure 7.8. One of the assets of the Texas coast is the Great Texas Coastal Birding Trail, which takes you from one end of the coast to another indicating the best places to observe birds adjacent to the road system.

environmental thinking in Houston. She and my mother-in-law had been friends in Fort Worth, and she took my wife, Garland, and me under her wing when we arrived in Houston. As soon as she found out I was an environmental lawyer, the next thing I knew I was on the board of directors of the Houston Audubon Society, as was Garland, the aspiring accountant, née Audubon bookkeeper.

Among the people I encountered in my fledgling days as a

member of the Audubon board was Ted Eubanks, well before he developed the Great Texas Coastal Birding Trail and went on to found his ecotourism consulting company, Fermata. I'll never forget being at a cocktail party that was attended primarily by birding types and hearing Ted talk about the gestalt of a bird, how you can tell certain birds by their appearance as a whole, by their character, more than by specific elements. Today I think I understand what Ted was saying over four decades ago, but I *do* remember that conversation. The conversation at birder parties can be a bit esoteric at times.

The Great Texas Coastal Birding Trail is divided into three sections with loops and stops that direct the user to specific points of interest along the roads where unique and lovely birds can often be seen. It is extremely well done and is a major tool in the enjoyment and utilization of our coast. But it is not enough. We can and should do more to integrate the enjoyment of our birds and the recreational potential they represent, and such an idea came out of Houston Wilderness and the SSPEED Center with the help of Elizabeth Winston Jones.

As discussed in the previous chapter, the SSPEED Center at Rice was interested in developing economic activities that could survive inundation from hurricanes. We discovered that our native ecosystems are resilient. They can absorb the physical blow from a very large hurricane surge and recover. Our SSPEED Center team worked to find ways to enhance the money-making potential of the natural system. We did not focus on creative regulation because, as I have maintained throughout this book, regulation is a nonstarter on the Texas coast. We felt that if we could develop an economy that could withstand inundation, then that would be a resilient economy, one that would last for many decades if not centuries. And we felt we had a much better chance to convince coastal residents to support money-making ideas as a path toward a more secure coast.

In searching for a way to exploit our ecological abundance and economic activity, we designed a concept for bringing together the various protected lands in and around Galveston Bay and the middle coast in a cooperative partnership called the Lone Star Coastal National Recreation Area (LSCNRA), a wonderful idea that may yet become manifest. Our research began after Hurricane Ike in 2008, and among the documents we reviewed was a recovery plan for the Bolivar Peninsula, which was devastated by the hurricane. While there was a focus on rebuilding beach houses higher and stronger, one section also talked about trying to get diverse recreational activities to come to the peninsula, and about the desire to find ways to make money off tourists who would enjoy the back side of the peninsula, the wetlands and shorelines of East Bay. That recovery plan was the genesis for the conceptual development of the proposed LSCNRA.

Initially, we focused on the ferry that connected Bolivar with Galveston Island, a unique gateway to the peninsula. We researched national seashores and studied various ways of creating a national seashore designation for Bolivar. We contracted with Lynn Scarlett, a former deputy secretary of the interior under President George W. Bush, and asked her to help us conceive of a way to structure a recreational development concept following the models of the National Park Service. We cautioned that anything that reeked of a federal takeover or federal control would be seriously opposed, but Lynn was already thinking that way anyway.

Lynn joined our Rice team, and we began to develop the concept that became the proposed LSCNRA. National recreation areas are different from national parks—they do not need to be owned by a single governmental entity, and they have flexibility not available with other designations. From our work, we determined that the national recreation area model had sufficient structural flexibility to work on the Texas coast.

During this time, we had been compiling a list of the lands owned by various public entities and we began to talk publicly about a concept for networking these land areas together to create a recreational magnet for the upper Texas coast. Matagorda County, which was outside our study area, asked to be included in the study because the county judge wanted jobs and ecotourism for his county. And then one day, Suzanne Dixon, the state director of an NGO called the National Parks Conservation Association (NPCA), showed up, joined us on a field trip, and announced that the NPCA had heard about our idea and was there to help. Along with Houston Wilderness and the NPCA and protected landowners who had agreed to participate in a meeting at the Texas Nature Conservancy Reserve near Texas City, the SSPEED Center continued to work on and develop this recreational proposal, which I believe to be absolutely perfect for Texas and for much of the rest of the United States.

With Lynn's help, all of us working together began to develop the framework, which was based on the Boston Harbor Islands and the Santa Monica Mountains National Recreation Areas. In these situations, the federal government—the National Park Service—did not own all the land. Instead, a partnership arrangement was negotiated whereby public lands owned by many different entities would work together in a partnership under the banner of the National Park Service. State land would remain state land. NGO property would remain in the ownership of these private entities. And private property would not be restricted in any way by its establishment. On the other hand, the excellent reputation, largesse, and importantly, the website of the National Park Service could be brought forward to aid in marketing this recreational jewel that so far had remained dull and unpolished.

The concept of the ecological jewels around Houston goes back to Houston Wilderness and one of our founding members, Beth Robertson, who had described the ecological abundance around Houston as a necklace of fine jewels surrounding our metropolitan area—an area known more for concrete than ecological value. The proposed LSCNRA was a way to join many of these jewels together in a functional arrangement that would allow them to be displayed and revealed—polished and mounted—for the public, who we hoped would come to see what we had to offer.

In order to create a national recreation area, an act of Congress is required. To make that happen, a local consortium needed to be formed to bring this issue before our Texas congressional delegation. For this, we needed public-spirited champions to take this concept forward and make it happen. In this regard, we were most fortunate. Former secretary of state James A. Baker III and Houston businessman John Nau stepped forward, along with a number of local businesspeople with an interest in the outdoors. Together, Secretary Baker and John Nau brought important credibility and seriousness of purpose to this fledgling endeavor.

One of the first suggestions from John Nau was that we commission a study documenting the economic development potential of the proposed LSCNRA. He knew that cash flow to coastal counties was an important key to gaining local support to ask Congress for the formation of an entity tied directly to the federal government. And although there were safeguards in the proposal to limit federal encroachment, more than one person was heard to question the need for any involvement of the federal government.

John's instinct about the importance of an economic study was right on target. This study left no doubt about the importance of the federal connection or about the strength of economic development potentially associated with the proposed LSCNRA. According to a report titled *Opportunity Knocks*, the LSCNRA after its tenth year could be responsible for bringing in 1.5 million visitors annually, generating almost $200 million in local sales, creating over five thousand new jobs, and increasing coastal employment by about 2 percent and local tourism-related jobs by 11 percent. In short, the LSCNRA was a major economic development opportunity without the vulnerability to storms often connected with coastal development. In short, it was demonstrated to be an ideal opportunity; hence the title of the report.

Victoria Herrin is a planner who has been working on the LSCNRA for the last five years, first in her role at Houston Wilderness and then as a staff member with the NPCA. It has been Victoria's job to go out into the coastal counties and introduce the LSCNRA concept to local communities and groups. She is also responsible for keeping together the coalition that has emerged to support and potentially implement the proposed LSCNRA, and that group is impressive. Advising Site Owners includes the US Fish and Wildlife Service, the US Army Corps of Engineers, and the Texas Parks and Wildlife Department. Participating Site Owners include Matagorda and Brazoria Counties; the cities of Galveston, Bay City, Freeport, Palacios, and Surfside Village; and NGOs including the Houston Audubon Society, Galveston Historical Foundation, Texas Nature Conservancy, Scenic Galveston, Galveston Bay Foundation, and the Bay Area Council, Boy Scouts of America, to name a few. The National Park Service owns no land within the proposed LSCNRA geographic boundaries at this time; though it is interested in the concept, it is not directly involved yet.

The basic idea of the partnership is that the legislation passed by Congress will create a framework in which federal, state, and local government agencies as well as NGOs and others can work together, identify priorities, and plan and leverage their resources in unison. In this way, the whole will become vastly greater and more effective than the sum of the parts. Once legislation is passed, site owners will create bylaws and flesh out the governing structure loosely described in the legislation. The legislation also identifies specific lands that local governments and NGOs are interested in transferring to the National Park Service, either in whole or in part. Of particular importance is partners' access to the peerless expertise of the National Park Service in education and interpretation for its sites, as well as personnel such as guides who will assist visitors in understanding the ecology of the region and help them learn how to enjoy these recreational jewels—a key to helping the many millions of people living in the Houston region who came here from other places to understand and learn to enjoy our ecological jewels, which are substantial.

So what are these jewels in the region of the proposed LSCNRA? A starting point is the reserves of the Houston Audubon Society at High Island and Bolivar Flats, two of the best places for bird-watching in the United States. These areas will become cornerstones, as will various historical properties in the city of Galveston, along with Galveston Island State Park. The bottomlands of the Brazos, San Bernard, and Colorado Rivers are the sites of the Brazoria, San Bernard, and Big Boggy National Wildlife Refuges as well as several newly acquired federal and NGO tracts that are great for bird-watching but are not yet open to the public. These will be combined with state wildlife management areas and Texas Nature Conservancy lands in both Texas City and at Mad Island. Together, these lands offer world-class birding and corresponding kayaking, two growth sports. A host of NGO properties near the Galveston causeway and Galveston Bay are also proposed for inclusion, as shown in figure 7.9. More recently, Calhoun County has indicated an interest in being included, and those protected lands, also shown in figure 7.9, include the wintering grounds for the whooping crane.

The LSCNRA concept is important in several respects. First, while these resources exist on the upper Texas coast, there is no organized way to access them. There is no formal infrastructure whereby guides are provided. Many of these properties are not open to the public, or if they are, special arrangements must be made. The proposed LSCNRA provides an opportunity to change this situation and open these ecological jewels up to the public of the United States as well as to Houston-area residents. As such, this is a perfect device for realizing our natural abundance by getting our residents outdoors.

Outdoor recreation is a major issue for corporate recruit-

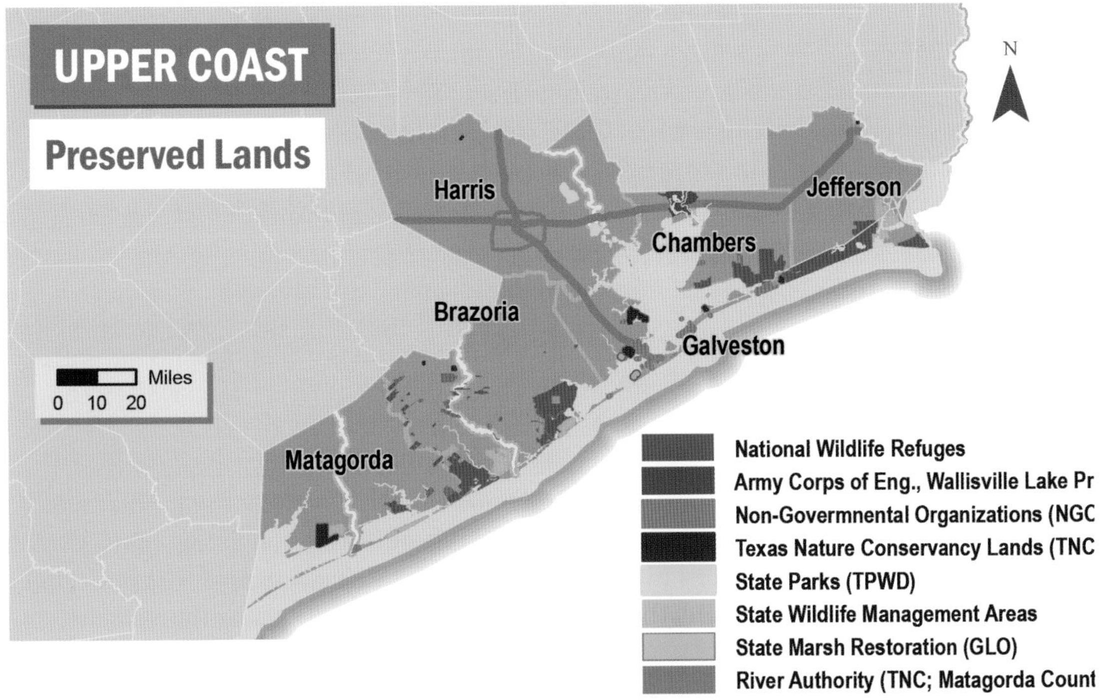

Figure 7.9. Most if not all of the lands shown here that are protected by federal, state, and local government and by nongovernmental organizations were proposed for inclusion in the LSCNRA as originally proposed.

ment to the Houston market. Houston is not considered an "ecological place" with excellent outdoor recreation, yet it is. Although this negative perception of the Houston-Galveston region is without merit, we have done little to change this image by recognizing and using our outdoor recreation asset in an effort to become more competitive. In this situation, ecology and outdoor recreation can become an advantage in the competitive market for young talent.

It is also interesting to consider the proposed LSCNRA in the context of the delivery of outdoor recreation in the future. The dominant thinking about national parks derives from President Theodore Roosevelt. Our national treasures such as Yellowstone and Yosemite were carved from the vast expanse of federal lands in the West and were beautiful, unique places worthy of protection and visitation from around the country. However, today most of the great opportunities for these federal land set-asides are in the system. In my opinion, the real need for outdoor recreation exists adjacent to population centers. For this need, a different type of national park is required, one that can be accessed by urban populations, one that is assembled from many parts that exist around many of our population centers as opposed to being created "whole cloth" like most of our popular national parks around the country. And there is no doubt that the concept and the reality of the proposed LSCNRA fit that need perfectly.

In order to help ensure that the proposed LSCNRA is successful, an NGO called the Lone Star Coastal Alliance has been formed. The purposes of this NGO include educating the public about and garnering public support for the creation of the proposed LSCNRA and funding a significant portion of its operation once established, given that many Texas politicians are extremely concerned about making further demands on the federal budget. Indeed, there has been concern about the word "national" in the title of the proposed LSCNRA, but this is the same "national" connection that will provide the marketing and branding to bring the ecotourists to the Texas coast. There are times in trying to implement these concepts that one truly questions the sanity of some of our politicians, if not of the political process in general. But then again, this is Texas.

The opportunities for ecoplay are not limited to the upper and middle coast. They exist throughout the coast, as evidenced by a wonderful trip a group of us took to the Fennessey Ranch near Copano Bay. We arrived at the gate just after sunrise on a blustery spring day. During the night, storms had come through Rockport, where we were staying, and it had rained bucketsfull, but for now we had caught a break in the weather and were determined to go on our ecotour of the ranch. We were met by Sally Crofutt, the ranch manager, as we entered the gate and parked on the roadside, where we saw the trailer lined with hay bales that was to be our ride through the coastal prairie, a hayride designed for ecoplay, a day of looking at birds and habitat along the way.

The Fennessey Ranch is located just off FM 2678 between Refugio and Bayside on the Mission River not far above where it flows into Copano Bay. The ranch set aside a 3,261-acre conservation easement to protect much of its important prairie, wetland, and riparian habitat. Like many ranches, the Fennessey is always trying to raise sufficient money and has been operated for the last decade or two as an environmentally friendly business with income from traditional sources such as cattle and oil and gas but also from wildlife tours, hunting and photography leases, and kayaking. We had signed up for a birding tour and were anxious to get underway, particularly with the ominous dark sky around us.

Our group was apprehensive about the weather and quite amusing to see, carrying every type and color of raingear and waterproof footwear (or not). Our group of friends included Jack, Sue, Isabelle, Sally, Carol, and two Johns from Houston, along with Bubba and Shelly from Austin, Diane from Marshall, Cheryl from California, and Garland and me. Just as we were beginning, our birding guide Nan Dietert pointed out a brown-crested flycatcher and golden-fronted woodpecker, two birds that most of the group had never seen before, or "life birds," as such birds are known to birders. We could not have asked for a better start for the day.

We jumped (some more so than others) up on the hay bales in the trailer and took off down the muddy roads, happy to be above it all. We saw a bald eagle's nest on the top of some transmission line poles and could see the eagle in the distance, but we were unable to drive closer due to the rains that had saturated the ground and left water standing across the pastures. A large wetland held numerous wading birds such as ibis and egrets and the last of the wintering ducks, primarily blue-winged teal. Although numerous neotropical migrants had been present on the property during the last week, they were relatively scarce due to the weather, making our experience similar to fishing in at least one way, as in, "you should have been here yesterday."

The vegetation and flowers were fabulous, with various hues of green in the brush and the grasslands, greens that only got more robust as we headed down into the bottomlands

Figure 7.10. Group enjoying ecoplay atop hay bales on a trailer being pulled down the roads and through the ecosystems of the Fennessey Ranch. Photo by Cheryl Overend.

of the Mission River, a really nice watercourse that rises in central Refugio County and flows along the edge of the Fennessey Ranch. It was here in this bottomland that the trip really came alive for us.

First, we met a group of birders engaged in a birdathon competition, a contest in which you count how many birds you can see in twenty-four hours. This group had come onto the ranch to find a green jay, among other birds, had just seen it, and were jumping into their car to dash off in search of more species. It was fun to get a glimpse of their fast-paced search for birds in contrast to our laid-back tour on the bales of hay, moving slowly, taking it all in, peaceful and blissful.

Then we came to the river, which was flowing a bit high with that dark tannin stain that comes with rainfall runoff from a forest. Looking down the river, we first saw a belted kingfisher, and then orioles decorating a tree hanging over the river from the other side, the orange and black a beautiful contrast to the newly greened trees and darkening sky that

Figure 7.11. Spring on the Fennessey Ranch near the Mission River and Copano Bay in Refugio County. Photo by Cheryl Overend.

Figure 7.12. Green jay attacking a barred owl in the forest next to the Mission River on the Fennessey Ranch ecotour. Photo by Alfred Lee Kaufman.

was building again. An owl hooted and our guide called back, bringing in a pair of beautiful barred owls so that all could see them, sitting perfectly still about fifty feet away in the large tree next to where we were standing.

And then all hell broke loose (fig. 7.12). Jays converged like attacking jet fighters, flashes of green, yellow, black, and purple accompanied by a cacophony of sounds. But the owls were unmoved, uncaring, unconcerned, stoic in all respects. Yet the jays were persistent, putting on a show, allowing us an unparalleled viewing of a green jay, one of the most beautiful birds in South Texas, followed shortly by a visit from a buff-bellied hummingbird visiting the flowers on the hanging vine while a flock of Franklin's gulls flew overhead, heading north.

When we were back in the hay wagon, the rain, which had held off all morning, slowly began. It seemed a good time for

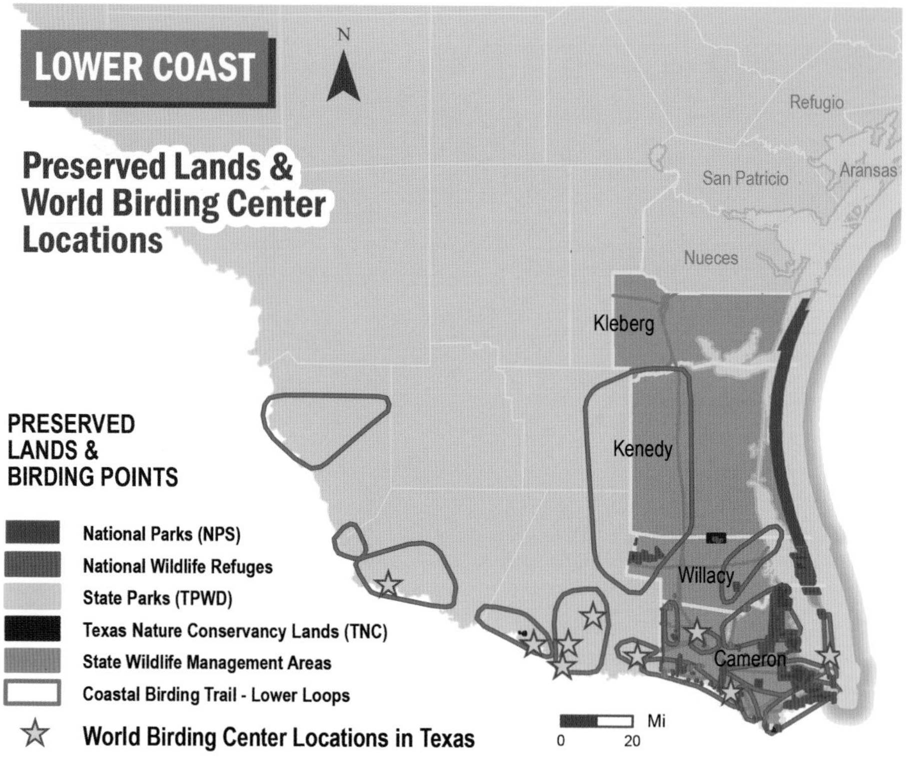

Figure 7.13. The southern leg of the Great Texas Coastal Birding Trail has numerous secondary loops that include World Birding Center locations and national wildlife refuge and NGO lands.

lunch, and we pulled up to an old camp house on the ranch and I had one of the best sandwiches I can remember, made so good by being able to watch the rain from beneath the roof of the garage where we sat in plastic chairs and relived the morning. We all agreed that the time had come to end our wonderful ecotour. Later that afternoon in Rockport just before dinner, we saw a painted bunting and a bronze cowbird in a local park, capping off a wonderful day.

The day recounted above is but one of many that I have spent at ecoplay on the Texas coast. I emphasize "play" because that is what it is—outdoor fun focused on ecology, our most underrated commodity. Tourism based on ecology, on the natural wealth of which the Texas coast has such an abundance, seems like a no-brainer for economic development, yet we are not very sophisticated in our understanding and development of this economic sector. We need to become much more so, and we can and we should.

The LSCNRA on the upper coast can and should be matched by similar concepts on the middle and lower coast. The Fen-

Figure 7.14. An Altamira oriole, a South Texas specialty bird. Photo by Kathy Adams Clark.

nessey Ranch, Welder Wildlife Refuge, Aransas National Wildlife Refuge, Rockport, Aransas Pass, and Port Aransas provide a wonderful opportunity for organized ecotourism, complete with whooping crane boat trips that allow views of sea ducks and whooping cranes during the winter and early spring, and later in the spring, rookery islands full of terns and gulls and herons and egrets and spoonbills.

Similarly, the Rio Grande Valley portion of the lower coast also has great potential. The World Birding Center was created by the Texas legislature at several venues, as shown by the stars in figure 7.13. There are also extensive national wildlife refuge holdings and several wonderful loops from the Great Texas Coastal Birding Trail that can be combined into a wonderful collection of ecoplay sites, including the beaches at South Padre and Boca Chica. In such places one might see South Texas specialty birds such as Altamira and Audubon's orioles, brown and green jays, clay-colored robins, elf and ferruginous pygmy owls, green and ringed kingfishers, plain chachalacas, olive sparrows, and northern jacanas, among several others.

The bottom line is that ecoplay is available to all who come to the Texas coast. It is about resources and it is also about mind-set. If you like getting outdoors and enjoying nature, the Texas coast has the ecological resources to provide a world-class adventure. What we need is organization and collaboration to make this happen, to realize a great economic as well as personal opportunity. We should simply do it.

CHAPTER 8

Fishing and Kayaking

Fishing instills passion for the coast in those that enjoy it, and passion for the coast will be a critical aspect of its positive future. Fishing and kayaking are among the best aspects of outdoor recreation on the Texas coast. I am a devoted fan of both and I recommend them to all. From as early as I can remember, my uncles, father, and grandfather took me fishing, mostly in central Louisiana in the creeks feeding the Cocodrie Swamp. Occasionally we would get up really early and drive down to the Atchafalaya Basin, returning with ice chests full of big, beautiful bream, which we scaled and fried along with hush puppies and French fries and served to the large extended family who gathered and ate with my Uncle L. E. and Aunt Kitty on their screened porch. Not exactly healthy, but definitely family friendly.

Later, I learned to fish the Texas coast, and I highly recommend it to anyone who enjoys the outdoors and a bit of adventure. Fishing to me is about friends and family, camaraderie, nature, and adventure. It's about going somewhere new and trying to understand it, seeing how the water moves, how the vegetation and physical features of the bay like reefs, points, and channels share space with the water, how the fish use that space. Fishing is about what is happening beneath the water, where you can't really see, particularly along the upper coast. It's about signs and movement, ripples and splashes, a mullet jumping here, a shrimp popping there, a tail revealed in the shallows.

Fishing is about stepping into the shallows, mounting a kayak, and paddling across water barely six inches deep. It's about wading in mushy bottoms where the mud climbs up over your ankles, sucking your shoes and making you question why you ventured into this corner of the marsh, when suddenly you see the telltale signs of feeding fish and forget about it.

Fishing is about ritual and repetition, about marking a spot where the last trip succeeded, about trying to relive past successes and avoid past failures. It's about a remembered wreck, or the corner of an oyster reef, or a nook within the marsh where the redfish and flounder wait to ambush the small ones that come into and leave the marsh with the tide.

Texas coastal fishing is about waking up at four in the morning, loading up and heading down to the coast, listening to Captain Mickey Eastman talk to the fishing guides on KILT AM 610, following a long tradition of weekend fishing shows that allow the guides to call in and talk about what they caught yesterday, how the wind seems to have changed, and how you should have been there. Fishing talk is about the one that got away, where it was caught or what it was caught on, often with a fair amount of misleading if not outright false information.

Coastal fishing is about rhythms—about the ebb and flow of the tide, about the moon phase and feeding cycles. Bays have a circular natural economy, with shrimp migrating into the Gulf to lay their eggs and the larvae floating with the tide back into the bay until they find the marsh that will be their nursery, where they settle and mature and then migrate back to the Gulf to do it all again. The bay is about flounder piling up near the passes in late fall, staging at the places where the Gulf and estuary meet, moving as a body together into the Gulf to spawn, with the fry returning to the nursery marsh. The bay is about the small finfish—the mullet and menhaden and anchovies—as well as the reds and trout moving back and forth through the passes to complete their life cycles, a fishery that we fishermen try to learn and interpret and intercept, often with only marginal success.

Fishing is about mental and physical agility, about being able to rebound from a fish totally outsmarting you as well as from the many ways you can end up feeling if not looking foolish in this noble pursuit. Fishing is about catching each other's lines at the critical moment when the fish are within casting range. Fishing is about dipping the net to capture the big one that somehow evades your thrust and throws the hook at your fishing buddy, who looks like he just lost a winning lottery ticket. Fishing is about humility, about life learning, about love for something bigger and more wonderful than yourself. And fishing is about forgetting all those travails and simply having fun.

If you want to learn to fish the Texas coast, hire a guide. I was lucky in that my uncles and my father were my early guides. Together we fished the swamps of central Louisiana and the marshes of coastal Texas, the bayous from small johnboats and the Gulf from the rock jetties that line our ship canals. Many people living in Texas today do not have family guides to open their minds and hearts to the Texas coast because they moved here from other places. For those of you from other places who want to know the Texas coast, here's a tip: hire a guide.

Now, there are some keys to using a guide. Ask a lot of questions. Do not pretend that you know what you are doing. The goal is to learn. Put your ego and your macho aside. I have found that women are often much better at this step than men. If you have youngsters you want to teach, teach yourself first. Learn about how to fish an area and then do it again and again. It is not necessary to own a motorboat. Let the guide own the boat. Let the guide do the hard work of navigating and finding fish. You will likely save much money in the long run if you pay the guide to own the boat and to squire you and your group around the bay, at least in the beginning. Hiring a guide is money well spent, and you will be helping build the economy that will save the future of the Texas coast, something you might consider feeling good about.

You can fish from the shoreline in many places, although you have to look for these, and you will find that they get crowded at certain times of the year. We have hundreds of

Figure 8.1. Guide pulling out of the Port Mansfield Marina with some prospective anglers. Photo by Larry Ditto.

miles of beaches, and the fishing is periodically great along these areas, which by law are open to the people of the state of Texas, although that right of public access has been taking a beating in the Texas court system lately. Beach fishing is best from late spring to early fall and can be excellent when atmospheric high pressure systems settle over the coast in late summer and flatten the surf and clear the water. In the Houston area, the key is "ozone days," because these conditions lead to elevated air pollution inland. So leave the dirty air in the city and go to the beach, where trout, redfish, Spanish mackerel, and occasionally pompano can all be caught on the same trip. Beach fishing is free and the air comes from above the clean Gulf.

If you think you want to buy a boat to fish on your own, first try a kayak. Kayak fishing is the sport of kings, at least as far as I am concerned, and a kayak is much cheaper than a good bay boat—much, much cheaper. Kayak fishing is a true adventure, one that puts the fisherman about six inches above the water in a craft that requires about three or four inches of water. It glides without a sound other than the water drops falling from the paddle (and the sound of your breathing).

Figure 8.2. Fisherman walking the marsh and using a cast net to catch finger mullet, an excellent live bait for redfish and speckled trout. Photo by Kathy Adams Clark.

You are immersed in the moment, senses engaged. True, your muscles will feel the strain after a while, but it's all good—really good.

I usually fish with a group of men collectively known as Team 11, a name based on our entry number at a fishing tournament many years ago. A fishing trip with Team 11 is about friendship—about Jack relating his latest adventure flying here or there to train engineers, and about the perils of the cold north and the hot southwest; about John F. discussing the ups and downs of the mortgage business and points, always talking points; about John C. bemoaning the lack of a future in real estate appraising, a tune he has been singing forever; and about me lamenting the latest environmental horror on the Texas coast, with new ones emerging more often than any of us would like.

Team 11 is owned by the auxiliary, our wives—Sue, Sally, Princie, and Garland. The auxiliary bet on us once in a Calcutta fishing tournament and won big because Team 11 actually managed to find some fish and win the tournament, a feat unlikely to be repeated, at least in part because we are not entering fishing tournaments anymore. Instead we are pursuing more relaxed fishing away from the crowds, being one with the water, the marsh, the air, and the sky, trying to find those that live beneath the surface but not worrying about it too much.

My favorite fishing trip with Team 11 is to hit the bay at daylight in our kayaks, a flotilla that launches into a bayou on the back side of Galveston Island rimmed by salt marsh and shallow seagrass flats. The water is still as the sun rises above the island, golden shafts lighting blue sky and dark water, our four kayaks moving gracefully, each of us heading in a slightly different direction, finding our spot, trying our luck. Here and there we hear the whisper or yelp of success, each of us in his own world, a world where roseate spoonbills fly over and egrets watch us pass by from their grassy hides where they stalk the marsh's edge, fishing with us, sharing space, sharing a system. This is fishing and being alive, enjoying nature, taking it into the deepest parts of our consciousness and absorbing it. Later, we gather together, Team 11 and its owners, good friends eating trout and reds and maybe flounder, sharing a bond forged yet again by a peaceful morning on a West Bay bayou in late summer.

The most difficult part of kayak fishing is finding a good

Figure 8.3. Kayak fisherman, alone and peaceful. Photo by Kathy Adams Clark.

place to launch and fish. Public accessibility is tricky in many areas of the coast. Public recreation areas often offer the best bet for access, along with public bridges and shoreline roads. Most of our bays are partially if not mainly ringed by private property, and kayak fishing from a car requires access by land. If you are able to load your kayak on a bay boat, then a whole world of opportunity opens up, but I limit myself to access by car.

Certain areas enjoy good accessibility, and they are worth knowing about. There is access to the Bessie Heights marsh on the east side of the Rainbow Bridge on US 87 between Port Arthur and Orange. A couple of boat ramps at the lower end of Sabine Lake near Sabine Pass offer access to both oyster reefs and marsh. The back side of the Bolivar Peninsula has numerous roads leading to the Gulf Intracoastal Waterway, with East Bay just across the twelve-foot-deep barge canal, and areas such as Rollover Pass where the water moves in from Gulf and out from the bay, at least until the Texas General Land Office moves forward with its plan to close the pass, the best public fishing place on the coast. And while on the Bolivar Peninsula, you might stop and eat at the Stingaree Marina, which has a wonderful panoramic view of the intracoastal waterway and East Bay. Smith Point in Chambers County offers excellent kayak access, and the backwaters of the Army Corps of Engineers Wallisville public recreation area offer great fishing at certain times of the year and a wonderful kayak adventure anytime.

The western shoreline of Galveston Bay has several boat ramps that can be used as access points, but much of the shoreline is developed for housing and is hard to access. However, places such as Sylvan Beach Park, Armand Bayou, and Taylor Bayou welcome kayakers and offer fishing opportunities. The Texas City dike and levee is an excellent public access point at the lower end of Galveston Bay, as is the back side of Galveston Island, particularly at Galveston Island State Park and San Luis Pass, which offer myriad opportunities. But be warned—San Luis Pass, particularly where it enters the Gulf, is dangerous. Wear a life vest when wading or kayaking the surf. Be smart. Stay alive. You may think you are a strong swimmer, but when you are loaded with fishing gear and lose your footing or flip out of your kayak, a life vest is your best friend.

There are numerous public access points south of San Luis Pass, including entry to Cold Pass and Tittlin' Tattlin' Bayou,

Figure 8.4. Public-access fishing is afforded by the rock jetties that line the deepwater channels at Sabine Pass, Bolivar Roads between the Bolivar Peninsula and Galveston Island, Freeport (shown here), Matagorda, Port Aransas, and South Padre Island/Boca Chica. Photo by Jim Olive.

which empties into Christmas Bay, as well as the Brazoria County boat ramp, which is midway on Christmas Bay and has seagrass flats nearby. The fishin' and paddlin' are superb but can vary tremendously based on wind conditions. Forget about it when there is a strong or perhaps even weak southwest wind, which blows nothing but ill for fishing, and a strong north wind can blow much of the water out of Christmas Bay. It is shallow. I have seen the water's edge several hundred feet farther out than normal after the passage of a strong cold front. Without question, one of my favorite kayak fishing places near Houston is where Christmas and Drum Bays come together, a gem of a place that lies between San Luis Pass and Freeport (see chapter 1).

The water where we fish is not generally deep, usually four feet or less, and our kayaks are stable fishing platforms, unlike river kayaks, which tip easily. Always take care. Wear a life vest. Pay attention to the wind and weather. Don't get caught out in your kayak during a storm. My wife and I almost got stranded on a mudflat in the delta of the Colorado River where we were watching wading birds and ducks and not the weather. On this occasion, the wind shifted and quickly blew the water off the flat, leaving us to work our way across the soft silt of the delta, slowly, ever so slowly, reaching paddleable water near sunset, barely making it back to our car before dark. This is a great sport, but be smart about it.

Down the coast, kayak fishing opportunities decline for a bit. Most of the prime fishing areas from Freeport to East Matagorda Bay are privately owned marshlands with only limited access through bayous with long paddles to the fishing areas, which I would advise novices to avoid. Start with the areas easier to access and work up to the harder ones. Go first with guided trips offered by canoe clubs or outdoor clubs. Groups such as Artist Boat in Galveston, the Houston Canoe Club, and the Sierra Club will take you out and teach you how to be comfortable in a kayak. Use them. They are a local resource. And Artist Boat might also help you learn to paint.

But back to the coast. The eastern and northern portions of East Matagorda Bay are relatively inaccessible to kayaks, other than locations within the community of Sargent. Again, much of the northern shoreline is privately owned. However, East and Matagorda Bays open up to car-borne kayaks at the town of Matagorda, particularly along the isthmus that runs along the old channel of the Colorado River to the Gulf. Here, the barrier island is accessible to automobiles and opens up the southern shoreline of East Matagorda Bay to paddlers, and FM 2031 provides excellent public access to the Colorado River and the marshes surrounding the isthmus, connecting the town of Matagorda to the beach. The Lower Colorado River Authority has a kayak trail at the southwestern corner of East Matagorda Bay that provides excellent marsh kayaking and fishing.

Farther south, again much of the northern shoreline of Matagorda Bay is privately owned, and the barrier beach is not accessible to cars and is also privately owned. Still farther south, there is excellent public access near the town of Palacios and along SH 35 where it crosses the top of Carancahua Bay, as well as where it crosses Lavaca Bay. Unfortunately, I do not recommend eating redfish (or crabs) from Lavaca Bay because of mercury contamination from the Alcoa facility at Port Comfort, one of three bay superfund sites along the Texas coast. This is a great place for catch-and-release reds, and while trout are not affected as much by the mercury as are redfish, consumption of all fish and crabs from near the bridge is prohibited by the Texas Department of State Health Services.

The southern shoreline of Matagorda Bay is home to the old town of Indianola, which was destroyed by two hurricanes in the 1870s. Here there is a public park along the bay that provides excellent access, and boat ramps provide access to Powderhorn Lake, a quality kayak fishing place. Farther south is the community of Port O'Connor, a wonderful launching point for fishing the islands and inlets of Espiritu Santo bay. This is a first-class fishing and bird-watching place, but it does require crossing the Gulf Intracoastal Waterway and can involve more serious paddling than many other venues. However, once you have become acquainted with kayaking, this is an excellent place to spend some time. Past Port O'Connor, there is an excellent access point at the bait camp about halfway down Espiritu Santo Bay with good parking and paddling. The next point is the town of Seadrift, which offers a nice bay front and launching place on San Antonio Bay, also accessible near the northern boundary of Aransas National Wildlife Refuge on the other side of the bay.

Down the coast toward Rockport, public accessibility increases substantially. As a kayaker and fisherman as well as a birder, I recommend paying attention to the stretch from the Lamar Peninsula to Aransas Pass and again from Aransas

Pass to Port Aransas. At the north end of this area, Cavazos Creek along SH 35 is a personal favorite, a lovely marsh-lined estuary connecting to Saint Charles Bay with great accessibility and good kayaking. The Lamar Peninsula is home to Goose Island State Park and many public access points, and both Aransas and Copano Bays are accessible at numerous locations in, behind, and around Rockport.

At Aransas Pass, the angler has a choice between going south to Port Aransas and Mustang and Padre Islands or staying on the north shoreline of Aransas and Corpus Christi Bays. The road from Aransas Pass to Port Aransas represents one of the finest public access areas anywhere on the coast. No place is better for kayaking than Lighthouse Lakes, with its trail threading through the mangroves and seagrass flats almost within sight of the Port Aransas ferry landing. There are definitely quality fish here as well.

The area from Port Aransas south down Mustang and Padre Islands also has great public fishing and access. There are numerous launch spots on the back side of these islands, with one of the best being along Packery Channel, cutting across Padre Island just north of the Kennedy Causeway, which

Figure 8.5. Nothing quite matches the serenity of fishing from a kayak in the marsh. Photo by Jim Olive

crosses the Upper Laguna Madre from Corpus Christi and Flour Bluff. The entire beach along Padre Island National Seashore is accessible down to the Mansfield Cut, but you need to be very careful, have four-wheel drive, and know what you are getting into. Check in with the National Park Service before making any serious plans. The boat basin on the Upper Laguna Madre side of the island is one of the finest public access fishing points in this area.

On the mainland shoreline, Aransas Pass offers several places to launch and kayak, as does Ingleside along the north shoreline of Corpus Christi Bay. One of my favorite places is the park area along the SH 35 crossing of Nueces and Corpus Christi Bays, with a reef on the Corpus Christi Bay side and marsh on the Nueces Bay side. The entire western shoreline of Corpus Christi Bay is open along the seawall and on occasion can offer great fishing, particularly closer to the channel coming into the Corpus Christi inner harbor. Farther southeast along the Corpus Christi Bay shoreline is Oso Bay, a surprising fishing opportunity immediately adjacent to the campus of Texas A&M University–Corpus Christi. Finally, there is a public turnaround and several boat launches at the Kennedy Causeway that offer great access to the Upper Laguna Madre and Gulf Intracoastal Waterway.

There is not much public access along the majority of the Upper and Lower Laguna Madre, with the exception of boat launches at Baffin Bay and Port Mansfield, both excellent fishing venues promising hard paddling to the better places. East out of Harlingen and Rio Hondo, access opens up along the Arroyo Colorado, an old channel of the Rio Grande now used for drainage and barge transportation. The Arroyo is accessible from several locations and can hold good fish at certain times of the year. With serious paddling, some of the best redfish water on the Texas coast is accessible where the Arroyo empties into the Laguna behind the Laguna Atascosa National Wildlife Refuge. Multiple opportunities exist in and around Port Isabel, where the Brownsville Ship Channel comes in through Brazos Santiago Pass and goes inland toward Brownsville. This channel holds good fish during certain times of the year.

I have found that you can get great information from the local bait shops, not to mention live bait. Live bait generally means shrimp, which is the meaning of the white flag blowing from the pole outside the bait shop, with yellow meaning croaker. Bait shops are great curiosities. Each is different and unique in its own way, and there is often an interesting array of cats hanging around. Check these fine places out. Talk to the people there. Strike up a conversation. All you have to lose is a bit of time.

Crossing the Queen Isabella Causeway to South Padre Island again opens multiple fishing opportunities. A park near the jetties offers great public access to either the deeper water channel or the Laguna Madre, and a healthy paddle gets one to South Bay, a really nice place to fish. The jetties themselves offer fine bank fishing at certain times of the year. Farther north up the island, the beach opens up to automobile traffic about five miles north of the causeway. Bay access is also provided near the convention center at about this location as well.

The last stopping point along the coast is Boca Chica, a spit of land lying between Brazos Santiago Pass and the mouth of the Rio Grande. Here there is excellent beach access as well as access to the south jetty for rock fishing. Kayak fishing along this jetty for snook is high sport under the right conditions, along with Spanish mackerel and speckled trout. It is also possible to access South Bay from this side of the Brownsville

Figure 8.6. Bait shops such as this one near Surfside are great curiosities, often have good information on where to fish and what's being caught, and are generally interesting places. Photo by Kathy Adams Clark.

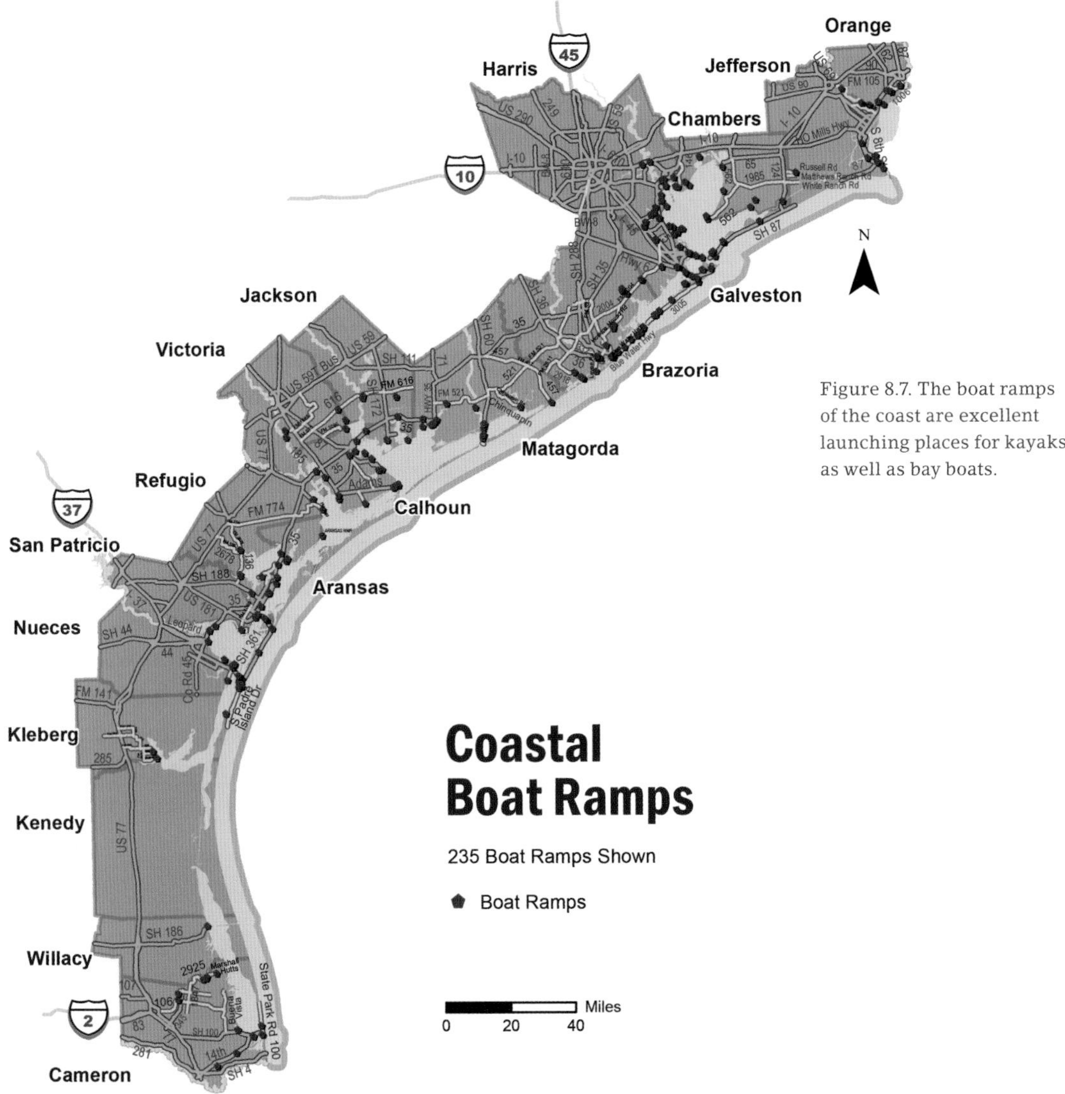

Figure 8.7. The boat ramps of the coast are excellent launching places for kayaks as well as bay boats.

Ship Channel. Figure 8.7 shows the location of boat ramps and some of the better access points on the Texas coast for kayakers and for those trailering their bay boats.

One of the high points of fishing is to understand and realize that birds are your friends. Birds can see and perceive what you cannot. But you can see and perceive them. So, as you learn to interpret the birds, your fishing success might increase.

Along the coast, I always look for bird activity. I like to see a formation of brown pelicans moving into my part of the bay, locating a school of finfish and diving headfirst into the water, and coming back up gulping down fish. I don't necessarily fish that location, but I consider diving pelicans to be a good sign that bait fish are in the area. And of course, when you see a mullet jumping out of the water, that is a great sign. I am convinced that they don't jump for pleasure. They have been frightened and are escaping. Throw where that action occurred and hope.

The best indicator birds are gulls, particularly in the summer and fall. Gulls locate schools of fish that are feeding on shrimp and follow them, diving down to pick up either wounded shrimp or those that jump out of the water to escape the predators, right into the mouth of the hungry gull. When you are in a motorboat, look out across the bay with a pair of field glasses for the telltale circle of laughing gulls that will locate the fish for you. The fun starts when you figure out which direction the school is moving and drift across its path. Often such fishing can yield a strike with every cast, at least until the school breaks up. But then, just wait and watch the birds until they show you where the school has formed again.

Often, you can locate one or more fish near where a single gull is sitting on the water. Sometimes these gulls tend to stay on top of a feeding fish, waiting for the action to reach the

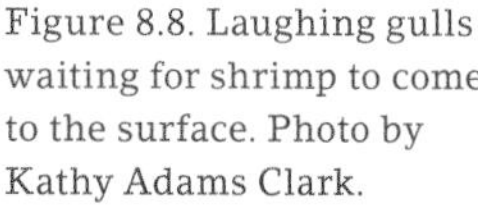

Figure 8.8. Laughing gulls waiting for shrimp to come to the surface. Photo by Kathy Adams Clark.

surface. More often than not I have caught reds under a single gull, whereas a large circle of birds more often indicates speckled trout or gaff-topsail catfish. Unfortunately, under the birds there are often many smaller trout that have to be released because they are under the Texas limit for size, which for trout is fifteen inches and for reds is twenty inches.

Then there are "liar" birds—most likely terns—that feed on smaller fish. These do not indicate a school of predators feeding on bait but rather highlight a school of very small fish that these particular birds like. I have been fishing with guides who got excited about bird action, only to disgustedly spit out, when we came closer, that these were "*** liar" birds. So, for fishermen (or would-be fishermen), it pays to learn the difference between a gull and a tern. But then about the time you are ready to never fish under a liar bird again, you catch a good fish below feeding terns and decide that maybe they don't lie all the time, which of course leaves you perplexed about what to do the next time you see them. Aargh. Such are the trials and tribulations—and the fun—of fishing.

The most interesting bird experience I have had while fishing was in the marsh in Matagorda Bay on an outgoing tide. Redfish often go way up marsh channels on the incoming high tide and into the grass in search of shrimp and other morsels that find sanctuary among the stalks and stems. As the tide falls, the shrimp and finger mullet, and the reds, fall back into the main marsh channels and the bay. One day when I was fishing with my guide and friend Al Garrison, we saw a number of large white birds seemingly dancing along the top of the marsh grass. Al pointed at the small flock of snowy egrets and slowly motored up the marsh channel to intersect them. As they neared our boat, you could see shrimp jumping out of the water and onto the mud to flee the school of reds, only to get captured by a dancing egret hopping up and down along the edge. I have never observed snowy egrets feeding like that since then, but I always look for them in the marsh on an outgoing tide. Of course, Jack and I got our lines tangled in the thrill of pursuit, but that was just part of the fun.

Similarly, one day I was wade fishing on the north side of Galveston Island and observed two white pelicans swimming into the marsh up a large channel. I followed behind them at some distance, and they led me deep into the marsh to a limit of reds. So when I see white pelicans swimming into the marsh, I go where they go.

So, where are the best places to fish on the Texas coast? I have my favorites, but where does the data tell us to fish? To assist you in understanding where you might want to fish, consider the Texas Parks and Wildlife charts in figures 8.9, 8.10, and 8.11 that identify the number of fish caught per hour of collecting fish by various techniques. These charts do not mean that you can catch fish at these rates, and they don't mean that these bays have these numbers of fish at all times of the year. There are many qualifications to charts like these, but it is fair to say that they indicate the relative abundance of fish over a year's worth of collection. The charts are presented first for redfish, second for speckled trout, and third for the two combined.

For red drum, the top five productive bays are Sabine Lake, Trinity Bay, West Bay, East Matagorda Bay, and Espiritu Santo Bay. For trout, the top five are Sabine Lake, Sabine Pass, Galveston Bay, Espiritu Santo Bay, and Baffin Bay. Sabine Lake and Espiritu Santo show up on both top five lists. When we combine the catch rates, a few changes appear, as can be seen in figure 8.11.

Espiritu Santo seems to be the overall winner, followed by East Matagorda Bay, Sabine Lake, and Trinity Bay. I would not have predicted that result. That's why we collect data, and that's also why we all have our best places that may defy the

Figure 8.9. Each bay is sampled by Texas Parks and Wildlife to show the rate at which various types of fish are caught. East Matagorda Bay has the highest catch rate for redfish.

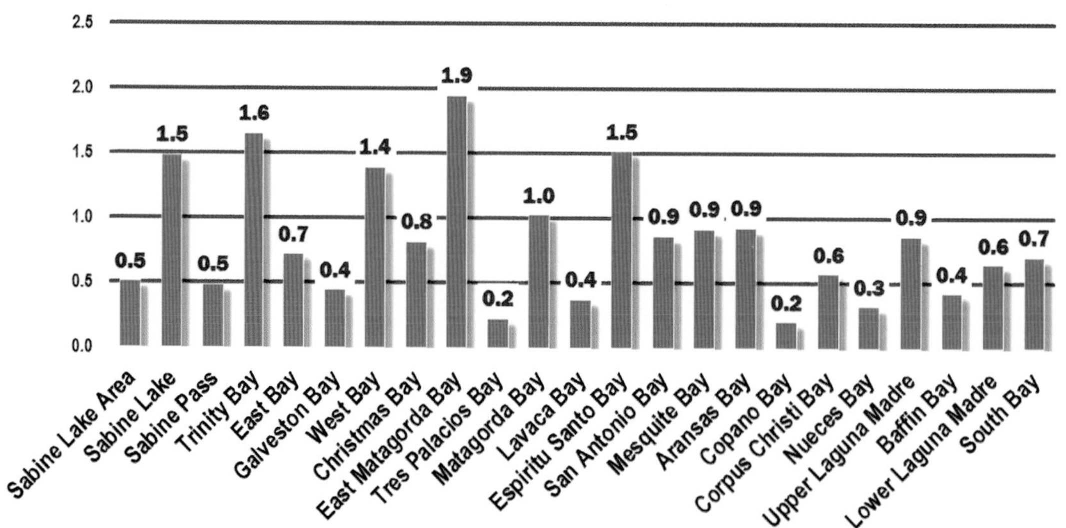

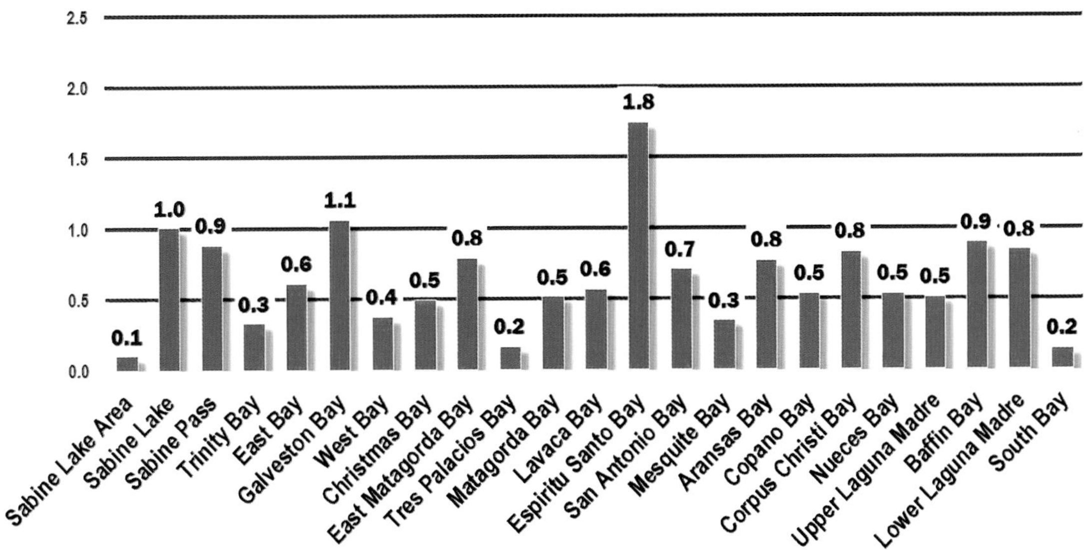

Figure 8.10. Espiritu Santo Bay emerges as the bay with the greatest catch rate for spotted sea trout, better known as speckled trout.

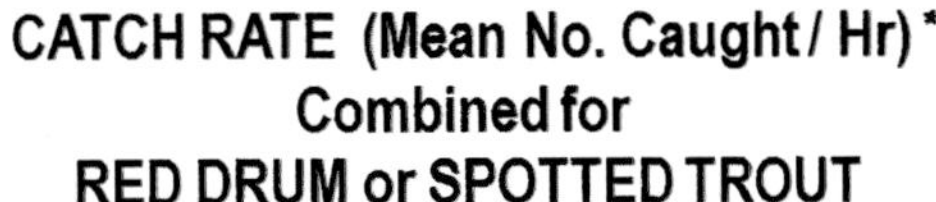

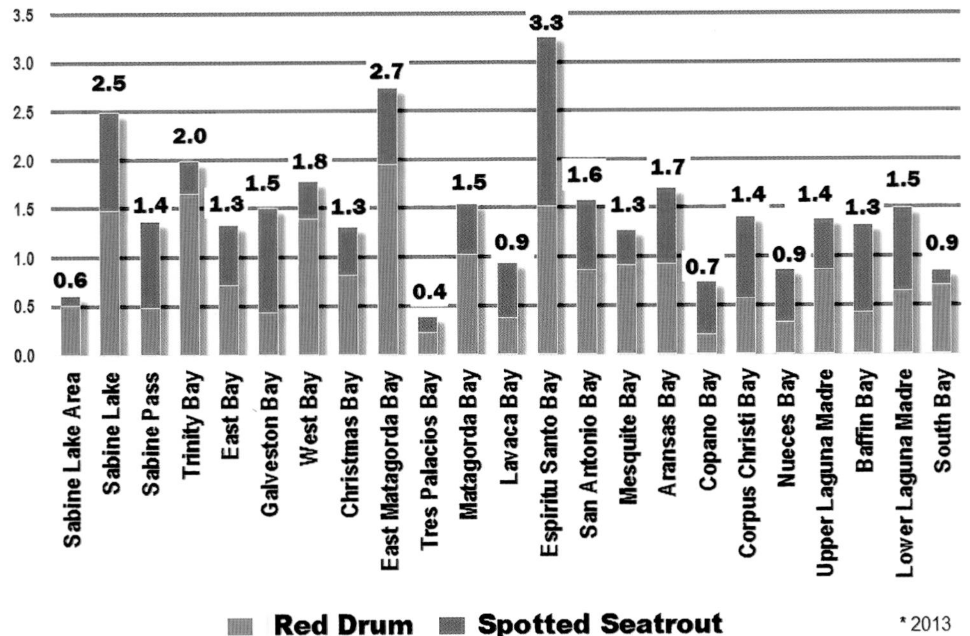

Figure 8.11. When both reds and specks are combined, Espiritu Santo has the highest combined catch rate, followed by East Matagorda Bay, Sabine Lake, and Trinity Bay.

data. It is also important to keep in mind that certain bays are better in wet times and others are better in drier times, and that reds are more tolerant of salinity variations, particularly low salinity, than are speckled trout, which prefer saltier conditions. The final hard truth is that some fishermen and women are just better than others. I have fished with Al Garrison and thrown to the exact same spot with the same bait or lure, and he catches more fish than I do. Every time. On the other hand, when I'm pitted against my Team 11 mates, that's a fair contest.

From an economic standpoint, recreational fishing is an underappreciated asset for the state. Serious money is spent on fishing equipment such as lures, bait, tackle, rods, and reels, and much bigger money is spent on boats and coastal homes. There are several hundred guides on the Texas coast, all making some amount of money. Together, these activities add up.

There is not much economic data or many studies that focus on the economics of coastal angling. A US Fish and Wildlife Service survey of fishing in Texas estimated that about 2.2 million Texans fished in 2011 out of a 2010 state population of about 25 million. At that time, the US Fish and Wildlife Service estimated that these Texas fishermen spent about $1.5 billion on supplies and equipment. It does not appear that this survey included information such as boat or home ownership. Texas Parks and Wildlife sold over 1.5 million saltwater fishing licenses or combination licenses in 2015. Also, according to Texas Parks and Wildlife, there are about 1,150 saltwater fishing guides in Texas.

Kayaking is one of the fastest-growing sports in the United States, with or without fishing. The Outdoor Foundation indicated that over twenty-three million people participated in paddling activities nationwide, generating $36 billion in economic activity. There is no separate data for Texas, although the coastal kayaking described in this chapter is only just beginning on the Texas coast.

Recreational fishing is part of the market solution to the future of the Texas coast. Commercial fishing is also a piece of that puzzle, representing about $250 million in income in 2014, as determined by the Coastal Research and Extension Center of Mississippi State University.

However, most of those landings were from offshore catches, because the commercial fishing use of our bays is declining rapidly as the state of Texas has increased regulation in an attempt to prevent overharvesting of important nursery areas and recreational species such as redfish and speckled trout. An unfortunate consequence of that political decision is that the number of voices willing to stand up and fight for the integrity of the coast has declined. Love 'em or hate 'em, but commercial fishermen are always willing to fight for the bays, something that cannot always be said for recreational fishermen. This decline in commercial voices must be countered by increased activism and serious political participation by coastal recreational anglers.

The dollar value of this coastal commercial and recreational fishery is one basis supporting the establishment of a dollar value for water taken from our rivers, as set out in chapter 3. The sooner we realize that the protection of this fishery for both commercial and recreational users is necessary, the better. So I repeat—coastal recreational fishermen and women need to step up and be counted and stick their necks out a bit to protect the coast.

As for myself, I am thinking about my next fishing trip. I think I will go to Christmas Bay or perhaps the back side of Galveston Island, or maybe I'll just call up Al. Regardless, it will be time well spent.

CHAPTER 9

Private Litigation

Passion engendered by birding, fishing, and ecoplay on the Texas coast, and a love of the land, your land in particular, is essential for the future of the Texas coast. You have to truly want something to fight for it—you have to be attached to it. And in times when nothing else works, you have to fight.

In the old days, when they said whiskey's for drinkin' and water's for fightin', guns were definitely involved. Today, the fight is more likely to involve the courtroom than firearms, although fisticuffs are still possible. And goin' to court is a time-honored private-sector action.

In Texas, we often talk publicly against private litigation and attack trial lawyers as greedy self-serving SOBs who need to be brought to heel with tort reform if not other actions. What is less well known is that corporations and corporate interest groups file more federal environmental lawsuits than any other entity. In my experience, the courts are perhaps the greatest equalizing entity when it comes to environmental law in Texas, particularly the federal courts. We may be at the mercy of state elected and appointed officials in the day-to-day oversight of environmental issues in Texas, but it is a different world when you walk into a federal courtroom having filed suit against state government officials. Sometimes you cannot foresee the result even if you make your best guess about a potential outcome.

Such was the case on February 22, 2016, when I found myself at the former Aquarena Springs in San Marcos, the current home of the Meadows Center for Water and the Environment at Texas State University. The Meadows Center is housed in a former hotel at the site of the springs that feed the San Marcos and Guadalupe Rivers. I had driven up from Houston that morning to meet Bill West and Todd Votteler, two key officials with the Guadalupe-Blanco River Authority (GBRA), an entity that had been on the other side of litigation from my client, The Aransas Project (TAP). TAP was formed to litigate for freshwater inflow for San Antonio Bay in order to keep the bay healthy so that there would be sufficient blue crabs to feed the wintering whooping cranes. On this day, we publicly announced that the GBRA and TAP were setting aside their differences and pursuing a shared vision for the Guadalupe River watershed and San Antonio Bay, a vision that included freshwater inflows for the bays and for the whoopers as well as for the human economy.

On one level, this agreement was a surprise ending to a very hard fought legal battle lasting from 2011 to 2015. On another level, however, unexpected results sometimes occur when two very determined entities clash legally and philosophically over a period of time, during which they learn a lot about each other, perhaps more than either wanted to know. But such is the nature of litigation. It brings the parties up close and personal.

Over the years, I have had many unexpected outcomes from legal clashes, such as settlements. Environmental cases are hard to win, and good lawyers lose environmental cases in Texas. It comes with the turf. On the other hand, it is important that those who believe in a point of view stand up and fight for it. I am convinced that if you are unwilling to go to court, your concerns—your claims—may not be taken seriously. You may not be liked for litigating, but you may well be respected. Without at least some element of respect, it is hard to convince opposing parties to work with you to solve problems. Such is the story behind the GBRA-TAP agreement regarding the future of water use and freshwater inflows in the Guadalupe River valley. And it is a story.

In March 2010, TAP was formed by ranchers, coastal fishermen, bird-watchers, and local elected officials and filed suit in federal court over the deaths of 23 of the 270 endangered whooping cranes that winter in Aransas County. Under Section 9 of the Endangered Species Act, it is illegal for any "person" to "take" an endangered species. In this case, we alleged that the actions of the commissioners of the Texas Commission on Environmental Quality (TCEQ), "persons" under the act, caused a "take" (e.g., death) of twenty-three whooping cranes by issuing and managing permits allowing withdrawals of surface water from the Guadalupe and San Antonio Rivers during the winter of 2008–2009.

Although the suit was filed under the Endangered Species Act over the deaths of the cranes, TAP was widely supported in Aransas County because of the negative economic effects associated with significantly reduced freshwater inflows. During the same period that the cranes died, recreational and commercial fishing suffered badly, vacation home rentals and home sales decreased, and retail business was way down. When bay productivity is harmed, the coastal economy suffers, creating a powerful alliance between economy and ecology.

Judge Janis Jack's courtroom is on the third floor of the federal courthouse in Corpus Christi, a beautiful modern building overlooking Corpus Christi Bay and the adjacent seawall promenade. It is hard to imagine a better venue for a lawsuit attempting to obtain freshwater inflows to keep San Antonio Bay, a neighbor to the north, healthy. I was the lead attorney representing TAP in a suit against the commissioners and executive director of the TCEQ. Our trial was a bench trial, meaning that there was no jury, only Judge Jack, a no-nonsense Corpus Christi lawyer who had been extremely well prepared during pretrial hearings and discussions.

The trial started auspiciously. As Austin lawyer Jeff Mundy, my cocounsel, and I walked to the courthouse for opening arguments early on that first Monday, Jeff, an expert bird-watcher, looked up and pointed to a bird fishing in the water next to the seawall. "Look, there's a loon. We will have good luck in the trial," he said. And he was correct.

This lawsuit was strongly opposed by the Texas attorney general's office, which represented the TCEQ officials, as well as by intervening affected parties such as the Texas Chemical Council, the San Antonio River Authority, and most visibly, the GBRA, which had taken the lead in defending this litigation. The GBRA had several large water diversion permits allowing withdrawals from the Guadalupe River and was interested in obtaining more. The GBRA was concerned that TAP's litigation could disrupt its water rights, and it committed significant resources to this fight.

And make no mistake about it—this was a fight, our legal team pitted against a courtroom full of defense lawyers. In addition to me and Jeff Mundy, an expert bird-watcher and trial lawyer, the legal team we brought to court included Charles Irvine, our crane and endangered species specialist who knew the case better than any of us; Mary Conner, our appellate ace; David Kahne, our constitutional and federal law expert, who handled the cross-examination of a key witness; and Patrick Waites, a lawyer who was in charge of visual presentation of evidence. My partner, Mary Carter, stayed back in Houston, keeping the firm together during this battle, which was critical to my peace of mind. We came to court fully prepared, feeling like we were part of that old legend about one riot, one ranger, hoping the trial would not turn into Custer's Last Stand.

Our case presentation started with an introduction to the life cycle of whooping cranes and their recovery so far by Dr. George Archibald, the world's leading expert on these cranes and founder of the International Crane Foundation. George was followed by Dr. Ron Sass of Rice University, who testified about his compelling analysis of the linkage between crane mortality over the years and freshwater inflows between July and December of various drought years. As can be seen in figure 9.2, a larger percentage of the crane wintering flock dies when the inflow drops, and the flock thrives when the inflows are higher. Dr. Sass found statistical significance in the linkage between mortality and inflow, a point that was emphasized and strengthened by the testimony of another expert, Dr. Kathy Ensor, chair of the Statistics Department at Rice. By the end of the first day, we were off to a good start.

There are several major themes and battles between opposing sides within a case, and one of those disputed themes in

Figure 9.1. A mature whooping crane and a cinnamon-streaked youngster fish together in a marsh pond on the Aransas National Wildlife Refuge. Note the small crab in the juvenile's beak. Photo by Kathy Adams Clark.

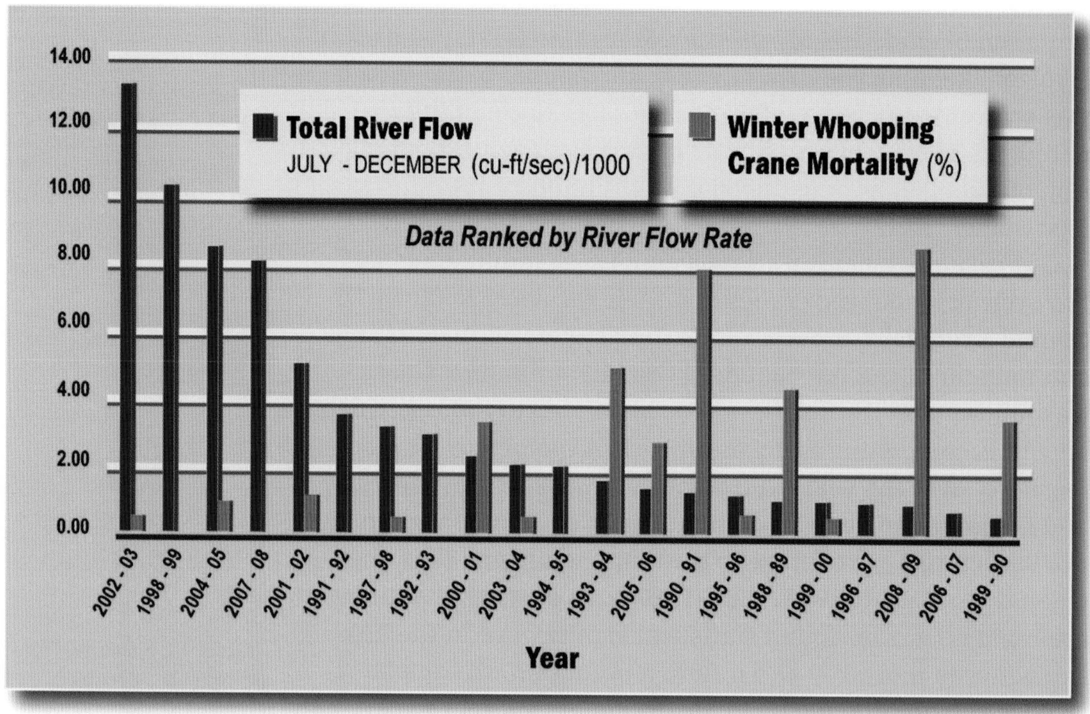

Figure 9.2. Graph prepared for the TAP trial by Dr. Ron Sass showing the relationship between decreases in freshwater inflows to San Antonio Bay and increases in the percentage of whooping crane mortality, based on data collected by Tom Stehn on the Aransas National Wildlife Refuge.

our case regarded the accuracy, reliability, and admissibility of data collected by Tom Stehn, an expert with the US Fish and Wildlife Service (USFWS) at the Aransas National Wildlife Refuge on the whooping cranes that winter there. Mr. Stehn had been meticulously recording data about the cranes for over two decades, and Dr. Sass had been analyzing this data regarding crane mortality over the years. Dr. Felipe Chavez-Ramirez, our expert on the cause of the crane mortality during the winter of 2008–2009, also relied on this data. If there were legal problems with the introduction of Mr. Stehn's mortality data, it would cripple the presentation of our case.

Early in the trial, the dispute over Mr. Stehn's data erupted. And while there was a basis for admitting Mr. Stehn's reports and data under various rules of evidence, it is always best to hear from the authority if possible. In response to objections raised by the defense counsel over TAP's use of Stehn's data, Judge Jack inquired whether we had tried to subpoena Tom for trial. Both the defendants and the plaintiffs did in fact try to gain access to Stehn, who at the time of pretrial discovery was an employee of the USFWS, but such requests had been denied by that federal agency, which did not participate in the trial. However, Judge Jack had a solution. She had the power to compel Mr. Stehn to appear and offered that if the parties wanted him to testify, she would subpoena him to appear. Both sides quickly agreed with that suggestion, and because Mr. Stehn had recently left the employ of the USFWS and was not officially a witness for either side, the plaintiffs and defendants also agreed to split a consulting fee for him to attend the trial.

As the plaintiffs were the party seeking to use his data, I as lead plaintiff's attorney took responsibility for presenting Mr. Stehn's testimony to the court. Lawyers generally have either worked with their own witnesses or deposed a neutral witness or one representing the other side. With Stehn, neither side had had that opportunity because our requests had been denied by the USFWS. As an attorney, it is truly frightening to examine an expert who can make or break your case without a clear understanding of what his or her testimony will be. Fortunately, upon direct questioning from me, Stehn was able to provide absolutely clear and convincing testimony about the deaths of the birds.

The GBRA had strongly insisted that there was no proof that twenty-three cranes had actually died, and that they

Figure 9.3. Tom Stehn holding an injured, sick whooping crane that later died, one of twenty-three that died during the winter of 2008–2009. Photo by US Fish and Wildlife Service.

had wandered off and were simply overlooked in Mr. Stehn's count. Only four bodies had been recovered, and only two of those were necropsied (underwent an avian autopsy). Tom testified that crane families, usually two adults and one juvenile, have clearly identifiable territories in which only they feed and roost, fighting off other cranes and returning to the same piece of marsh year after year. Mr. Stehn conducted periodic counts during the winter of 2008–2009 and identified a decline in the number of birds on these territories. Of the twenty-three birds that died, he testified that sixteen were juveniles (clearly identifiable by their cinnamon-streaked plumage rather than the all-white of adult birds). From a map he had prepared and from notes that he summarized in his year-end report, he identified all the missing birds. His map of territories and found dead birds (in red) and missing birds (in yellow) is shown in figure 9.4. This map covers the Blackjack Peninsula of Aransas County and the Aransas National Wildlife Refuge, portions of Matagorda and San Jose Islands, and the Welder Flats area of Calhoun County, all of which make up the prime wintering grounds for the whooping cranes.

Back to the trial. I finally got to the critical question of whether or not Mr. Stehn would testify that in his opinion, twenty-three cranes had died during the winter of 2008–2009. Lawyers hate to ask questions that they do not know, for sure, how the witness will answer. After I asked the question about whether or not twenty-three cranes died, Tom paused, really thinking about it, and my heart fell to my toes. And then he said, "Yes, at least twenty-three cranes died. There may have been more but twenty-three dead is all I feel confident about." Whew. I do not need any more courtroom moments such as that.

The remainder of our case unfurled like clockwork. Dr. Chavez-Ramirez testified that the crane necropsies showed that the two bodies examined were emaciated, indicating food stress. Dr. Chavez-Ramirez was present on the refuge during the winter of 2008–2009 at the request of refuge personnel to assess the conditions and found the birds to be showing evidence of food stress in their appearance and behavior. His conclusion was that food stress and starvation were the causes of the crane mortality.

Joe Trungale, our computer modeler, testified as to (1) what the inflows into San Antonio Bay would have been during the drought with no permitted diversions, along with the result-

Figure 2. Whooping crane territories at Aransas during the 2008-09 winter.

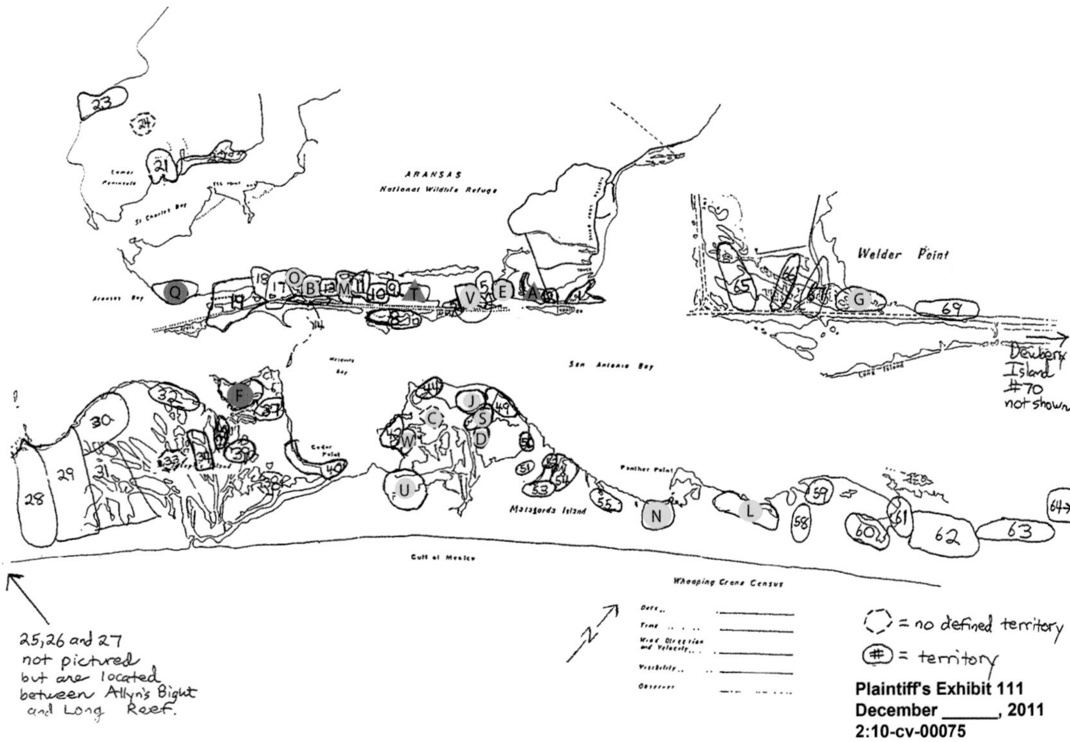

Figure 9.4. Hand-drawn map by Tom Stehn showing the location of missing whooping cranes in yellow and the location of the four bodies found in red.

ing salinity levels, (2) what actually occurred with reported withdrawals and salinity in 2008–2009, and (3) what would have occurred if all of the permitted water diversions had actually occurred. As bad as 2008–2009 was, it definitely could have been worse. Mr. Trungale was followed by Dr. Paul Montagna of Texas A&M University–Corpus Christi and the Harte Research Institute, who testified about two important aspects. First, he testified that recent studies by the TCEQ had confirmed that Nueces Bay had been killed by the absence of freshwater inflow, showing that a bay could in fact lose productivity because of the impacts of water diversions. Second, he testified that the abundance of blue crabs, the major food for the cranes, was directly related to salinity, and that when salinity reached twenty-five parts per thousand and higher (seawater is about thirty-four parts per thousand), blue crab abundance dropped appreciably. Because Joe Trungale's computer modeling showed that San Antonio, Carlos, Mesquite, and Espiritu Santo Bays adjacent to the whooper territories suffered salinities greater than twenty-five parts per thousand, the conclusion was warranted that the major food supply

Figure 9.5. Whooping crane grabbing blue crab with its beak. Each whooper eats up to eighty crabs per day. Photo by Kathy Adams Clark.

for the cranes—the blue crab—was largely absent during the period when the cranes died.

Our case concluded with three policy experts. Larry Soward, a former commissioner of the TCEQ, testified that there was more than ample authority within the TCEQ to alter water rights permits to protect endangered species if it desired to do so because of the water being publicly owned and because of emergency provisions regarding suspension of water rights. This point of adequate authority had been heavily contested by the TCEQ officials. Then Dave Frederick, an expert on the Endangered Species Act, testified that a permit could be issued by the USFWS to allow the involuntary "take" of an endangered species, but only if the entity wishing to "take" the species had prepared and adopted a Habitat Conservation Plan (HCP) that set out steps that the permittee would take to try to avoid harm, such as providing freshwater inflows to the bay in our case.

Our final expert was Dr. Andy Sansom, the former director of Texas Parks and Wildlife, who is now the head of the Meadows Center for Water and the Environment at Texas State University. Dr. Sansom testified that this was not the first time that endangered species and water issues had arisen in Texas.

About a decade previously, a federal endangered species suit had been filed over the endangered species in Comal Springs in New Braunfels, and in San Marcos springs where the Meadows Center now resides. Dr. Sansom indicated that Texas found a way to provide spring flows (and groundwater control) to protect the endangered species at the springs with the help of a lot of stakeholders and interested people. In his opinion, Texas could find a similar solution regarding the whooping crane with the same approach. That, plus the testimony of several TAP members, including Aransas county judge Burt Mills and Al Johnson, the owner of the Crane House, ended our case.

In contrast to our case, the defense case came unhinged early and often. The defense case and the problems associated with it were thoroughly discussed in Judge Janis Jack's 123-page opinion, which was issued about a year after the conclusion of the case. Judge Jack had listened to every word of testimony. She had reviewed hours of videotape of cranes in the field. And she was strong in her rejection of the case put forward by the GBRA, stating that the witnesses the GBRA put forward were not credible or reliable.

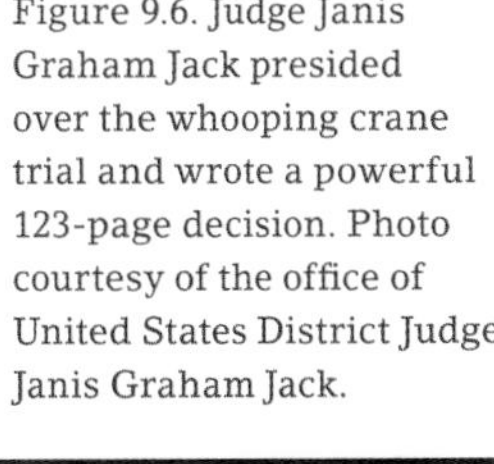

Figure 9.6. Judge Janis Graham Jack presided over the whooping crane trial and wrote a powerful 123-page decision. Photo courtesy of the office of United States District Judge Janis Graham Jack.

Judge Jack ended her written decision by ruling in TAP's favor and issuing an order enjoining state officials from issuing further permits to allow water to be removed from the San Antonio and Guadalupe Rivers and compelling the development of an HCP to protect the whooping cranes. This decision was a stunning victory for environmental flows for the bays and estuaries, and a hard blow to the traditions of Texas water law.

We were not, however, fooled into thinking we had won. We knew that the case would be appealed to the Fifth Circuit Court of Appeals in New Orleans, the hardest of all federal appeals circuits on environmental cases. To make matters worse, the lawyers for the other side changed prior to the appeal. The solicitor general of Texas—the state's chief lawyer—took over for the TCEQ officials, and perhaps more importantly, the GBRA hired Molly Cagle of the

Houston power law firm of Baker and Botts, who assembled an excellent team of former US Supreme Court clerks. And they were really good. The briefing was excellent on both sides, and argument was set for August 2013.

The Fifth Circuit is housed in a courthouse of its own just east of Canal and Poydras Streets in New Orleans. The building is grand and imposing. Its long halls and really high ceilings leave no doubt that you are in a place where serious business is conducted. It is intended to convey seriousness and power, and it does. At the Fifth Circuit, a panel of three judges was assigned and we drew two of the most conservative, Judge Edith Jones, an intellectually and philosophically fierce former chief judge, and Judge Jerry Smith, a hard-line conservative interpreter of the role of the courts and statutes. I was not optimistic about our panel. I can vividly remember jogging around Rice University right after our panel was announced and passing a disheveled-looking male grackle, standing in the shade with its mouth open and tongue hanging out, looking like a man having a bad day, and thinking, "Hello, my brother, I feel your pain."

The night before the argument, I did not sleep. We arrived at the courthouse when it opened, making sure that we were at least on time. The other side went first and they were solid, good. And then it was my turn. The court had moved our case from Monday to Thursday so that we could be the only case on the docket and would have more time for argument and questions, a change that brought Judge Jones to the panel. The argument went fast, with most of my time spent responding to Judge Jones, who was well prepared and agile. It was clear that she and the other two judges were concerned with Judge Jack's decision. They discussed with me whether the decision would leave Texans without water. They were concerned that the state agency was too far removed, both physically and actionwise, from the harm, and that the causation was too remote. They were concerned that the constitutional rights of the state of Texas might be trampled by Judge Jack's interpretation.

I left the oral argument exhausted but exuberant. I had held my own. I did not lose the case on oral argument, a key goal for a lawyer with few cases before the Fifth Circuit, all the while remembering the admonition of Mark Rose, TAP's policy adviser, to not **** it up, advice given with a wry smile when the decision was made to initially file in federal court back in 2010.

The wait for the decision was a long one. It arrived via

e-mail notice, with another e-mail on the screen. When it came, we were not surprised to learn that we had lost, that our three-judge panel had ruled against us. And perhaps most importantly, they had done so in a very narrow ruling that supposedly addressed the theory of legal causation applicable to our case.

Our case was filed under Section 9 of the Endangered Species Act, which prohibits a "take" of an endangered species. "Take" is defined to include killing or interfering with feeding or use of habitat. A prior Supreme Court case had upheld the regulations under which we sued, and several other appellate courts had determined that actions by a governmental entity that permits the behavior that causes the "take" in and of itself constitutes a "take"; hence our suit against the TCEQ officials. Judge Jack made extensive fact findings about the TCEQ's role in causing the "take," which was her responsibility as a district court judge in a bench (nonjury) trial. The Fifth Circuit, by contrast, is not supposed to retry the factual evidence but instead to interpret the legal standards applicable to the case.

The decision by the Fifth Circuit hinged on the concept of proximate cause—about whether or not the state action "caused" the death of the whooping cranes, in a legal sense. However, it seemed that in the decision, which was very carefully and artfully drafted, the Fifth Circuit had rewritten Judge Jack's fact findings rather than purely interpreting the law. In theory, these judges should have deferred to the trial judge rather than substituting their own factual judgment, although they stated that they were, in fact, working with Judge Jack's fact findings. We were all a bit confused by this logic, but one thing was clear—the decision had been written narrowly and specifically in an attempt to keep us from framing an appeal that the US Supreme Court would accept and evaluate.

Prior to petitioning the Supreme Court, we filed a motion for rehearing, asking that the case be reheard by all fifteen judges of the Fifth Circuit, sitting as a single panel. This is an extraordinary form of relief, seldom granted, but we felt we had to try. Although our motion was refused by an 11–4 vote, Judge Prado of San Antonio did write a dissent blistering our three-judge panel for substituting their factual judgment for that of Judge Jack.

The US Supreme Court accepts relatively few cases each year. An aggrieved party seeking Supreme Court review must file a petition for certiorari, an extremely serious legal filing that requires upward of $10,000 in printing costs alone for the bound copies that must be filed with the court. We hoped that Judge Prado's dissent and the votes of three other Fifth Circuit judges against the decision might be enough to catch the attention of the Supreme Court. We learned from Judge Prado's dissent that the Fifth Circuit had been out of line in the past with respect to its circuit judges substituting their factual judgment for the trial judge's fact findings in other cases, and we hoped that the Supreme Court would act to bring the Fifth Circuit back into conformance with the rules of appellate practice. Unfortunately for us, as well as for the cranes and the ecology of San Antonio Bay, our petition, like over 95 percent of them, was denied, and the case was ended.

However, this loss remained a win in many respects. A federal judge had ruled that the evidence brought before her by a private organization was sufficient to find a violation of the federal Endangered Species Act. On the other hand, the ruling by the Court of Appeals was based on a technicality under the legal definition of "take," a very narrow issue. So while our case may have failed, the vulnerability of the state water system to a federal court challenge was clearly revealed by this case. In many respects, Texas water law may never be the same after this case, particularly after Judge Jack's fact findings related to the impact of water withdrawals authorized by the state of Texas on the bay as well as on crabs and whooping cranes.

Then the improbable happened. Months after the Supreme Court had denied our appeal, I was talking with Molly Cagle, the excellent lead attorney for the GBRA, and I asked whether there was any interest on the GBRA's part in discussing a path forward in which the issues of both the GBRA and TAP might be integrated and worked on in a joint manner. Molly took this issue to Bill West, the general manager of the GBRA, and a few weeks later I met Bill and Molly at a restaurant in Seguin, Texas, for a lunch discussion about our long-term goals and hopes for the Guadalupe River watershed and San Antonio Bay. Perhaps surprisingly, many of our differences were not as great as they had seemed during litigation, where even in settlement discussions they had been insurmountable.

That meeting led to another, after which we produced a draft document that became the agreement signed by the GBRA and TAP and presented to the public at the February 22, 2016, meeting at the Meadows Center in San Marcos, as shown in figure 9.7. The day was perfect—blue skies, cool but not cold, and the water at the springs was sparkling. I will remember that day for years to come.

The agreement is both historic and nonbinding. We agreed on much, yet neither of us gave up anything. We were stepping forward carefully, each aware of past insults and hard feelings. We agreed that we needed to find a way to protect existing and future water users, the bay, and the whooping cranes. But the important thing is that Bill West and I did shake hands and agree that it was in the interest of both organizations to work together in the long term rather than to continue to fight and hurt each other. I must admit, in the context of an agreement like this, I believe that an honest handshake is worth ten supposedly binding agreements.

The agreement provided a break from the ingrained positions that the water community and environmental community have taken for years. It is an attempt to address an incredibly difficult problem together, by jointly studying issues as diverse as

Figure 9.7. Jim Blackburn, representing TAP, stands between Bill West and Todd Votteler of the GBRA at the signing of the TAP-GBRA agreement at Aquarena Springs in San Marcos, home of the Meadows Center for Water and the Environment at Texas State University, which hosted the signing event. Photo courtesy of GBRA.

1. long-term water supply, future demand, and where we might find additional water,

2. the cost of state water and the future role of full-cost pricing (see chapter 3),

3. the ability of restored prairies to generate additional stream and river flows and renew the farm economy in the Guadalupe River watershed through the sale of ecosystem services (see chapter 6),

4. the role of climate change in future water flows (see chapter 5),

5. the role of sea level rise in future whooping crane habitat (see chapter 5),

6. Guadalupe delta evaluation and restoration,

7. expansion of whooping crane habitat,

8. evaluation of the presence and needs of endangered sea turtles,

9. evaluation of freshwater mussels and potential management issues for mussel protection, and

10. the potential for utilizing desalination for future water supplies.

Then this story took another turn. Bill West retired as general manager shortly after signing this agreement, and the GBRA board selected a new general manager, Kevin Patteson, a former head of the Texas Water Development Board. While the agreement remained in force, I was struck by the fact that this was Bill's agreement, but Bill was leaving and Kevin was inheriting it. So it was clear that there was still much work to be done.

In mid-September 2016, TAP and the GBRA met at the ranch of Lucie Wray Todd in Columbus to talk about the future of this agreement. By now, I had moved from TAP attorney to board member, and I was joined by another TAP and International Crane Foundation board member, Ann Hamilton. Ann had attended the trial and the appeal and was my chief adviser, along with Charles Irvine, who was now TAP's lawyer. Kevin Patteson attended, as did Todd Votteler and Jonathan Stinson, two of Kevin's key advisers.

Once again, fate smiled on us. Kevin affirmed the commitment of the GBRA to the agreement and indicated that he wanted to turn it into "his" agreement, something that Ann and I also wanted. After about three intense hours, we agreed to redraft the original agreement, attempting to simplify it and break it into two parts, with the first part addressing habitat-related issues and the second part addressing water-related issues. The revised agreement reads as follows:

Affirmation and Restructuring of the Shared Vision for the Guadalupe River System and San Antonio Bay

On February 22, 2016, the Guadalupe Blanco River Authority (GBRA) and The Aransas Project (TAP) reached agreement on a shared vision for the future of the Guadalupe River System and San Antonio Bay. This document affirms the vision by restructuring that agreement to outline both habitat-related and water-related studies needed to reach our mutually agreed-upon goals.

This agreement grows from past conflicts between development of water supplies to meet the needs of a growing population and economy and finding a balance for the environment and lower Guadalupe Basin ecosystem, the San Antonio Bay fishery, the only wild flock of whooping cranes in the world and other rare and endangered species. It is a conflict that can be resolved if all parties work together to find such solutions. This affirmation and restructuring is a joint resolution by GBRA and TAP of good faith intent to work together to solve these difficult and critical issues.

We believe that by working together we can find ways to meet the long-term water use needs within the basin and protect the natural ecosystem of the Guadalupe River system and San Antonio Bay. We envision a future where economic development and ecologic protection are both achieved within the watershed and San Antonio Bay, a vision that includes people and industry, whooping cranes and recreational fishing.

We have identified two major topic areas for research and collaboration. One is related to habitat, endangered species, and land stewardship. The second is related to the future of water supply and water development within the watershed. Of the two, water availability and supply is more difficult and will require more time and financing than habitat analysis and evaluation, although neither is easy or inexpensive to address. For that reason, we have divided this agreement into two parts—habitat and water.

In approaching these problems, we believe three

issues are worthy of special mention. First, by working together and with stakeholders, that the chances of successful resolution are increased significantly. Second, market-based solutions offer a great opportunity for innovation. Third, creativity demands that all issues and solutions are considered from the outset.

Under this agreement, we are asking for help and input from others. There are groups and individuals potentially affected by this agreement and many possess important expertise. We will have two primary levels of stakeholder involvement, one at a more general advisory level and at least two at the more specific project level. We hope that through these stakeholder involvement processes, we can enhance the quality of the work and ensure that our ideas are well considered, that the work is well vetted, and that solutions developed will be successful.

Several issues in the original GBRA-TAP agreement can be generally identified as habitat-related rather than water-related. Part 1 of this agreement sets out the combined study areas that comprise the habitat-related portion of this affirmation and restructuring. Part 2 of this agreement focuses on the water supply issues on the Guadalupe River system emphasizing understanding and evaluating ideas and concepts for solving long-term issues that must be addressed to achieve this vision.

Part 1: Habitat Investigations

Conservation and enhancement of habitat is a key goal. Our primary focus of habitat investigation under this agreement is to evaluate and then provide for adequate future territories and expansion areas for whooping cranes as the wild flock expands toward the goal of 1000 birds. A second focal point is understanding and planning to realize the potential of the Guadalupe Delta as habitat as well as a channel for freshwater delivery to the upper portion of San Antonio Bay. This includes better understanding of improvement in estuarine as well as terrestrial habitat for cranes and other wildlife and fisheries. Third, the potential for improvement of habitat throughout the watershed, both for water supply and fish and wildlife purposes, will be investigated. In all studies, extensive effort will be expended developing market mechanisms as well as traditional means for bringing revenue to landowners in exchange for habitat improvement. Fourth, several species of mussel are under consideration for listing as endangered species. The habitat needs and requirements of these unique species must be understood and addressed.

Each of these three areas will be researched in detail. The U.S. Fish and Wildlife Service and the International Crane Foundation (ICF) have both conducted extensive work on existing and projected future whooping crane habitat taking future sea level rise into consideration. The ICF information is currently available and the U.S. Fish and Wildlife Service will release their analysis soon. Here, there is the potential in working with various landowners to utilize market-based contractual systems to expedite habitat conservation. The ICF and USFWS information along with additional studies on expansion and market opportunities will be integrated with stakeholders and landowners to understand potential future habitat needs and the opportunities and problems that lie ahead.

The Guadalupe Delta is a unique area with interesting physical features, including multiple bayous and channels that complicate full understanding of its current functioning, resources, and potential future role from a habitat perspective given potential sea level rise. A geographic information system is needed for the delta that identifies both existing and potential habitat, water surface elevation, topography, land ownership and physical features. A better understanding of the manner in which water flows into and through the delta in both low flow and higher flow circumstances needs to be developed. A complete understanding of the operation of the salt water barrier during droughts and relationship to the delta and bay system are needed, in addition to the performance of the delta during river-flooding, drought, and storm-surge events. Relative to bay habitat, the potential creation of a low-flow sanctuary in the upper half of San Antonio Bay will be evaluated as a nursery for blue crab and other juvenile species. Among other issues, the need for and/or availability of minimal inflows to maintain this nursery reserve area will be evaluated.

Potential habitat restoration for the watershed as

a whole is both a fish and wildlife and water supply enhancement concept that will be fueled by the market system and buying and selling ecological services. The structure of this market system and quantitative information about the potential for habitat improvement to increase base flows during dry times needs to be fully researched and understood in order to evaluate the potential benefit from this conceptual approach.

Finally, there is a need to understand the habitat requirements of certain species of mussels that are candidate species for listing as either endangered or threatened. The Comptroller's office has money set aside to research this issue and is considering funding research for mussels in the Guadalupe River system. This research would be integrated with the research to be funded directly through this agreement.

Part 2: Water Investigation

In the long term, water supply for the watershed and freshwater inflows for the San Antonio Bay complex must be addressed in a sustainable manner. Here, several different areas will require study and evaluation. There are also a number of ongoing conflicts in need of solutions and potentially others in the not-too-distant future. There are many ways to organize and approach this research and several key topics warrant research and better understanding. The following are ways to consider and organize this research and study effort. Again, our intent here is to further develop these concepts with the assistance of a stakeholder group.

GBRA and TAP plan to investigate options regarding the potential re-allocation of existing water supplies for environmental use, dependent on timely replacement and supplementation so that inventory is maintained for human needs and the additional supplies needed to meet future demands are developed in a relatively cost-neutral manner. To this end, several specific water re-allocation and management strategies should be evaluated, and all holders of permits for both surface water and hydrologically-connected groundwater will be invited to participate in these discussions. These substitute supplies are typically not considered to be needed new supplies of water, but the cost will be new water cost, and the price or charge for a re-allocation generally should be based on that cost.

There are several aspects of long-term water supply that require better computer modeling and understanding. The water availability model (WAM) for the Guadalupe River System has not been updated to reflect the period of record including the recent drought. Updates in this tool should be carefully evaluated, with a goal of understanding domestic and livestock usage along with a full understanding of the role of return flows and groundwater flow through springs and seeps in the long term health of both the river and estuary. Also, the role of a changing climate on future rainfall and base flows should be evaluated. Similarly, the freshwater inflow modeling work completed to date for the SB3 freshwater inflow studies has not incorporated blue crabs, a key food source for whooping cranes, into the modeling, nor has the creation of a nursery sanctuary in the upper half of San Antonio Bay during severe drought conditions. This task envisions both water availability and bay and estuarine modeling.

GBRA and TAP also plan to evaluate the ability of market tools to assist in water allocation and availability will be evaluated. The State of Texas owns the surface water in all watercourses. To date, Texas has not charged for this water even though there is an innate "value" to it. To date, we are unaware of any study that establishes a dollar value for water that stays in the river and flows into the bay, fueling bay and estuarine shrimp and oyster production as well as recreational and commercial fishing. If the "true cost" of this water were agreed to, then it could be used in developing alternative water supplies as well as supporting efforts to bring water to the bay. Similarly, the idea of "purchasing" water for bay and estuarine inflows should be considered. Research work currently being undertaken on purchasing inflows for bay and estuarine enhancement should be fully integrated into this work.

The various water management strategies to enhance water availability will be evaluated. Here there are several issues to be considered, including the impacts of full utilization of permitted water rights, future re-use projects, off-channel reservoir construction, aquifer storage and recovery, and domestic and livestock water usage. These evaluations could easily become controversial and full stakeholder participation is essential. Fully evaluating and discussing these issues will test the ability of our groups to work together to achieve mutual goals. We are committed to this effort.

3. Conclusory Statement

If we are successful under the process set out in this white paper, GBRA and TAP, with the assistance of vested stakeholders, will create an action plan for ensuring water supply, a healthy bay and protected endangered species, including whooping cranes and mussels. We believe that hard work, creativity and openness will give us the ability to solve what may seem initially to be an impossible task.

There is much work to be done to flesh out and make this agreement live up to its potential. We have a lot of work ahead of us, and we need the help of many people, corporations, and governments. But to me, the potential for change is palpable, within our grasp. People on the coast and in Austin are now thinking differently about the future of the whooping cranes and water supply issues in the Guadalupe River Basin. We are now openly discussing issues that we could not broach prior to Judge Jack's decision. I have no doubt that the agreement finally reached between TAP and the GBRA would not have occurred but for Judge Jack's decision and the years of legal fighting. And I have been told that it might not have happened if the TCEQ and GBRA had lost on appeal. The important point is that we fought over important issues, and I believe that we have succeeded in changing the dialogue. If this agreement is successful, it could transform the future of water in Texas.

Litigation should be and will be a key part of the Texas coastal future. There are many battles in many places yet to be fought. But litigation cannot occur if it is not funded. Many environmental groups in Austin and on the Texas coast shy away from litigation because funds can disappear if nonprofits litigate. We need to consciously raise money to support litigation. I am not saying this to put money in my own pocket, as I am effectively retired as an active litigator. I am saying this to support the young environmental litigators of the coast, young lawyers able and ready to take environmental issues forward, lawyers like Charles Irvine, Mary Conner, Kristen Schlemmer, and Michael McEvilly of the Irvine and Conner law firm, and Jen Powis of the Powis law firm, all in Houston. What we need is bold groups that are willing to use and fund them, groups that believe that fighting for our green assets is good for all of us, groups that are both wise and willing.

Finally, litigation alone is nothing but a stopgap measure. Litigation without an end game is less likely to be successful in the long term. Environmental litigation, as good as it may feel or seem to feel, is not about punishment. Instead, it should be about vision, and the willingness to fight for that vision.

Today, several new suits have been filed. A lawyer from Austin, David Smith of the Graves, Doherty law firm, sued the Corps of Engineers over allowing pilings to be placed in the Gulf Intracoastal Waterway along a portion called the Lydia Ann Channel, just north of Port Aransas. Judge Jack ruled that the pilings that allowed the mooring of barges near whooping crane feeding areas should be removed because of errors in the issuance of a "letter of permission," a unique form of permit rarely, and in this case wrongly, issued. A federal suit has recently been filed by the Matagorda Bay Foundation (MBF) against the US Department of Commerce for failing to issue rules to protect "essential fish habitat" on the Texas coast, which includes all our major estuaries. The MBF has also filed suit against the Lower Colorado River Authority under the Texas Open Records Act for failing to make available computer models developed with state funds that identify the impact of building an off-site reservoir near Lane City, south of Wharton, just off the Colorado River.

There are many lawsuits that can and should be filed in the future. There are many battles yet to come over water, for the bays specifically and for coastal issues generally. The Corps of Engineers gets many things right, but it does make mistakes, and these mistakes can be costly. There will likely be contamination issues. There will be chemical plants and refineries that will foul our coastal air and water. There will be conflicts between those with power and those without, and the federal courts will be there to even the playing field. That makes me grateful and leaves me smiling, happy that there is a new generation coming along, of both lawyers and clients. And don't forget—if you are not willing to fight for it, you will lose it.

CHAPTER 10

Coastal Spirituality

The will to stand up and act to protect the coast comes from many places. For some it comes from use and appreciation, such as fishing or birding. For others it comes from land ownership. For others, either faith or philosophy or both—what I call spirituality—will propel them to act. Whether based on organized religion, environmental philosophy and ethics, or a personal derivative, spirituality will form a core set of values and ethics that will come to epitomize private-sector concern for and appreciation of the Texas coast and will represent yet another manifestation of our migration to the full world.

On a hot afternoon in early June, my wife, Garland, and I drove down to White Heron Estates in Chambers County on the banks of Trinity Bay to participate in the unveiling of a rookery dedicated to the memory of Cynthia Pickett-Stevenson's mother. Cynthia's mom, Katy Lloyd-Pickett, had passed away earlier in the year, and Cynthia, a steward of Galveston Bay and Chambers County, decided to create a natural area—a rookery, a plot of trees on an island within a wetland and lake complex—in memory of her mom.

Cynthia and her husband, Don, had purchased this tract of land along Trinity Bay and had been working to improve and restore the land where the rookery was created. A young Eagle Scout named Justin Rearick had created a project in 2015 that involved planting a marsh behind a constructed breakwater along the Trinity Bay shoreline of this property, and the rookery was a continuation of the effort to restore the natural system on this piece of property.

Sunday morning dawned bright and clear. We were staying with my wife's sister Carolyn Kerr and her husband, Doyle Perkinson, at their bay house overlooking Trinity Bay adjacent to Cynthia's property. We watched as the crowd began to arrive and walked over to join the group gathered to dedicate the rookery. A line of four-wheelers pulling trailers with hay bales waited along the road, and we jumped aboard for a short hayride to our destination.

The created rookery was in the early stages of its development. A pond had been excavated and the dirt had been piled in the middle to create an island, which was planted with willow and yaupon and a few larger trees. The water was edged by freshwater wetland vegetation that gradated to slightly higher ground where native plants had been planted to bring diversity to the monoculture that had grown over the land left fallow, land that had been invaded by tallow and other nonnative species and that was now being reclaimed and restored. Benches and chairs and a portable microphone had been placed so that we could look out at the rookery while we listened to the dedication ceremony.

Cynthia started by talking about her mom and her own religious base, which grounded her and gave her hope and strength through the difficult time that had recently passed. Then she introduced Cynthia Kostas, a Greek Orthodox lay minister who counsels people about life's challenges and the strength that can be found through spiritual assistance, a trained theologian within the church led by the Green Patriarch Bartholomew. On this fine day, Kostas spoke of Christian stewardship, about the necessity of protecting God's creation, about how we need to keep from destroying the gifts of God. She spoke of other living things and how we share the Earth,

Figure 10.1. Cynthia Pickett-Stevenson speaks at the dedication of the Katy L Rookery (in the background) on the banks of Trinity Bay after a presentation on stewardship and keeping the Earth by Cynthia Kostas, in the orange blouse. Photo by Mari Ibrahim.

about how the example set by Cynthia Pickett was one we should embrace and support. She spoke of creation as a gift to be passed on to future generations, and she spoke of the duty and responsibility that falls on all of us.

Lightly, she ad-libbed about the monarch butterfly that dropped in to join the dedication, flitting among the blossoms of the butterfly weed recently placed in this sacred ground, smiling as she talked about the creation. During her presentation, a great-tailed grackle started singing from a perch within the trees—trees that were not here a few months before—the singing bird accompanying the lay minister as she ended by inviting all to walk to the entrance sign for the Katy L Rookery and drink a glass of champagne to Cynthia's mom and to this act of stewardship, a form of Christian witness on the banks of Trinity Bay.

More and more I encounter examples of religious connection to nature preservation and protection. Over the last several decades, the Christian community has been developing and expanding the connections between biblical scripture and the environment. This movement started, it seems, in response to a highly critical article written in 1967 by a scholar named Lynn White, published in the journal *Science*, wherein he opined that western theology (Christianity, Judaism) was the root cause for the ecological crisis facing the world. This article led to numerous personal attacks against Dr. White, but it also stimulated intense and ultimately very creative debate within the Christian community—debate that ultimately led to some of the most profound change that I have seen in my life, showing a movement from empty-world thinking toward full-world thinking in a manner beyond my wildest imagination. And it is happening today.

I was raised a Southern Baptist and can remember tent revivals on a riverbank in central Louisiana. I have seen people talking in tongues (or perhaps trying to), but during my youth I never experienced a Baptist preacher teaching about stewardship for the creation, yet that is where Christianity arrived in the late 1980s and early 1990s.

Before the Rio Earth Summit in 1992 (perhaps the most important international environmental conference ever held), most denominations of Christianity and other religions had adopted various resolutions and statements about religion and the environment, discovering biblical passages in support of Earth-keeping and stewardship. The Presbyterian denomination of Christianity has been among the most active and is responsible for the seminal publication "Keeping and Healing the Creation," published in 1989. Indeed, creation theology has been at the center of Christian environmental thinking, emphasizing as it does the biblical writing that God made the Earth and "behold, it was good" (Genesis 1:31). Episcopalians, Methodists, Baptists, and Catholics all have strong writings about God and the environment. Jews cite passages about planting trees, about care for the garden. Muslims quote from the Hadith. Hindus have long protected various living things, and many Hindu gods are of animistic origins. Buddhism is circular and organic in its views of humans and the Earth.

I have followed the development of much of this literature for use in my teaching, and I have done some lecturing on this subject. I remember a presentation I made at Penn State in which I talked about how passages from the Bible regarding dominion of nature had been reinterpreted in light of the concept of stewardship from the New Testament. After that lecture, I was approached by a young woman who said she was Jewish and asked if I had ever read the original Hebrew version of the dominion of nature phrase. I had not and said so, and she then told me that it literally translated as "place your foot on the neck and push." She was very impressed that the scholars had gotten from that point to stewardship, as, frankly, am I, although in the Old Testament context, humans and nature were often at odds, a reality that has changed today, leading to the empty world–full world tension.

Like many aspects of Texas, our local practices are not totally in step with national trends and consensus. Although many denominations of Christianity active on the Texas coast have adopted these strong national positions about the environment, local churches and congregations have often failed to adopt these national frameworks. There is much local autonomy, and local pastors, ministers, and priests often speak what the community wishes to hear. For this reason and perhaps others, the environmental side of Christianity or Judaism is not seen or heard as much in our community as it is in other parts of the United States. But it certainly exists at the national level. Many groups of different faith traditions have emerged that are devoted to religion and the environment, including GreenFaith, Interfaith Power and Light, the National Religious Partnership for the Environment, the Shalom Center, the Evangelical Environmental Network, EcoSikh, Green

Muslims, the Coalition on the Environment and Jewish Life, the US Conference of Catholic Bishops Environmental Justice Program, and the Buddhist Peace Fellowship, among many others.

If these environmental scriptures and policy positions gain more recognition and acceptance, there is a very strong organized religious faith community along the Texas coast to receive them. In a 2010 survey, 3.6 million people, representing 59 percent of the coastal population of 6.1 million, identified themselves as being associated with one faith community or another. Of these, 36 percent identified as Catholic, 25 percent as Baptist, 7 percent as Methodist, 4 percent as Muslim, and about 25 percent as "other." This is a large group of coastal Texans.

From the standpoint of the future of the Texas coast, this spiritual component could be very powerful, representing the private sector—the faith community—acting to support the long-term protection of the Texas coast, tossing the money changers from the coastal temple, protecting the lush coastal garden, or simply singing Psalms in praise of natural beauty and life. It all works, and it all fits within the emerging religious environmental fabric.

No spiritual leader has taken as much of a stand for environmental issues as has Pope Francis. With the publication in June 2015 of the papal encyclical "Laudato Si'," Pope Fran-

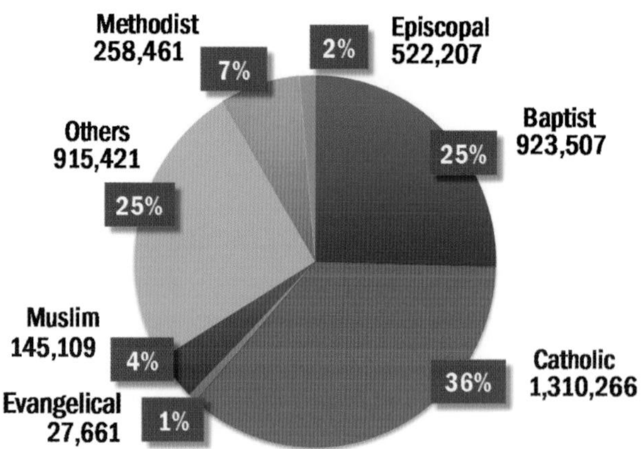

Figure 10.2. Religious affiliations of residents of the Texas coast.

cis threw down the spiritual gauntlet in support of care for the creation of God (e.g., the Earth), of humans taking responsibility for climate change, and of all of us seeking equity for the people of the world who are getting hurt by environmental impact and change. It is a powerful incorporation of science and religion, perhaps unlike any document in existence before now. With this one document, 1.2 billion Catholics around the world (and about 1.3 million on the Texas coast) were challenged to add care and concern for the environment to their code of ethics, to their moral code of behavior, to what the Catholic Church expected of each of them.

It is impossible to overstate the power of this document. It reads as an ecological, climate change, and environmental justice manifesto. Pope Francis captured in this one document the essence of the challenge posed by human impact on the environment and recast environmental thinking as spiritual thinking. Consider some of the statements from this document:

> 2. This sister [Earth] now cries out to us because of the harm we have inflicted on her by our irresponsible use and abuse of the goods with which God has endowed her. We have come to see ourselves as her lords and masters, entitled to plunder her at will. The violence present in our hearts, wounded by sin, is also reflected in the symptoms of sickness evident in the soil, in the water, in the air and in all forms of life. This is why the earth herself, burdened and laid waste, is among the most abandoned and maltreated of our poor; she "groans in travail" (Rom 8:22). We have forgotten that we ourselves are dust of the earth (cf. Gen 2:7); our very bodies are made up of her elements, we breathe her air and we receive life and refreshment from her waters.

> 12. What is more, Saint Francis, faithful to Scripture, invites us to see nature as a magnificent book in which God speaks to us and grants us a glimpse of his infinite beauty and goodness. "Through the greatness and the beauty of creatures one comes to know by analogy their maker" (Wis 13:5); indeed, "his eternal power and divinity have been made known through his works since the creation of the world" (Rom 1:20). For this reason, Francis asked that part of the friary garden always be left

untouched, so that wild flowers and herbs could grow there, and those who saw them could raise their minds to God, the Creator of such beauty. [21] Rather than a problem to be solved, the world is a joyful mystery to be contemplated with gladness and praise.

My appeal

13. The urgent challenge to protect our common home includes a concern to bring the whole human family together to seek a sustainable and integral development, for we know that things can change. The Creator does not abandon us; he never forsakes his loving plan or repents of having created us. Humanity still has the ability to work together in building our common home. Here I want to recognize, encourage and thank all those striving in countless ways to guarantee the protection of the home which we share. Particular appreciation is owed to those who tirelessly seek to resolve the tragic effects of environmental degradation on the lives of the world's poorest. Young people demand change. They wonder how anyone can claim to be building a better future without thinking of the environmental crisis and the sufferings of the excluded.

14. I urgently appeal, then, for a new dialogue about how we are shaping the future of our planet. We need a conversation which includes everyone, since the environmental challenge we are undergoing, and its human roots, concern and affect us all. The worldwide ecological movement has already made considerable progress and led to the establishment of numerous organizations committed to raising awareness of these challenges. Regrettably, many efforts to seek concrete solutions to the environmental crisis have proved ineffective, not only because of powerful opposition but also because of a more general lack of interest. Obstructionist attitudes, even on the part of believers, can range from denial of the problem to indifference, nonchalant resignation or blind confidence in technical solutions. We require a new and universal solidarity. As the bishops of Southern Africa have stated: "Everyone's talents and involvement are needed to redress the damage caused by human abuse of God's creation". [22] All of us can cooperate as instruments of God for the care of creation, each accord-

ing to his or her own culture, experience, involvements and talents.

From that point in the encyclical letter, Pope Francis proceeds to lay out the scientific case for climate change and environmental impact throughout the world and then sets out the ethical and spiritual response to the science. To use an overused phrase, it is a game changer. It is a new articulation of important concepts from the Old and New Testament as well as historical Catholic writings. And it does not mince words. It is clear. And strong.

Now, many of you reading this may say that you are not Catholic. Fair enough. My grandmother was a Southern Baptist who thought that a good day's work included converting Catholics to become Baptists. But the theology of care for the creation, for Earth-keeping, is well established and building in all Christian denominations.

Recently, I met Rev. Duane Larson, the leader of Christ the King Lutheran Church, for lunch at the faculty club at Rice. Rev. Larson had heard me speak about ecological values and transactions at a Saturday morning presentation I made to a group at his church, and he and I talked a bit afterward and agreed to meet. At lunch, I quizzed him about modern thinking about creation and was impressed both with his background and his knowledge about this subject. It turned out that Rev. Larson was a scholar of ecology and religion and was able to afford me one of the best explanations of the underlying theological basis for care for creation that I have heard so far.

In Christianity, there is the concept of the Trinity—God the father, God the son, and God the Holy Spirit. Of the three aspects of the Trinity, the Holy Spirit had always been the most difficult for me to grasp, and irreverent young Baptists often talked of the "Holy Ghost," as did my mother. However, Rev. Larson explained that in the creation, God extended the Holy Spirit throughout creation, breathing life, infusing the Trinity and God throughout creation, rather than simply creating a planet with plants and other living things. Now that is indeed powerful, to protect the coast because the Holy Spirit pervades it, something I have felt in my own way many times but have never really heard articulated by a theologian. Thank you, Rev. Larson. That was a great gift over lunch.

On the other hand, many people do not believe in a God

or have perhaps lost faith, or at least faith in organized religion. Many discover inspiration and hope in the environmental writers and ethicists that helped frame the environmental movement of the United States. Although I greatly respect Henry David Thoreau, Ralph Waldo Emerson, and John Muir, I find the best expression of what I feel through the writings of Aldo Leopold and Rachel Carson, two people who have contributed substantially to the spiritual and ethical underpinnings of much modern environmental thinking. *A Sand County Almanac* and *Silent Spring* are both excellent pieces of literature that convey ethical grounding and spiritual connections between humans and the natural system.

Aldo Leopold's *A Sand County Almanac*, published in 1949, is a fabulous book of environmental awakening and knowledge, of discourse about how humans and nature do and should coexist. Leopold was a trained land manager who knew ecological concepts and was able to present them cogently and literately. *A Sand County Almanac* documents the destruction of the natural system and human dominance over nature while stating and restating the premise that humans are within the ecological system, not above it. *A Sand County Almanac* expresses a reverence for life, articulates the existence of humans in a system of relationships and partnerships with nature, and expresses the concept that human changes to nature are of a different magnitude and rate than evolutionary changes.

To Leopold, a "land ethic" was an ethic focused on the Earth and its ecosystems. Leopold specifically advocated reducing the violence of the interaction between humans and nature and stated his conviction of the individual's responsibility for the health of the land. He concluded that an ethical relationship was one that included love, respect, and admiration for the land (e.g., ecosystem). Leopold was a trained scientist who had observed the impacts—and failures—of the science that he had studied and practiced. He recognized the gaps that science left as it reduced the elements of nature to specific studies and examinations. He complained of professors who were experts on the various instruments of the orchestra but did not hear the music of the symphony.

Leopold wrote with the conviction of one who had pursued truth and found it only after reconsidering and rejecting the concepts by which he had practiced land management in the early twentieth century. Just as historians are revisionists, so was Leopold. By discovering the ecosystem and the human role within that ecosystem, Leopold found both a scientific and an ethical basis for human action.

A Sand County Almanac is literature that makes valid scientific points with beautifully written prose. The essay "Thinking like a Mountain" is riveting in its description of the killing of a mother wolf, detailing Leopold's first doubts about the accepted rationale for humans to kill wolves. More generally, the essay demonstrates what an ecological view is, revealing the importance of predator-prey relationships and the counterintuitive aspects of ecology. Killing wolves does not mean more deer; instead, when the wolves are gone, the deer population expands to the point that the vegetation is denuded and the deer die from starvation, leaving the mountain barren and eroding, suggesting that we should indeed "think like a mountain."

Several ethical concepts emerge from *A Sand County Almanac* that are components of an Earth-focused philosophy. These can be summarized in the following points regarding Leopold's land ethic:

1. Land does not simply equate to property. Instead, a land ethic is concerned with the ecological system, with the whole. From this ecological perspective, a unique position is accorded to native vegetation with its ecological adaptations and niches. In Leopold's view, the development of a land ethic is an evolutionary possibility and an ecological necessity, one of the most powerful thoughts I have encountered, epitomizing the transition to full-world thinking.
2. The individual is a member of a community of interdependent parts. While our instinct and cultural bias may be to compete, the ethic is to cooperate.
3. Human-caused change is recognized as being of a different order and rate than evolutionary change. Further, human-caused change often has effects that are more comprehensive than is intended or foreseen. At the least, alterations of the land should be accomplished with less violence.
4. An ecological conscience exists with the conviction of individual responsibility for the ecological health of the land. In this context, health is the ability for self-renewal or sustainability. Here, we have a responsibility to understand and preserve this sustainability.

5. Several paradoxes exist, including the cultural "man the conqueror" versus Leopold's "man the biotic citizen"; "science the sword sharpener" versus "science the searchlight"; and "land the slave and servant" versus "land the collective organism."

6. An ethical relationship must exist between humans and the ecosystem and other organisms. In this view, a thing is right when it tends to preserve the integrity, stability, and beauty of the biotic community, and there is a fallacy in the view that economics determines the appropriateness of all actions.

7. There is a concept of appropriate technology and appropriate scale. Leopold writes of the wisdom (or lack thereof) of remodeling the Alhambra with a steam shovel.

Over a decade later, a second major work articulating elements of an Earth-based philosophy and ethic was published. Rachel Carson's *Silent Spring* is a masterpiece of literature and science, a powerful denunciation of the use of pesticides such as chlorinated hydrocarbons and organophosphates. But *Silent Spring* is much more than a book about chemicals. It is a book of ethical and moral guidance, a description of a tragedy that can be corrected, ultimately, only by a change in cultural mores.

It is important to note that *Silent Spring* was published in 1962, following a decade of post–World War II industrial and technological expansion. During the 1950s, there had been a tremendous growth in the use of pesticides and herbicides as part of this expansion. There had also been extensive atmospheric testing of nuclear and thermonuclear devices. *Silent Spring* incorporated, in a subtle manner, the legacy of the nuclear age into a book about chemicals and ecology.

By 1962, the danger of "fallout" had become widely known. In the early 1950s, the "Bravo" test of a US superbomb in the Pacific went awry, leading to the death of the Japanese seaman Aikichi Kuboyama from the Japanese vessel *Lucky Dragon*. This became one of the first global environmental disasters and served as a platform for further concern about the dangers of atmospheric testing of nuclear weapons, which was prevalent in the late 1950s into the early 1960s. Among these dangers was the fallout of strontium-90 (Sr-90), a radioactive isotope with a relatively long, twenty-eight-year half-life. In the 1950s, the presence of Sr-90 was documented in the bones of all human beings worldwide, regardless of age or location.

It was against this backdrop of concern about radioactivity that Rachel Carson positioned *Silent Spring*. In the opening chapter, she established the thrust of the book—that some "evil spell had settled on the community." The "shadow of death" was over the community. In the chapters that followed, Carson, a trained marine biologist and ecologist, wrote of the ecological terror occurring from the indiscriminate use of pesticides and herbicides. Carson documented the human war against insects and weeds, the so-called pests of civilization. On page 37, in the chapter titled "Elixirs of Death," she wrote that "we are rightly appalled by the genetic effects of radiation; how then, can we be indifferent to the same effect in chemicals that we disseminate widely in our environment?"

The remainder of her book is filled with documented situation after documented situation identifying how these chemicals are destroying birds and other organisms and ultimately threatening humans. The magnification of pesticides through the food chain is documented with examples of bird deaths in Clear Lake, California. The random killing of robins, squirrels, and other organisms is documented in Michigan and Illinois, as is the death of fish in the Miramichi River of New Brunswick, Canada, as well as in Maine and Oklahoma and in the Colorado River of Texas. In all cases, the killing agent was a chlorinated organic pesticide.

Rachel Carson did not stop with the documentation of impacts to the natural system. She also documented the contamination of the food we eat and the concentrations of pesticides within our bodies. Just as food chain impacts had killed the robin that ate the earthworm that picked up the DDT from the elm leaf dropping to the soil, so also might humans be affected. "For each of us, as for the robin in Michigan or the salmon in the Miramichi, this is a problem of ecology, of interrelationships, of interdependence" (p. 189). Carson then proceeded to discuss chemically caused cancers and, ultimately, the adaptive capabilities of pests to render pesticides ineffective.

Silent Spring transformed the public's view of chemicals and the chemical industry as well as the economics of the use of certain chemicals. Rachel Carson exposed the complacency and ignorance of the government officials that many people had trusted. *Silent Spring* led to the enactment of pesticide and herbicide legislation in the early 1970s, and to the regulation and ultimate prohibition of the usage of many chlorinated hydrocarbons in the United States. However, *Silent Spring* is much more than an attack on chemical usage and manufacturing. It is basically about ethics and morality and the consequences of human actions. The following is a synthesis of some of the ethical principles from *Silent Spring*:

1. The magnitude of change generated by humans in the last century is far beyond past experience. Nature lacks the capability to comprehensively adapt to these rapid changes. The public has the right to know the type and magnitude of the changes wreaked by these chemicals and has the right to be free from "sugarcoated half-truths."

2. Ecological impacts affect all members of the web of life, humans included. As shown in the concentration of chemicals up the food chain, a relationship exists between all members of the ecological system. In nature, "nothing exists alone." Humans are not above the ecological system but are instead merged with it.

3. Humans often destroy other living organisms when there is no need for such destruction. Alternative methods often exist to address various types of "pest" problems, yet these alternatives are seldom chosen. Human actions should be considered judiciously and with forethought rather than indiscriminately and without regard for their impacts. Needless destruction should not occur.

4. Humans must develop an ethic of reverence for life and other living organisms. "The question is whether any civilization can wage relentless war on life without destroying itself, and without losing the right to be called civilized."

5. Humans have deluded themselves with terminology such as "control of nature." This term supposes that nature exists for the convenience of humans and is born of "the Neanderthal age of biology and philosophy." Rather than control nature through indiscriminate tools and actions, we must establish a relationship with the natural system, a bona fide full-world concept.

Rachel Carson's legacy is extensive. Without doubt she initiated major alterations in the regulation of chemicals. But her more lasting contribution is her Earth-based philosophy and ethical insights.

I became seriously interested in the Earth and spirituality when I was trying to stop drinking. As I wandered my own personal wilderness in the early and mid-1980s, I came to attend meetings of Alcoholics Anonymous and was told that I needed to find a higher power. Now that was a problem. I had been raised a Baptist and had fled from the church as soon as I left home for college. I felt I could not return to that path and was distraught until I heard a young man discussing his higher power, a Metro bus, which was "bigger than he was and beyond his control." That piece of "AA wisdom" allowed me to relax and become more open and accepting in my search for and vision of a higher power. It allowed me to smile.

Ultimately, I discovered my higher power and a true sense of spirituality in the natural system of Galveston Bay. I would go to the edge of Galveston Bay—to the marshes, to the rookeries, to the oyster reefs—to find serenity and hope, and a vision of the future that has guided me since. These revelations changed life and living for me, and I have not looked back. It was a turning point in my life, and I am grateful for it.

I have had the opportunity to present my thinking about "Earth Church" at the Rothko Chapel, a wonderful spiritual place in Houston built by Dominique de Menil. Earth Church is my construct, my place. It is personal, yet many who have heard me talk about it have connected with the thoughts, the concepts, and the vision. It is about life and living. It is about the Earth. It is about a way of life. It is about scientific principles and ethical and moral duties. It is about truth, honesty, and hope. Along the way, I developed the ten principles of Earth Church.

Principle 1 is respect for life and other living things, which are part of the Earth and inherent in the Earth. Life is what makes the Earth unique. It seems to me that we must embrace other living things if we are to understand and maintain this planet of life. Earth and life. Together. We should include other living things in some way within our value set. We should include protection of life and living things of the Texas coast in our value set.

Principle 2 is population reduction through education and reproductive choice for women. Population control is a tough issue that must be addressed head-on. Earth Church must embrace both the education and empowerment of women everywhere. Across the world the pattern is clear—educated

(Following page) Figure 10.3. Some find spirituality in nature and some find the manifestation of God in nature. And some just feel at peace looking out over a salt marsh at sunset. Photo by Jim Olive.

women have fewer children. And education must be followed by access to contraception. Humans consume disproportionately compared to other species. As a species, we take too much. We may not be able to survive ourselves as we transition to a world that is full of people and impacts. It is also interesting to note that about 75 percent of my clients over the years who have fought for protection of home and ecosystem as well as for the coast have been women.

Principle 3 is that the basic needs of all people of the world should be met. All of us have a fundamental right to food, water, and shelter. We all need some path, some process, some hope to meet these needs, whether it be by farming or by being employed or by owning a business. If people do not have access to basic needs, chaos will result. It is both self-serving and necessary for the Earth's future to ensure that all people's needs are met.

Principle 4 is the identification and realization of "enough," of placing limits on our "wants." It is unrealistic for me as a human living in the United States to assume that the rest of the world's population does not aspire to consume to our standard. Yet that goal cannot be met within the limits of the Earth with existing production practices. It simply cannot. We in the West seek satisfaction through material goods, through immediate gratification of our wants, yet we seem perpetually unsatisfied. We must restore satisfaction to the human self while using less. There is not enough Earth for all wants to be met. My Earth Church mantra is—I use enough, I have enough. And for that I am grateful. I do not need to further expand. I am content with what I am.

Principle 5 is that human economic principles over time should conform to the Earth's ecological principles, thereby becoming circular. In this way, we will create a society that exhibits balance between economy and ecology. Here, it makes sense to challenge the concept of economic growth as practiced today—an idol that that we practically bow to—the false God of unmitigated growth. If nothing else, principle 5 is a cry for efficiency—for reduction in the material and energy content in every product we make and consume. This is true regarding energy and water and all forms of matter. It is true regarding carbon dioxide and climate. Less will enable more within limits. The efficiency goal of Earth Church is to produce every product with less footprint—with less impact—with a long-term goal of keeping that footprint to the absolute minimum and at least offsetting that which we cannot reduce. And as members of Earth Church, we should consume with this goal in mind.

Principle 6 is that our society should empower all and seek equity. Fundamental to Earth Church is that we humans each have a voice and a right to be heard. We also have a right to know about certain things—to have access to information. We have a right to be governed by a system that empowers us to participate in the decision-making process, and we have a right to be governed by a system that seeks to minimize human impacts and protect our air, water, and land. We have a fundamental right as humans to not have one sector of society exposed to greater health risks than other sectors. We have a right to life and to conditions that support life equally.

Principle 7 is a mandate to celebrate and learn about your place—your geographic center on the Earth. Earth Church is about the Earth, about embracing and understanding our place within the Earth, about its rhythms and patterns, its beauty and spirit. Understanding place is essential to who and what I am. Without understanding the characteristics of the Earth in the place where I live, I am without context. I would be lost but for my place on Earth.

Principle 8 holds cooperation as the highest form of social interaction. Success within Earth Church is defined by the whole and not the pieces. If we all don't succeed, then we all fail, and no issue epitomizes this more than does addressing climate change. Earth Church is about the Earth and all of its living community succeeding. It is larger than the individual, although the individual is a key part. I as a member of Earth Church have a duty to cooperate, to work with others to achieve these principles, even as I maintain my own identity and pursue my personal goals.

Principle 9 is the adoption of creative conflict resolution concepts, ultimately including the elimination of warfare. We can and should do better as individuals and as societies in resolving disputes. As a society, we are nowhere close to being beyond physical and emotional violence as a solution to our disputes. It is a fact that now and in the future, we are going to disagree as humans. It will happen. Most of the biblical Ten Commandments are about behaving in a manner that will prevent us from killing each other or otherwise becoming involved in disputes. But we do become involved in disputes, and we simply have to get better at resolving them.

Principle 10 is to try to accept change. Change is an essential core aspect of Earth Church. Earth Church is not "business as usual," as indicated by the previous nine principles. Earth Church is about seeing the Earth, about seeing me differently and acting accordingly. I smile as I write about change because it is easier to write these words than to live them. However, the commitment is not to change immediately but to simply be open to change and try to change.

These principles are not right for all people. I know that various leaders in various other religions and denominations would not agree, and that is good. That is as it should be. We do not need to agree on all aspects to work in a common direction. The important thing is that if we agree on a common goal, we can find various ways of achieving that goal. We do not all have to believe exactly the same things to get to the same place—a healthier Earth, one that will be here for future generations, one that meets the needs of all people. Such is Earth Church, however you get there.

Spirituality alone may not save the Texas coast. But it is a powerful force on the Texas coast and in Texas generally, one that offers a solid backdrop from which to try to save this magnificent piece of the church that is the Earth, one that should not be overlooked, and one that should be nourished.

So I paddle into the church that is Christmas Bay on a cool, crisp spring day, accompanied by shorebirds in various hues of breeding plumage, green eye patches visible on the great egrets, purple bills evident on the reddish egrets, and I follow the black-crowned night heron as she guides me into the marsh channels where I connect with something larger than myself, something strong, something mystical, something real. The draw of the coast for me is at its core a spiritual draw. I come back to keep myself nourished with the stuff of life, the ether that connects all living things, all matter. And I feel better.

CHAPTER 11

Entrepreneurship and Competition

LEED, SITES, Envision, and the Living Building Challenge

Another formative aspect of the future of the coast will involve two familiar concepts—entrepreneurship and competition, two private-sector hallmarks. We know that these attributes exist and we hold them in extremely high regard on the Texas coast. But I have heard little discussion of the role of entrepreneurship and competition as powerful engines for change, engines that have been at work on the Texas coast for quite some time and that will propel us from doing business in the empty world to doing business in the full world.

I'll never forget my friend Bud Payne from South Texas talking about how many of the ranchers in South Texas were nervous about owning high-quality wildlife habitat like native brush and wetlands, about how some even cut or otherwise modified some of this habitat for fear of it being taken over by the federal government, perhaps by condemnation or some other perceived horror. But then a funny thing happened.

A nonprofit organization in the Rio Grande Valley called the Valley Land Fund was formed, with the goal of conserving important habitat in South Texas. John Martin, the initial executive director of the fund, decided in the mid-1990s that a photography contest to showcase the wonderful wildlife of South Texas would be a great idea for emphasizing the resources that existed there. The concept was straightforward. Ranch owners were paired with photographers who would spend countless hours in blinds on these properties, looking for prize-winning shots of various types of birds, mammals, reptiles, amphibians, spiders, plants, and landscapes.

From the beginning, the competition to have a winning photo was heated among the ranchers, but it began to be clear that certain ranches always seemed to do better than others. What also became clear is that the winning ranches were those with the best and most diverse habitats, the ones with beautiful wetland ponds with shelves full of water-tolerant grasses and forbs rather than dug-out holes in the ground without water-loving plants, the ones with native brush patches rather than all improved pasture. Winning the contest was about high-quality habitat.

When that became known, the competition entered a new era. Now, in addition to pursuing quality photographers as partners, certain landowners began to improve the habitat on their property. Some constructed better wetlands. Others allowed native grasses and brush to come back. And they began producing winners in the photo contest, each winner hooting as the announcement was made over drinks after dinner. Imagine management practices and stewardship ethics resulting from competition to win a photo contest. By the way, Bud's ranch has been a winner in the contest, an eloquent testimonial to good stewardship. A prize-winning photo of two caracaras taken on the Payne Ranch by Greg Lasley is shown in figure 11.1.

A somewhat similar phenomenon has emerged regarding "human habitat." One major game changer for the built environment was the Leadership in Energy and Environmental Design (LEED) certification process, which certifies the energy and environmental soundness of buildings. This initial certification effort has generated a form of competition among building owners and architects, with the result that our urban environment is steadily getting greener. The LEED process and its progeny, the Sustainable Sites Initiative (SITES) for certifying landscapes, the Envision process for certifying engineering infrastructure projects, and the most difficult of all, the Living Building Challenge, are changing the norms and best management practices of the built environment. And just as in the photo contest, all of this change has been accomplished without regulation. In fact, in some ways, the change has been impeded by regulation.

The message has penetrated the business community that it needs to make progress in incorporating important issues such as energy use, carbon emissions, climate change, and water into the design of buildings and products. Corporate websites are full of these issues, and most major corporations dedicate both time and attention to issues such as sustainability, resource consumption, environmental metrics, and corporate social responsibility. If anything, there has been a revolution in corporate thinking on these issues since we have

Figure 11.1. Valley Land Fund prize-winning photograph of caracaras on a dead cow on the Payne Ranch south of Falfurrias. Note the full craw bulging from the breast of the bird on the left. Photo by Greg Lasley.

entered the twenty-first century, and nowhere is it more evident than in the adoption of building certification standards as set forth by the LEED program.

LEED was the first of these certification processes to be initiated, with its origin dating back to 1994. LEED has different standards for five categories of built environments—new construction, interior construction, building operation and maintenance, neighborhood development, and homes. In each category, four levels of certification—certified, silver, gold, and platinum—may be achieved based on points awarded for the use of best practices in various subcategories. The LEED process is administrated by the US Green Building Council.

It is difficult to appreciate the extent to which LEED has changed building construction practices in the United States by adopting a set of best management practices and then rating a building on how well it meets these standards. Most major corporations today have a policy that any new construction will be LEED certified. Many universities, federal, state, and local governments, and nongovernmental organizations have similar requirements. Today, LEED construction is the norm for new buildings, but it wasn't always that way. The success of the LEED certification process bears witness to the power of creativity, marketing, and good design, which, by the way, is changing the way we build our cities, and Houston is an exclamation point on that success story.

John Kirksey is a successful architect in Houston who has built Kirksey and Associates into a top-flight design firm. Kirksey and I go way back to high school in Harlingen, Texas, in the Rio Grande Valley. Our paths diverged for many years before coming back together through various groups and activities like the Galveston Bay Foundation and Trees for Houston, and I am proud to know him.

Kirksey is a man of the coast, a guy who likes to fish and enjoy the ecological abundance of the bays and estuaries, and he was looking for a way to both brand his architecture company and express his interest in trees and the environment through his work. John had always been interested in the concept of sustainability, a way of thinking to make sure the business world and the natural system were both protected into the future.

Kirksey's answer was to lead his company to become a leading green-design firm that practiced what it espoused. He embraced the LEED program before it was well established, making him one of the real design visionaries of the Texas coast. He planted trees in the name of his clients and friends. Ultimately, he set up a system by which he gave ownership in his firm to key employees, but most importantly for this chapter, he became a leader in green design and has helped make Houston better.

Houston is not known for land-use planning. Although cities in Texas are authorized to enact zoning ordinances, the City of Houston has chosen not to allow zoning, clearly distinguishing itself from other Texas cities such as Dallas, San Antonio, Austin, and Corpus Christi (and the list goes on and on). Houston has a different style about it, and green design would seem not to fit, yet nothing could be further from the truth. And John Kirksey was there for the beginning of this strange revolution.

Although Kirksey and his firm had been focused on green design since the early 2000s, he remembers a seminal moment in his career when he heard a major official of Shell Oil proclaim that from that time on, Shell would be renting or buying only buildings that met LEED criteria. According to Kirksey, when developers such as Gerald Hines and others heard that message, they decided that their new buildings would meet those criteria and provide for this new, emerging market. When that group of developers made the LEED commitment, the competitive nature of the development world and those that design it kicked in, and the Houston architectural market has not really been the same since, as indicated by the large number of LEED-certified buildings now in existence within the city.

John Kirksey tends to deflect credit for the accomplishments of his firm, instead focusing on the excellent staff that helped him with this LEED effort, including Bryan Malarkey and Julie Hendricks. It turns out that Houston ranks fourth in the United States in LEED-certified buildings, a remarkable metric for a city not generally known for its green accomplishments. Kirksey Ecoservices was involved in certifying about 22 percent of those LEED buildings, a major accomplishment. Further, Houston leads the United States in LEED for existing buildings, and Kirksey Ecoservices has certified about 68 percent of those buildings. That is impressive for the city and for the firm. And it is about leadership and entrepreneurship.

As can be seen from figure 11.2, the LEED rating system gives credit for eight different categories. These categories were chosen because they represent issues and concerns about either energy or the environment. A checklist and point system correspond to receiving credits in each category. If the design addresses the various requirements, then points are awarded. The total number of points is 110. A platinum certification (the highest) requires 80–110 points, a gold certification is given for 60–79 points, a silver for 50–59 points, and a LEED certification for 40–49 points.

Within each of the subcategories identified in figure 11.2, there are various topics with associated points. For example,

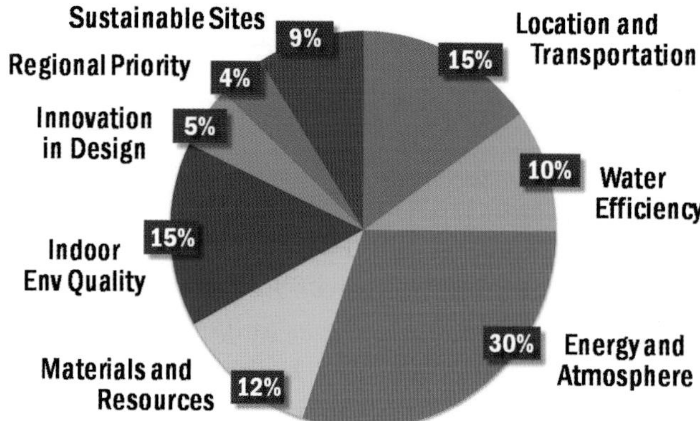

Figure 11.2. Point allocation by subject area for new-building LEED certification.

under the sustainable sites category, points are awarded for protection of habitat, use of a brownfield (previously used) site, and development of a soil erosion plan and light pollution reduction plan. Under the water efficiency category, points are awarded for percentage reduction below baseline water use, water-efficient landscaping, and water-efficient toilets and sinks. Under the energy and atmosphere category, the focus is on efficiency of products used within the building, energy-efficient design, use of on-site renewables, and other similar requirements. When LEED first came along, such requirements were revolutionary. Today, more likely than not they define the norm for major corporations and the developers that serve them.

LEED has evolved over the years, becoming more rigorous along the way. However, it is important in that it found a niche for green design—an opening for architects to make their buildings more responsive to current problems, problems that have led to inefficient and decaying urban development that can and should be built for the long term, with an eye toward operation and maintenance as well as initial capital cost. This program has done much good and has spawned related methodologies in other design disciplines.

Entrepreneurship can change the complexion of a city, not only in its skyline but in its development philosophy. Green buildings have caught on because they make sense—they save money, people enjoy working in them, and companies like them. Today websites for most major corporations around the country specify that all new buildings will be LEED certified, but that was not the case when LEED began. It required commitment and risk to lead an architectural firm in a new direction, the same type of leadership that we need from many directions today. So thank you, Kirksey. We need more businesspeople like you.

Susan Rieff and I have known each other since she came to Texas to work for the Texas Parks and Wildlife Department as the head of its Resource Protection Division. Susan worked with one of the best sets of commissioners ever, in my opinion—led by chair Ed Cox and commissioners George Bolin, Dick Morrison, and Billy Wheless. Susan was the first woman to have such a position at Texas Parks and Wildlife and was a trailblazer for environmental policy in many ways here in Texas.

After working with Texas Parks and Wildlife and in several other notable positions involving one form or another of public service, Susan became head of the Lady Bird Johnson Wildflower Center and was at the helm when this organization changed in many important ways. In addition to getting the center added to the University of Texas at Austin, Susan also led it into conservation biology and sustainable landscape design, expanding its scope of interest and influence substantially.

One of the most important initiatives implemented during Susan's tenure was the Sustainable Sites Initiative, the landscape-architecture equivalent of the LEED certification program. This program is now implemented by the US Green Building Council as the SITES program. Here, instead of certifying the energy, water, and resource sustainability of buildings, SITES establishes a standard for landscape certification. And nothing may be more important from a water perspective in Texas in the future than landscaping.

In Texas today, landscaping—yard watering—consumes about 50 percent of urban water. When we plant and maintain yards in a manner better suited to England than to Texas, we expose nonnative lawn grass to Texas droughts and insects. When we cut this grass every other week if not every week, we expose the internal organs of this grass to the hot Texas sun and our pests, causing the loss of more water and energy, which we offset by watering and fertilizing in a continuing cycle that would be almost comical if it were not causing such negative environmental impacts.

The bottom line is that we commonly use nonnative plants for landscaping that should not be here—plants that should be replaced by native plants. The SITES initiative attempts to remedy this situation by setting forth criteria for evaluating and rewarding appropriate landscaping adapted to the climate and place of the project. SITES is a major step forward. Just as the LEED certification project reset social and business norms for buildings, so will SITES reset social and business norms for landscaping.

SITES began as a joint project of the Wildflower Center, the American Society of Landscape Architects, and the US Botanic Garden. SITES is "an interdisciplinary effort to create voluntary national guidelines and a rating system for sustainable land design, construction and maintenance practices for landscapes of all types, with or without buildings." While it shares many similarities with the LEED process, it is also quite different, reflecting at least in part a greater focus on ecology and a later creation date. More recently, the US Green Building Council became the administrator of the SITES program and it is now side by side with LEED certification.

Years ago, Susan came to Rice and spoke to the students in my sustainable design course about the Sustainable Sites Initiative, as it was known at that time. As presented by Susan, the methodology was about ecology—about knowing information about the place where you were constructing, selecting plants that fit with the climate and soils and treating the soil as a resource. Soil was not just a foundation, but instead the base of the ecosystem, the heart of landscape thinking, and the SITES methodology takes you into stewardship of the soil, water, plants, birds, and butterflies. It is about merging the built and the natural environment.

What impressed me most about this effort was that it went well beyond reducing degradation (minimizing impact) and was more about stewardship of the land, focusing on issues such as improving soil, reducing runoff, increasing rainfall infiltration, increasing vegetative cover, and ultimately improving air and water in our community. As such, SITES was about moving from conservation to regeneration of ecosystems. That caught my attention. Regeneration is a great goal for development—restoring and maintaining rather than simply minimizing impact. In fact, that will be the design standard for the future—projects that actually help enhance environmental quality. That is a huge change from environ-

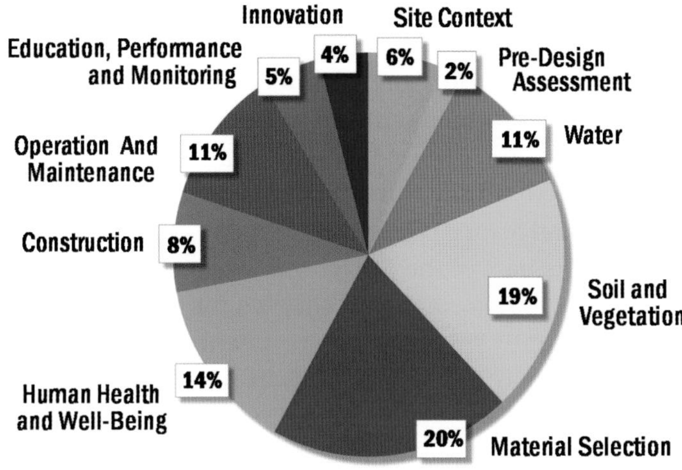

Figure 11.3. Point allocation by subject area for the SITES certification process.

mental thinking during the 1970s through the 1990s and represents a transition to full-world thinking.

Susan is very clear about the team aspect of the SITES initiative, but I am clear that leadership is important, and Susan, in my opinion, led the Lady Bird Johnson Wildflower Center into the middle of one of the key issues for the future of Texas, namely fitting the human built environment and the human landscape to the realities of the Texas environment. Wildflowers are both a metaphor for this effort and directly on point. We are not taming this land, we are living within it, an important message for all of us. Working with nature, not against it, makes sense. Just as nature has a circular economy, so will we in the future, and those circular systems are fully represented in the SITES evaluation criteria.

As with the LEED process, the SITES process has a number of categories within which points are awarded. As can be seen in figure 11.3, the focus is on design relative to water, soil and vegetation, material selection, and human health and well-being. Again, points are required for various levels of certification. SITES has a potential score of 200 points, with certification requiring at least 70, silver being awarded for 85–99 points, gold for 100–134, and platinum above 135. One difference between SITES and LEED is that SITES has certain required elements without a point structure, meaning that they must be addressed affirmatively. This distinction begins to address one of the criticisms of the LEED process, which can allow certain issues to be ignored and still award certification. SITES addresses this concern to some extent. The SITES process is just beginning to be implemented, but I believe it will become successful in the same manner that LEED has.

The SITES process brings important aspects of landscape quality together. In this way, the impact of human landscapes on the natural system is reduced. When combined across cities and across Texas, these changes will make a huge difference, reducing both the water and carbon footprint of yards and public landscapes. We brought traditions with us when we settled this part of the Earth, but we do not have to maintain practices that are not well adapted for life here. Learning to live intelligently in our place—respecting its boundaries, its limits—may be the most important element of human development.

Susan is a leader, one who takes us where we need to go. In terms of water in Texas, nothing may be more important than getting our development practices aligned toward the reality that water in Texas is in short supply, not only for human needs but for the health of the bays and rivers. We can have it all, but we need to be smart. Thank you, Susan, for helping us be smarter about living in Texas, and thank you, Lady Bird Johnson, for liking wildflowers.

As first the architects and then the landscape architects were developing their certification processes (and in the case of architects, developing business), the engineering community was left behind. But in about 2009, the Envision process was developed by the Institute for Sustainable Infrastructure (ISI) in connection with the Zofnass Program for Sustainable Infrastructure at the Harvard Graduate School of Design. The Envision process was developed for major infrastructure projects such as roads and freeways, pipelines, water supply facilities, wastewater treatment plants, and other similar large-scale projects.

At Rice, I use the Envision process as a teaching and design tool. Here, I have enjoyed the help and assistance of Michael Bloom, an engineer with R. G. Miller in Houston. Envision is relatively new and has not yet been widely accepted, but there is no doubt in my mind that this certification concept, or something very similar to it, will emerge and become as well known for engineering infrastructure projects as LEED is for buildings, particularly where these projects are undertaken by the private sector or by governmental entities concerned with environmental impact and ecological service issues. Michael is certified in the Envision methodology, which has as of early 2016 certified only about nine projects in the United States, including one in Texas. However, these numbers will climb in the future.

As seen in figure 11.4, Envision awards points for five general categories—quality of life, leadership, resource allocation, natural world, and climate. Each of these areas has a series of specific inquiries, ultimately totaling fifty. Each inquiry has several different levels of attainment, from the low end, which generally entails developing information about an issue (e.g., calculating a carbon footprint), to affirmatively minimizing or mitigating the impact, to taking steps to regenerate the natural system relative to the issue of concern, a process called restorative. The Envision process has five categories of attainment—improved, enhanced, superior, conserving, and restorative. These five categories are the equivalent of the certified, silver, gold, and platinum of the LEED process. However, the Envision process goes beyond the LEED process with its emphasis on restoration, an emphasis that also emerges in the SITES process. And restoration is the direction in which all development in the United States is likely to proceed over the next several decades. Design is changing to reflect the realities of climate, carbon budgets, and water supply issues. Design is leading us into the full world.

The restorative level of engineering design is the big advancement by the Envision process. In the case of the climate evaluation, a restorative project must be net carbon negative, meaning that more carbon must be offset than just the carbon footprint of the project, including the footprint of

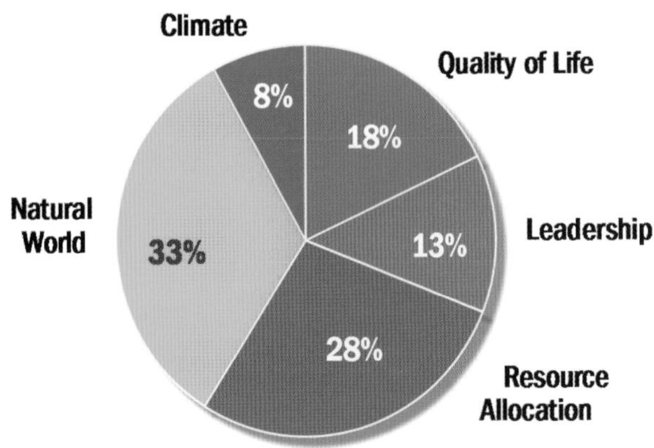

Figure 11.4. Point allocation by subject area for the ISI Envision certification process for engineering and infrastructure projects. Note that this certification process is beginning to directly address climate change as well as some of the more social issues, as represented by the quality of life category.

materials used in the project. In other words, for a project to be considered restorative, it must make the project site better from a natural resource (e.g., water and vegetation) and carbon sequestration standpoint than it was before the project was begun. This is quite a task.

In our class, Michael Bloom and I asked the students to evaluate aspects of three structural alternatives to protect Galveston Bay. Each of these projects involved a large gate across the Houston Ship Channel and either concrete or clay structures to intercept and hopefully repel hurricane storm surge of about seventeen feet at the coastline. These three projects each calculated a carbon footprint for the various structures they evaluated, and the resulting carbon footprints were quite large. They then evaluated how many acres of various types of habitat would need to be created to offset these impacts and reach the restorative level. If this system were adopted for all future engineering projects, there would be significant restoration of the Texas coast from these projects alone.

Perhaps one day soon, an enterprising and competitive engineering firm will suggest a design based on these principles and will emerge as the selected entity, an action that will lead others to seek this knowledge, this design process, in order to compete for future jobs. One of my students has already been certified in the Envision process, although he is finding that as of 2016, that certification is not yet valued by Houston-based engineering firms. My student might find himself creating his own company because the existing ones are moving too slowly, and that is how change happens. Innovate or die, as my friend Jack Matson says. And there is truth in that statement.

However, of all the voluntary certification programs, the Living Building Challenge (LBC) is in a league of its own. It is simply great. Rather than allowing various levels of certification, the LBC requires that certified projects meet all of its rigorous requirements, although exceptions can be made under unusual circumstances. But the differences go beyond the certification protocol. The LBC is changing the way we think of buildings and the built environment, making them about life and living rather than about enclosure and escape from the elements. The LBC is about designing for future generations. It is the next big step forward.

I first met Robert Potts when he was a lawyer at Baker and Botts in Houston volunteering to help the Galveston Bay Foundation evaluate a piece of property on the Bolivar Peninsula. Over the years, we have maintained a friendship as he moved to central Texas and became involved in work with the Texas Nature Conservancy and then with the Edwards Aquifer Authority. Today, Robert is the executive director of the Dixon Water Foundation, which is interested in the future of water and ranching.

The Dixon Water Foundation maintains three working ranches on which native prairie has been restored. Robert smiles when he describes how these lands perform during a drought compared to neighboring properties, about how their grass "greens up" quicker than that of the neighbors, about how their livestock tanks are slower to fill up but last much longer, about how the water system has been restored. The Dixon Water Foundation wanted to develop a meeting place on one of its ranches and wanted a design that blended with the ranch, that understood and reflected the ranch. For that design, it turned to Lake Flato in San Antonio, a premier group of design architects.

Tenna Florian was the Lake Flato designer charged with meeting the criteria of the Dixon Water Foundation, and after getting started on the project, she realized that this building at this site was an excellent candidate for the LBC. According to Tenna, the firm approached the foundation with the idea and offered to incorporate the LBC requirements into the design at no additional cost to the foundation, indicating the true entrepreneurial spirit at work. In turn, Tenna produced the first building in Texas that became certified as meeting the requirements of the LBC, and the ninth in the world.

You can tell that the LBC is different upon your first encounter with it. Rather than categories, the LBC has "petals," emphasizing that it focuses more on life than does the LEED process, for example. There are seven petals—energy, water, equity, site, health, materials, and beauty, and the requirements of all seven must be met to have a project certified as meeting the LBC. The goal here is to integrate all seven of these important aspects of a sustainable future into the design.

I invited Tenna to come and discuss the LBC and the associated design process with my class at Rice. It was interesting to hear her speak of the key differences between a living building and one that meets certain LEED requirements. While elements are similar, the scope and holistic nature of the LBC take the design team far beyond normal design.

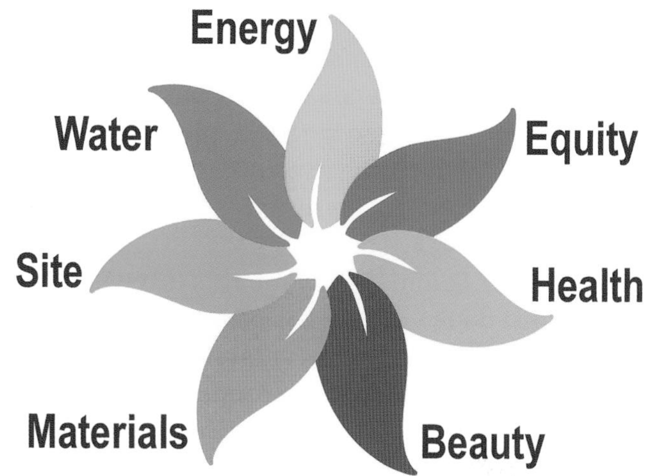

Figure 11.5. The Living Building Challenge logo clearly indicates it is different from the other certification concepts; the requirements of each of its seven petals must be met for certification.

According to Tenna, the most striking difference between the LBC and the LEED process, for example, is the "red list" of materials that are banned from Living Buildings. Now think about it—a private-sector voluntary process has banned products containing chemicals that are acceptable to the government. This goes well beyond existing regulations. These red-list materials include a number of chlorinated hydrocarbons, halogenated flame retardants, phthalates (plasticizers), formaldehyde, neoprene, and more traditional substances such as lead (above certain levels) and asbestos. It is often difficult to obtain information about the chemical composition of building materials, and the architect or builder is required to provide proof that these substances are not present. A new website called Declare by the International Living Future Institute is now offering disclosure information about the content of various materials from various vendors.

In many respects, this concept of a red list is a radical departure from past programs and indicates the potential power of these certification processes. If a product cannot be used because of its chemical content, and if demand for "clean" products becomes strong enough, then entire markets will swing away from red-list materials. This is consumer selection of product through certification requirements that are being pursued because of competitive instincts, a desire to be the best.

The red list is not the only controversial aspect about the Living Building Challenge. The building has to be energy and water positive by generating more energy than it consumes and by capturing rainfall and storm water runoff, among other requirements. Some Living Buildings have trouble meeting building codes that require water and sewage to meet certain standards set fifty to one hundred years ago. The Living Building must be carbon neutral. It has to incorporate biophilic, or nature-loving, thinking into the design. Urban agriculture has to be part of the design. Mobility to and from the building by bike, mass transit, and walking are important criteria, and equity must be incorporated into the design. In this context, equity means making a donation to a charity based on a proportion of the project cost as well as creating a more equitable society through transparent social practices within the corporations and businesses working on the project. To top it all off, unlike other certification programs, which are based on design representations and computer modeling, the LBC requires that the building be constructed and its performance monitored and verified for one year prior to becoming eligible for certification.

Among other things, the LBC requires that the designer submit an essay about how the building design exemplifies beauty. In her beauty narrative submitted for the certification, Tenna speaks about the beauty of the native prairie and how this low-slung building complements this landscape. She talks about the beauty of the live oak that is a key component of the site and building design. She speaks of beauty from the standpoint of integrating the human and natural in a form and manner in which they complement one another, becoming part of the same landscape. She speaks of the porches and overhangs as safe places, as gathering places—places that frame nature from various points within the structure. While she describes her concept of beauty, she also provides an interesting narrative about biophilic design.

The LBC is not for all buildings or owners. It is a rigorous and powerful force for change. When we understand that our human structures should replicate nature and natural systems, that they should have no net impact, that they should express love for and appreciation of nature, we will have made much progress toward a world that Aldo Leopold and Rachel Carson would applaud, perhaps realizing an evolutionary possibility and an ecological necessity. Such is the nature of the innovation occurring today in the design world, and it is fueled by competition, a desire to be the best, to excel, to get it right.

These four programs—LEED, SITES, Envision, and the Living Building Challenge—have changed and will continue

Figure 11.6. Tenna Florian of Lake Flato Architects in San Antonio designed the first Living Building certified in Texas for the Dixon Water Foundation. Photo by Casey Dunn.

to change the ways our built environment impacts the natural environment. That in itself is important, and the fact that these systems are being utilized voluntarily is also important. But perhaps most important is that these buildings are beginning to incorporate certain economic development concepts that are different from those of the past. This, I believe, can be viewed as the first step in moving from a straight-line growth society to one that is more circular.

Our economy has always been focused on straight-line growth, with the growth lines extending off the page, into the stratosphere and beyond, endless. Our consumption of natural resources and our emission of pollutants such as carbon dioxide have followed these same straight-line trends. We are beginning, however, to realize that these trends cannot be sustained and that we need to conform these straight lines to the circular patterns of nature. This transition from straight-line to circular thinking has begun and has been moved forward by these certification programs.

These programs mark a significant change in the status quo, one that has escaped attention for its larger implications. Competition—the desire to do something better than someone else, the desire to be recognized as the best in a class—is a powerful engine, one that can take us to unexpected places, much like a photo contest in South Texas has led to better habitat. Human nature is a funny beast, one that can work for the common good on a good day. And as with the South Texas photographic contest, our competitive desire might take us where our rational minds fail to go, a concept that makes me smile.

PART 4

The Future of the Texas Coast

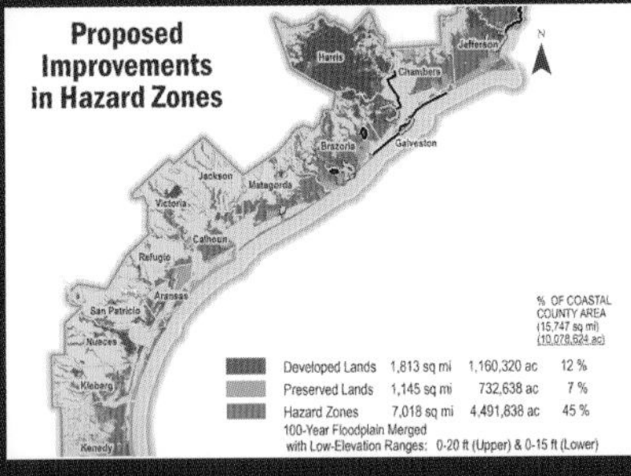

CHAPTER 12

Moving Forward

For twelve chapters, I have set out assets, challenges, and concepts for moving forward into the full world while protecting the Texas coast. I have tried to do this without depending on the government and regulation, instead focusing on private-sector initiative, creativity, entrepreneurship, and the power of money and spirituality and human nature. So many attempts to protect things that we care about are framed as negatives—don't do this, you are prohibited from that. Seldom do we frame the future in terms of positive thinking and positive outcomes. Yet as we move into the full world, there are positives upon which to draw, several of which have been highlighted in prior chapters. There are emerging leaders and many yet to be born who will take us forward. And that thought makes me smile.

A few years back in Port Arthur, a native son named Hilton Kelley returned home after spending time in the navy and then on the West Coast. When Hilton returned to his hometown neighborhood of West Port Arthur in 2000, he was shocked at the way it had fallen into disrepair. Many long-time Anglo citizens of Port Arthur had moved to mid-Jefferson County—to Port Neches and Groves and Nederland—away from the town where they were raised. Most downtown buildings were either boarded up or about to close down. Most of the residents of West Port Arthur that remained were relatively poor, mainly African American, and unemployed. It was a community living in the shadow of two refineries and two chemical plants and their illegal flares, surrounded by oil storage tanks. Hilton found what he considered to be a community under siege.

After settling in and taking stock of the situation, Hilton decided he needed to do something to make things better. He formed a citizens' group called Community In-Power and Development Association (CIDA) and sought the counsel and support of several of the ministers serving West Port Arthur, among others. With the help of his counselors, he reached out into the community and began to understand the situation,

Figure 12.1. Hilton Kelley with process units and storage tanks in the background. Photo courtesy of CIDA, Inc.

coming to the conclusion that the environmental problems in West Port Arthur had to be solved before any other improvements could occur. And there were major environmental problems.

From about 2000 to 2005, the use of flares increased substantially. Flares are supposed to be used for emergencies in the big plants, an escape valve of last resort to prevent a major fire or explosion. Flares are not supposed to be used on a routine basis, yet industry, aided and abetted by government, had fallen into a pattern in which flares were abused and accidental releases were excessive. And no one but Hilton Kelley was willing to stand up and fight for the citizens and the community.

Through the newspapers and my sister, Ann, who lives in Beaumont, I had heard about Hilton Kelley, and one day I saw a request from Hilton for a lawyer willing to undertake pro bono work to help him fight the expansion of the Motiva Refinery, which was proposing to double its capacity from almost three hundred thousand to about six hundred thousand barrels per day. Motiva had filed for an air pollution permit and Hilton wanted to challenge that permit. I agreed to help.

Hilton Kelley is a force of nature, a truly charismatic character who wins people over with sincerity and a huge smile. We filed the opposition papers and Hilton convinced Dr. Neil Carmen of the Lone Star Chapter of the Sierra Club out of Austin and Eric Schaeffer of the Environmental Integrity Project out of Washington, DC, to help us analyze and understand the air pollution issues arising from this expansion. These issues included meeting the ozone national air quality standard, complying with new source performance standards, and making sure that the design levels for air toxics at the property line of the plant did not exceed applicable screening levels set by the state. Over time, we developed a set of recommendations and were prepared to move forward in opposition to the expansion.

Once again, another excellent lawyer from the Baker Botts law firm was on the other side. Pam Giblin has permitted more refineries and chemical plants than anyone else I know, and she and I had worked against each other many times in the past. Together, we developed the settlement concepts that led to major changes in the performance at Formosa Plastics down the coast, and we rolled our sleeves up with Hilton and the Motiva environmental manager and worked out an agreement on both air pollution issues and some of the social issues that were at the heart of the problems of West Port Arthur. This agreement settled the dispute over the expansion of the plant, which was allowed to go forward without further opposition. On the citizen side, not only were substantial pollution controls installed in the plant as a result of the agreement, but Hilton and his nonprofit, CIDA, also got several provisions related to employment, health studies, copay assistance, and community improvement written into the agreement. In addition, a fund was set up with a governing board to award money for important civic improvement projects in West Port Arthur. For the first time to my knowledge, social issues were included in an environmental settlement on the Texas coast, and these social provisions laid the groundwork for major changes in West Port Arthur.

Shortly after the agreement with Motiva was reached, Hilton also negotiated a settlement with Valero Refining and its environmental manager, Rich Walsh. Here, an interesting exchange took place. Rich approached me and said that Valero was willing to make a major investment in West Port Arthur where it had a refinery, but the company had some questions that it wanted resolved. Hilton had come back from the West Coast and had become active in the community, saying, among other things, that he was a member of the Screen Actors Guild (SAG). Rich told me that Valero had been told that this was not true, and he wanted me to ask Hilton to show them his SAG card. On the one hand, this could be interpreted as questioning Hilton's integrity. On the other hand, those who opposed Hilton, namely people in local government, were very jealous of Hilton and his success. So in many respects, it was a chance to establish bona fides, to prove he was what he said he was.

This was a pivotal moment. I can clearly see Hilton and myself sitting in a booth at a restaurant and me asking Hilton if he would be willing to produce his SAG card. Hilton smiled, reached into his back pocket, pulled out his SAG card, and the negotiations went smoothly thereafter. The final Valero agreement went further than the Motiva agreement in terms of providing Hilton with significantly more discretion in how various funds were used within the community, including the development of job training opportunities and even a community video project that ended up on local public television, helping the community develop a spirit that had been missing for many years. Trust is hard to establish, but once it is there, miraculous things can happen.

Hilton was rightly recognized for his efforts at revitalizing the West Port Arthur community when he received the Goldman Environmental Prize in 2011, one of the highest environmental awards in the world. And while that is wonderful and well-justified recognition, the award is not the most important part of this story. Instead, it is that one person can and did make a difference. Our system does reward initiative and creative thinking and willpower. Hilton had a vision for his community and he was willing to take chances to get things done. And he certainly made a difference.

We have many people on the Texas coast who can make a difference. We have wonderful nonprofits up and down the coast. We have statewide and local groups. And we have countless people who donate extensive time and effort to bring their issues to the forefront, who try to make a difference. What we need, however, is a coherent vision of what is possible, what might work, and how to achieve these things.

The lesson of West Port Arthur is that the refineries and Hilton came to an understanding about an alternative way to proceed. Both sides agreed to "change the dance." We have to change the dance on the Texas coast, and we need to do it sooner rather than later if we are going to have an ecologically productive coast in the future. The question is how to do this. And of course, the challenge is to do it.

"Changing the dance" is an interesting concept. We seem to have evolved a way of doing things that is locked in place, although many of us would be hard pressed to describe the system we are locked into. We have city, county, state, and federal politicians that dance a certain way. We have businesses that dance a certain way. We have citizens that dance a certain way, and activists that dance a certain way. In their own way, each group is comfortable with the dance, but we need to move forward toward a new way of thinking, and that is not always comfortable. In fact, when really good work is being done, it can feel uncomfortable.

We all need to dance a different step to a different tune. Hilton changed the dance in Port Arthur. The challenge is for all of us to change the dance on the coast.

This book has described the resources and opportunities that exist before us. There is a convergence of forces both within and beyond the Texas coast that makes the time right for action. We just have to be smart enough to recognize opportunities and prepared enough to act on those opportunities. Here are some thoughts.

Partnerships and cooperation are going to be a key to future success, even if it might take litigation to get these systems initiated. Three key areas lie before us relative to partnerships—water, ecosystem restoration, and ecoplay. In the first two of these cases, crises provide the incentive to act, one due to the reduced dependability of surface and groundwater and the other due to climate change. The third—ecoplay—requires partnerships to fully utilize the resources we have.

The first partnership for the coast is a water partnership for the watershed of each major river emptying into a coastal bay. The GBRA-TAP agreement mentioned in chapter 9 is a good model, and I urge all of you to pay attention to this agreement, its implementation, and its success or failure. If you can, follow this agreement and the studies to be done under it. If the promise of this agreement is realized, it has the potential to transform the reality of freshwater inflows for the future of our bays and estuaries. The agreement recognizes that problems and issues cannot be solved by thinking the way we were thinking when we created them, to paraphrase Albert Einstein.

Our water system is an old one, based on empty-world thinking. We need a better one, one focused on current realities and without the roadblocks that prevent creativity and change. There is a willingness on the part of one river authority—the GBRA—to take a fresh look at its watershed with a citizens' group—TAP—as its partner. This agreement will take a hard look at two key subjects—habitat and water, keys to the future of the midcoast region. Under habitat, we will be looking for new areas for the cranes, and we are considering a view of freshwater inflows that allows the establishment of a nursery zone within San Antonio Bay to get the system through droughts without losing its fishery seed stock. Under the water category, we are looking to find water for the bay any way we can. We plan to study the permits from top to bottom. We will consider methods to enhance stream flow, perhaps by utilizing ecological service transactions. We are open to any new ideas that have a chance to work. If we are successful, we might hope to set in motion a new system that will work better as the watershed continues to fill up with people.

The potential importance of this agreement is hard to overstate. In the long run, the goal is get sufficient water to the bays and estuaries to keep them healthy while meeting the water supply requirements for current and future water use. If the parties to this agreement and the many other interested parties can find a way to undertake this work and find pathways to solutions, they will likely be followed by every major watershed on the Texas coast. If you care about the coast, get involved in the implementation of this agreement. It is going to be hard. It is going to demand attention, time, and money. But it has the potential to truly make a difference. And that is all we need—the chance to make a difference.

Another key partnership will be coastal landowners (the sellers) and the oil and gas industry as well as all of us (the buyers) working together to implement a system of buying and selling ecosystem services on the Texas coast if not throughout all of Texas and the United States. The oil and gas industry, along with the rest of us, is in the process of altering our thinking about and our approaches to climate change, and those changes need to start now. The buying and selling of ecosystem services has the chance to be a "win-win" in that sequestering carbon begins to implement action to address climate change and also has the potential to transform the economics of farming and ranching. The groundwork is being done at Rice and in many other places to aid and abet these ecosystem transactions, which may go well beyond carbon dioxide to include water supply enhancement, fish and wildlife production, property protection, and beef and shellfish production.

The Texas Coastal Exchange, the transaction assistance system set up by the SSPEED Center at Rice, has a goal to complete up to ten major ecosystem service transactions by 2020. In order to get there, a number of things need to happen, including the emergence of a voluntary market. But whether it happens by 2020 or not, it will happen eventually. When it does, Texas coastal landowners will be able, through free-market transactions, to achieve personal needs and goals just as society as a whole will benefit. And we can hope that the oil and gas industry will find its way before it is too late for it if not for all of us.

It is not unreasonable to foresee that much of the private land in Texas coastal counties will become involved in ecosystem service transactions, particularly the hazard-prone areas that are uniquely suited to natural production. In this manner, four important coastal goals can be accomplished—private farms and ranches will enjoy sufficient cash flow to stay on their land, carbon dioxide will be sequestered in meaningful amounts, high-risk hazard zones will be used in a manner compatible with that risk, and native ecosystems will be restored. That is an excellent outcome for the future of the coast. But that is not all.

Yet another partnership will emerge to implement the recreational, recruitment, and money-making potential of ecoplay. Along the upper coast, the Lone Star Coastal National Recreation Area is already in the creation and implementation stage. There is no reason a similar effort could not exist along the middle coast and lower coast. In all three cases, the natural resources are there to support birding, kayaking, and fishing as well as more general hiking and beach activities. We have the assets. Now all we have to do is develop them and help people prosper as we do these things.

Make no mistake about it. There will be a new economy associated with these partnerships. Jobs will be created by this "green" or, perhaps more aptly, "creative" or circular economy. We will be working to create ecosystems and collect seeds, measure success and create the contracts to implement these deals. We will be working to find ways to make freshwater out of salty or brackish water. We will be guiding birders and fishermen and kayakers and leading urban kids out into the nature reserves that will surround many urbanized areas. At the same time, we will be helping the oil and gas industry bridge from the past where it was the leader to a future where it will be fighting for relevance, perhaps the most important challenge in the history of the industry.

A fourth aspect of this future is the provision of excellent information so that the market system can function correctly, so that buyers and sellers can act on the same information. All buyers in hurricane evacuation areas should be made aware of the risk into which they are buying. No buyer should find out after the fact that he or she is moving into a high-risk hurricane surge or wind damage zone. We should provide accurate and honest information so that all of us can understand the risk. If we choose to accept that risk after being informed, so be it. However, if we choose to move into high-risk areas after being informed, we should not expect to be bailed out by the government when we get flooded or get our roof ripped off. Responsibility comes with freedom to choose.

We should also be providing information about our resources, including keys to using and enjoying them. Those who have never enjoyed coastal resources will likely not act to protect them. We need to make the information about these opportunities available and we need to find ways to get people out and enjoying these resources. I am convinced that once people learn about our abundant resources and how to enjoy them, they will come back time and again and will ultimately act to protect them. But if they cannot find accessible opportunities, it may not make any difference how excellent the resources are.

We should also be talking about and understanding climate change. Our climate is changing. Our storms are getting worse. Our sea level is rising. Our droughts will become more severe. To date, we on the Texas coast as well as in Texas generally have refused to publicly acknowledge climate change, much less our role in causing this change. This denial must end. Many things can be done to address climate change, starting with understanding what a changing climate means to life on the Texas coast. We will see more and more high tides coming over roads, particularly when low pressure systems move through with spring and fall fronts, not to mention hurricanes. If we acknowledge climate change, we may start trying to reduce our footprint and offset what we cannot reduce. If we citizens do that, we can perhaps show the oil and gas industry the way. Without honest conversation and information, we will fail.

Future development will occur on the Texas coast. One hope is that it will move away from the tidelands and focus on higher ground. As we move further into the twenty-first century, rising sea level and larger storms will worsen our coastal living conditions. Development north and west and even southwest of Houston makes more sense than expansion to the south or southeast. Development to the south and west of Corpus makes sense. Coastal industry, if not protected by some master system, should make sure it has sufficient levees in place.

Private-sector activity has led the implementation of the LEED program. However, nothing will transform water usage to the extent of the SITES program for landscaping. Given that 50 percent of urban water is consumed by yard watering, significant water savings are available for the future. That will make a major difference. Similarly, if we develop an Envision-like program for the chemical and refining industries, we should see significant improvement in plant performance as well as reductions in water and energy use and even carbon offsets as best management practices become articulated and implemented voluntarily.

From an infrastructure standpoint, the major improvements that are needed are flood protection structures. I am generally opposed to structural interventions, and I hate to see the government tapped to pay for these improvements, but the potential environmental and economic harm that lies ahead in Galveston Bay poses a risk that can and should be avoided. No doubt several billion dollars will be required. But if we are smart, we can pay for these improvements with local or state bonds rather than federal money. A map of the proposed improvements overlaid on the flood hazard risk map is shown in figure 12.2.

I have no doubt that litigation fits into this future, although exactly how is not clear. If the GBRA-TAP agreement fails or is not implemented in other watersheds, then certainly further litigation will be necessary under various provisions of the Endangered Species Act as well as under other federal environmental laws. The water needs of the bays are too important to be left to the same institutions that up to this point have failed to meet them despite Herculean efforts by many wonderful people. Sometimes you simply have to ask the courts for help.

The threat of litigation might also be important in getting

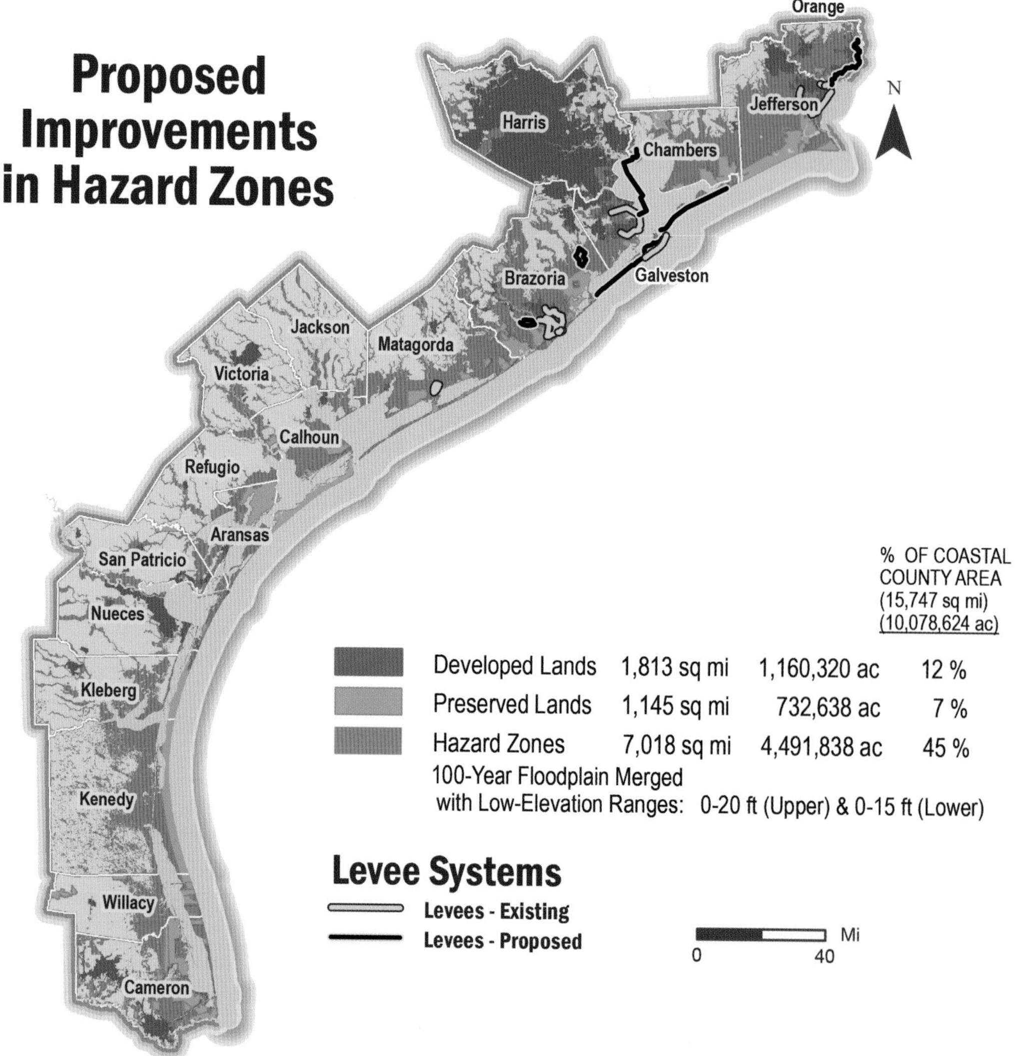

Figure 12.2. The high-risk flood hazard area is shown juxtaposed with developed lands and protected lands. The protected lands, which represent 7 percent of the coastal counties, play a major role in absorbing these various flooding rainfalls and storm surges.

Texas coastal industries to acknowledge the risk posed by hurricanes and the need for better surge protection. To date, industry has been very silent about whether it needs better protection from storm surge. I believe it is reluctant to step forward because it is afraid that either (1) it will be made to pay for the improvements or (2) it will be opening itself up for future liability if it admits there is a problem and it fails to do something about it. Unfortunately, there is a problem and we, if not industry, do need to do something about it. All of the research on surge risk and climate change indicates that industry could be found liable for failing to exhibit reasonable care by conducting its business without adequate consideration of the danger posed by these huge storms, which will definitely be part of our future.

The faith community has a role in the future of the coast of Texas. So far, it has been missing in action. It is simply not participating in the dialogue about any of the issues described in this book, yet its writings and philosophies set out a path that would lead these important institutions to the forefront of the effort to secure water for the bays, to sequester carbon, to take our children out into the garden that is the Texas coast.

Finally, I call on the fishermen of the coast, particularly the recreational fishermen, to step up and be counted. You are among the prime beneficiaries of this plan, a plan that the recreational fishing community has the ability to implement in part. Coastal fishermen have money to spend. Coastal fishing nonprofit organizations could create programs whereby members could buy habitat and support restoration activities; they could buy water rights created by innovative restoration or they could find and purchase unused water rights. And they could litigate the hard issues of the Texas coast.

Together, we can make this plan work. It is fueled by money working alongside spirituality. It is supported by sound science and good policy. With all of us coming together and helping each other, we can realize a different future for the Texas coast.

In closing, keep in mind the power of one or more committed individuals. I started this chapter with Hilton Kelley and I want to end it with Suzette Chapman. Suzette hired me to come down to the Columbia Bottomlands of Brazoria County, where she had moved after living for many years in the Houston area. Suzette wanted solitude, and she found it among the oaks and hickories and elms of the Columbia Bottomlands

Figure 12.3. To find a good place to think about doing things differently or about whatever you have on your mind, get in a kayak and find a marsh. Photograph by Jim Olive.

alongside Cedar Lakes Creek, the boundary between Matagorda and Brazoria Counties.

Suzette called me over a dispute with a local drainage district that wanted to destroy the plant life along Cedar Lakes Creek and a small tributary running into it. She explained to me that she had told the drainage district representatives that she did not want to cut down her trees along the two creeks, that she would work with them to try to make sure that the water could flow as it needed to. But the good ol' boys of the bottomlands didn't want to work with a fussy woman from Houston, and they illegally sprayed herbicide on her property without permission, trying to kill her opposition by killing her trees.

That was the wrong move by the district, yet I have seen such strong-arm tactics more times than I care to remember. Rather than killing her opposition, the tactics enraged her, causing her to find me and to take any step she could in court and in the political process to fight to save these trees. Pure passion fueled her, passion for the forest, passion for her privacy and security, passion for nature. She thereby also became a force of nature.

By the end of the battle, Suzette had managed to protect her creeks and her property. She fought condemnation and she countersued for damages. She negotiated a conservation easement with the US Fish and Wildlife Service. She went to the district meetings. She campaigned for those who would do

Figure 12.4. Suzette Chapman lives in and loves the Columbia Bottomlands, where she walks in the woods along Cedar Lake Creek with her dog and trusty machete. Over the years, Suzette has fought long and hard to protect these bottomlands, drawing grudging respect from those who wished to denude her creek bank of vegetation. Photo by Jim Olive.

things differently. And she ultimately earned the respect of all those who had initially dismissed her.

Spirituality, passion, smarts, and a willingness to stand up to bullies—all of these describe Suzette and Hilton and countless others along the coast. We need to cultivate those among us who "get it." We need leaders who can find the way into the future by making two seemingly opposite forces come to an agreed position. It can be done. It has been done. But it is hard.

You need to want it. And you need to be committed to making it happen.

In this book, I have described the assets and the concepts to protect them into the future to the best of my ability. I and my generation of conservationists and lawyers will be gone in the not-too-distant future. Others will need to step up, take these ideas and add to them, and help realize a full-world future where the Texas coast benefits and thrives from the combination of our economic, ecological, recreational, spiritual, and entrepreneurial thinking—the body, mind, and soul of the Texas coast united. Remember, we are not going to solve our problems by thinking the way we were thinking when we created them.

PART 5

A Poetic Tribute to the Texas Coast

CHAPTER 13

Poetry of the Coast

Over the years, I have found peace and personal satisfaction from writing poems about my experiences on the Texas coast. These poems have become special places of refuge for me, places where I explore who and what I am and what the coast means to me. This poetry may offer a slightly different viewpoint of the coast, or it may be considered as Psalms. I title each poem after a bird I have seen that somehow relates to some subject that has bubbled to the top of my consciousness that day. I hope you enjoy them as a conclusion to this book of hope for the future of the Texas coast.

THE BLACK SKIMMER

On the Gulf Intracoastal Waterway
On a late spring day in the 1970s.

Sailing down the Texas coast—
Young and easy and without cares—
Breathing it, digesting it, bio-accumulating it
In every living cell of my body.

The sun hung low in the June sky,
Heavy, glowing near the horizon,
The water calm, reflective, green
In the cove where we anchored.

They came from over the marsh grass,
Seeming to lope rather than fly,
Each glued to the other, close knit
As they descended to the water's surface.

We watched as their beaks spread apart,
The lower mandibles penetrating the surface,
Liquid flowing across like a waterfall,
Two water lines left as proof of passage.
The orange beak was brilliant,

The black and white body reflecting
The purple light that glowed
On a good day to be alive.

The herons and egrets rose from the grass
To depart to their rookery homes nearby.
The blue-tipped tail of the redfish
Flopped as it nosed among the roots.
The sun waned and then disappeared
Calling out the mosquitoes to play,
Ending the day that was the beginning
Of my love affair with the Texas coast.

THE OYSTERCATCHER

On the GIWW in the late spring
Near Freeport.

The water is asleep.
The tide has not yet begun
To move through the pass
To fill the bay.

The birds loll complacently
On low exposed sand flats,
Waiting, ever waiting
As am I in my kayak,
Watching for the movement,
Waiting for the moment.

The reef is above the water surface,
The oysters gray-black and shiny.
A squirt of liquid shoots skyward,
Proof of life within the shells.
A pair of oystercatchers sit together,
Orange beaks like neon lights
In the dying afternoon sunlight,
Waiting, patiently waiting,
For the tide.

And then it happens.
An alarm has rung that I
Cannot hear.

Two snowy egrets glide before me,
Extending black legs with yellow boots
To claim their fishing spot.
A great egret joins the reef fishers,
Followed by two fussing willets,
All coming to fish the pools
Within the oyster lattice
Slowly, ever slowly, being filled.

Soon, I perceive it,
The changing water line,
The tidal current
That the birds perceived
In ways beyond me
Long before me
On Christmas Bay in my kayak.

THE WHITE IBIS

In the marsh on the West End of Galveston Island
In a remote cove in my kayak.

The tide is high,
The Spartina marsh green-gold,
The sky clear blue.
As I glide down a marsh channel,
A white shrimp leaps from the water,
And beside me, a school of finger mullet
Bolts into the stalks,
Causing a blue crab to shuffle aside,
Orange claws pointed up,
Jagged daggers warning me to stay away.

The white ibis raises her head
From the grassy edge of the marsh pond,
Makes eye contact with me,
Determines I am no threat, and returns
To ramming her long curved beak
Into the soft mud deposited by
Runoff from storms long past.

I hear the whoosh and then see.
The flight of blue-wing teal flares up,
Startled by my lime green boat,

And then darts back down,
Setting their wings, settling in to feed.

A thought penetrates my consciousness.
I am part of a living system and
Experiencing other living things.
Life is not just being alive—
Life is about being alive
Amongst other living things
In a living system.

Energy flows through me,
A pulse of connectedness with those
With whom we share the planet.
This is life.
I am living it—
I am perceiving it—
I am getting it in every cell of my body.
Primal. Forceful. Clear.

THE REDDISH EGRET
Fishing in the Lower Laguna Madre
In the heart of winter on a good day.

The motor is off.
The boat slides in
And secures itself to the mud.
I step into the December water
Encircled by uprooted ducks
Settling back in to graze
The grassy flats of the Laguna,
Buffleheads and mergansers,
Pintails and widgeons,
Whistling as they gather.

I move toward the blue tail
That lazily flips in the crisp air,
Fly rod poised, stealth-mode engaged
As the reddish egret lands
On the shallow ledge beside me,
Me slowly walking beside the ledge
In knee-deep water,
She striding up on the ledge

To my right and slightly to my rear
In inch-deep water,
Mirroring my footsteps,
Moving when I move,
Then lurching with her beak
To grab the unsuspecting mullet
Fleeing me.

We fish together for most of an hour,
She and me working together,
Physical proof of the partnership
That we have with other living things
Such as an egret on a water ledge
In the Lower Laguna Madre
In South Texas.

THE REDHEAD

At Port Mansfield
Wade fishing in the fall.

Stillness surrounds me,
The quiet disrupted only by the whirr
Of my reel as I fish the edge
Where bright green seagrass
Comes near the surface,
Revealed by the rays from the orange globe
Rising slowly over the sand dunes of Padre Island.

The tails appear as lace flippers,
Casually moving from side to side,
Inviting me to try my luck.
The line spools off the reel
As the rod catapults the imitation close,
And then BAM,
Experiencing the power of the strike,
Pulling, feeling and then losing the swift red.

In frustration I turn to the heavens,
Where three redhead ducks flare away,
Spooked by the sudden movement,
Rising up before me—
The red brilliant against the clear blue sky,
So clear—so bright—so perfect.

Years later I close my eyes
And there they are,
The redheads and the tailing redfish,
Captured forever in my mind.

ROSEATE SPOONBILL

I am in the church of the Earth
And the pink bishop is in residence,
Striding across the shallow flat
Head down, moving to and fro.

I come to Earth Church for services that renew my soul.
The sunrise starts the service by allowing me to see,
A gift for which I am grateful.
I listen to the chorus of the redwing blackbirds
Greeting the sun, welcoming me.

The pink bishops rise, painting the blue sky
With a pink ribbon of undulating life,
Speaking to my very essence of the nature of life
On this rare and precious planet,
Of the relationship between all living things,
Of our duty as stewards, of the responsibility
That comes with being one of the living.

The congregation gathers in celebration,
The ibis, the willet, the sandpipers all
Chirping praise to the glorious day
That I celebrate by enjoying it,
By living it to the fullest.

The benediction is laid down by the
Presence of the caracara, my special keeper,
Who comes to tell me that it is good that I came
To church today, asking me if I want to be a deacon?

I leave church with a smile,
Unlike many of my childhood visits
To a church of another type
And I pray to the pink ones
That I live to attend again.

WHITE FACED GLOSSY IBIS

In the wetlands behind the chenier
On the north side of East Bay.

The freshwater wetland glistens in the October sun,
Blue water interrupted by green and greener grasses
Populated by wading birds of all description—
The pink roseates, the white ibis,
The yellow footed snowy and the delicate tri-color—
But the star today is the thin dark ibis
With the lovely scimitar beak that probes the soft mud
For delicacies of the soil,
Gifts of the natural wonder that is a functioning wetland.

There are those who believe that the Earth
Is the manifestation of God—a part of the Trinity—
The breath of what my mother called the Holy Ghost,
The essence of God pervading creation,
And there are those who simply consider the Earth
As a church—a place where they come
To find spiritual food for mind and soul,
Nutrition to fuel the life spirit within us all,
Life epitomized by the wavering V
Of black, curve-beaked waterbirds floating on air
Above the green grass beyond the chenier.

THE LOON

Walking toward federal district court
Along the seawall in Corpus Christi
On the first day of the whooping crane trial,
Jeff Mundy beside me
His federal rules ever-present.

The loon fishes in the calm morning sea
Diving and staying down for seeming minutes,
Only to bob up and show the white bib
That flashes to our anxious eyes
Where it is seen by Jeff
Who quickly whispers that luck will be ours today,
The loon telling us that the cranes are hopeful
Of our success.

How can we lose when the loon wishes us well?
When the caracara meets me on my drive south
And tips its wings to note my passing,
Asking how well prepared are we
Who dare to bring the State of Texas to task?
Promising that all of the bird world
Will be with us, wishing us well,
Sending greetings and love and hope for the future.

THE RUBY-THROATED HUMMINGBIRD

At my law office
Planning the defense of the whooper
Before the Fifth Circuit Court of Appeals
In New Orleans.

I can feel the fear
Working the edges of my consciousness,
Looking for my weakness,
Looking for points of vulnerability,
Looking for the points of entry
Into the essence of me.

To fight the fear
I accept that it exists,
That it is real,
Much like the fear
That the tiny hummingbird must feel
As it strikes off to fly
Across the Gulf of Mexico
To complete its migration,
To complete its life.

I smile to myself.
Why do I let fear bother me
When it doesn't stop my little friend?
It is simply another obstacle
That I must accept and defeat.

And so I start on my migration
To the banks of the Mississippi
To the Fifth Circuit Court of Appeals
To continue my quest
To protect the Whooping Crane.

THE BLACK-CROWNED NIGHT HERON

It is late evening on Christmas Bay
On the longest day of the year.

As I paddle past the rookery,
The black-crowned night herons
Become active,
Moving about shadow-like
Among the branches,
Anticipating another night of foraging
In the Spartina marsh
In the lights of the night sky
Beginning to emerge
As the sun leaves behind the dark.

Slow paddling and thinking—
Reflecting on the stars sending lumens
From millions of light years away,
Light that I see today,
Evidence of what was
A million light years ago,
Stars once alive, burning,
Stars that I believe I see
But yet may be no more.

The night heron flies overhead,
A darker shade of dark
Revealed before the flickering lights,
Reminding me of what is real,
And that what I know is now.

I know that at this moment,
She and I are together
In time and space.
At this moment,
She and I are both alive.
And beyond that
On a good day like today
She helps me understand
That I need to know no more.

THE BELTED KINGFISHER

Off of Teichman Road on Galveston Island
After Hurricane Ike.

The blue and white kingfisher
Hangs suspended over the marsh pond
Surrounded by debris from the relentless surge.
The sailboat lies on its side, sailing not
On the bay but on marsh hay cordgrass,
Its keel buried in the mud, cowbirds sitting
On the mast that will never fly canvas again.

So where did the kingfisher fly
When Ike came pounding ashore?
Did it go with the wind and come back
To this prime fishing ground?
Or did it move in from afar,
Sucked in by the northern gale
That rushed behind the roaring vortex?
Sucked like the bay water
Into the backside of Galveston,
Water that chose not to attack
The fortified wall against the sea
But rather like a coward,
Seeping into the sewers,
Climbing over the marsh edge,
Bringing with it the stoves
And golf carts and refrigerators
That supported life on the bay.

The kingfisher drops to the glassy surface
Of the pond and pops back up to the air,
Gulping down a morsel,
Unfazed by the destruction,
Needing no rebuilding,
Simply living after Ike.

THE FRIGATE BIRD

At the Bolivar ferry landing
The frigate bird sits atop the steel girder,
Guarding the ruin brought on by Hurricane Ike.

The frigate looks toward a road lined with debris,
Pile after pile of demolished dreams—
The ceramic toilet piled alongside the broken roof
Alongside wood parts of every shape, color and origin—
Roadside pyres of what will never be again.

The landscape is covered with plastic,
Hanging everywhere—suspended
From the brown salt-burned grasses
And the skeleton-like leafless trees,
Draped across barbed wire strands that separate
His worthless tract from hers,
Plastic that does not decompose,
A permanent reminder that we are not
As smart as we think in many ways.

The Gulf water laps at the road beyond Rollover Pass,
Each high tide taking one more millimeter
Of precious sand away from the beach,
Setting the stage for the next big storm
That will rip up the asphalt and
Toss it into East Bay,
Severing the domain of the frigate from easy access.

The frigate sits immobile, head scrunched into its body,
Scissortail barely visible, beak prominent
Like the faded scepter of an Old Testament ruler
Presiding over Bolivar's return to its native owners.

THE CATBIRD

It is cold and drizzling in the deep woods
Adjacent to Jones Creek
In the Columbia Bottomlands.
Trekking through searching for birds,
Part of the annual tallying at Freeport.

Large petroleum storage tanks stand
Mute guard over the gates,
Testament to the pervasive influence
Of oil and gas on the Texas coast.
The large oaks reach for the sky,
Making our necks weary as we search
The upper limbs to try to pin down

The flittering, twittering bird party
Chip, chip, chipping in the treetops.
A rabbit scatters as we approach the thicket,
A tangle of yaupon and holly and briars
That obscures the edge of a small pond
That sits like a jewel in the shadows.

We stand still in the forest
That is quiet except for bird sounds,
Eyes focused, trying to make contact
With the stealthy form that has stopped,
Pausing in the darkest of dark shadows.
And then it moves into the light
That peeps into an opening,
A gray bird with a sly eye
That is directed to my soul.

The "meow" comes as a shy greeting,
A hello from another living thing
With which I share the Earth,
Welcoming me to peaceably walk
Within her home,
To meet her neighbors on this special day
When we celebrate our birds.

Later that day we humans gather
For a hot meal and reports
Of birds seen and maybe not,
But I am focused elsewhere,
Simply basking in the glow
Of the knowledge of another living thing—
Of an experience that touched my soul,
That altered my life ether,
That made me more.

THE BLUE GROSBEAK

On Galveston Island in a field of flowers
Next to an oak motte in the spring.

The small group of birds
Hop across the sandy soil,
Looking for seeds,
The blue of their feathers

Fitting into the mosaic
Of green and pink and orange flowers
On a dreary spring day
On the Texas coast.

This small band of grosbeaks
Is part of a river of birds—
A river flowing each spring—
Carrying immigrants from south
To north and back again,
A river formed by repeated habits,
A river based on the will to survive,
A river that is not known
To many of my kind.

My place is the Texas coast—
A place within the banks of this river,
Making me a part of the river
That flows the energy of life through me,
Finding an eddy
In the deepest chambers of my soul,
Filling me with connection—
With purpose—with contentment—
On a flowered little patch of prairie
On Galveston Island in the spring.

THE BLACKBURNIAN WARBLER

In a hedgerow on the West End of Galveston Island
In the spring.

The small black and orange warbler moves to and fro
Among the thorny bushes and small shrubs,
A bird that carries my family name,
A bird I see only during migration after it has flown
Across the Gulf or up the coast from Veracruz,
Having made it through the trials of another year
In the era of climate change.

I am proprietary about this beautiful, vulnerable bird.
I look for hope and help for its future
And find the brightest light coming from
The least expected source—praise be—
For Pope Francis has thrown down the gauntlet

And issued the encyclical Laudato Si', a challenge
To my species to be respectful of nature, of climate,
Warning that we can and do harm others by our acts,
Informing us that we have duties and responsibilities
To the poor and other living things.

The fallen Baptist in me wishes for this leadership
In other denominations, in other faith ministries,
That stewardship and Earthcare could become one
With concepts of self, of right and wrong, and of success.

The Blackburnian warbler in me sings
"Laudato Si', Pope Frances,"
Praise be to you holy man
For being that which a spiritual leader should be,
A spokesman for the Earth that is my church,
A purveyor of hope for many more encounters
With my own special warbler
On the West End of Galveston Island in the spring.

THE BOB WHITE QUAIL

In Aransas County at the cut at Cedar Bayou
Fishing with JC and Marshal.

"Bob White"—"Bob White"—"Bob White."
The two-note whistle cuts through the clear salty sea air,
A resounding affirmation of life after the rains of May,
Historic rains that caused the parched brown landscape
To remember how to smile in hues of green,
A gift from the child El Niño of the Pacific.

The inquiring "Bob White" from Matagorda Island
Is immediately received and acknowledged
By the "Bob White" from St. Joseph Island,
Two living things communicating across the water,
Talking to one another, seeking covey,
Seeking company,
Seeking food and safety,
Living life a moment at a time.
Immediate. Now.

Floating on the incoming tide I am adrift
In emotion about life restored,

About second chances,
About the rain that brought life to Matagorda
After years of drought,
About the rain that cleansed my inner self,
A gift of La Natura, the child that is nature,
A gift for which I am appreciative and often
Struck with awe,
Grateful that I can live life
A day at a time
With peace in my soul.

And I am grateful for my friends with whom
I have shared the last two days.
"Bob White"—"Bob White"—"Bob White."

THE PROTHONOTARY WARBLER

My father called it a swamp canary,
The little yellow bird
That would accompany us
As we paddled
Back into the Cypress Swamp,
Looking for fish, watching for snakes,
Passing the day together,
Forming impressions lasting a lifetime,
Impressions that guide me today
As I seek to balance
Ecology and jobs,
Life and development.

The Great Depression struck my parents
When they were in their early teens,
Hitting them like an anvil—
Hard, direct, meaningfully.
They never forgot those times,
Of being caught by forces
Beyond their control,
The fear of no work,
The demise of an economy.

Later we debated the spotted owl,
My mother concerned.
Was I more for the owls
Than for jobs?

Me wanting to reassure them
That scenarios existed for win/win,
Hoping the combatants
Would be facile enough and persistent
Enough to find their way.

Today I carry that two-edged sword,
An economy with meaning,
A circular economy with jobs that protect
That needed for life on the planet,
Principles for meeting human needs,
Principles that include
Protecting the Cypress Swamp
Where I can still see the swamp canary
From my kayak in the summer
Deep in the Texas Bottomlands
On the Trinity River in Chambers County.

THE BLACK AND WHITE WARBLER

She calls them pig bastards—
The elected drainage commissioners
And their minions
Who joyfully destroy life
In the bottomlands,
Gleefully denuding the banks
Of secret watercourses incised in the Pleistocene mud,
Spraying herbicides across the creek
To kill her opposition,
Bullying, blustering, sputtering, spitting,
Hating, hurting elected czars,
Flicking away concerns,
Ripping plants and streams asunder,
Acting with deep intent
And malice aforethought,
Acting from fear and hatred of things
They don't understand

Such as a woman who enjoys walking
In the late evening light,
Delighting in the revealed spider webs
Spun from sapling to sapling,
A woman who smiles
At the native shrubs that hold

The precariously placed stream bank soil in place,
Providing the cranny for the frog
And clean water for the fish,
A woman who marvels
At the black and white warblers
Working the insects in the craggy oaks
And sheltering yaupons
On the flood plain bench,
A woman celebrating life
That has escaped the pig bastards
For another day.

THE SAVANNAH SPARROW

On a Christmas bird count on the Stringfellow Ranch
In Brazoria County on a cold December day.

The small brown bird with the yellow eye patch
Rises up and lands on the ancient wire fence,
Giving us one of what will become a record
Number of species on this day of bird counting,
Species that abound due to the variety of native plants
Found in the systems of forest, prairie and wetland,
Plants that are an integral part of the Church of the Earth,
A church where we humans share services
With the savannah sparrow
Nibbling seeds with its flock,
Moving from one stand of grass to another,
Taking in the day, living life.

The morning light reflects off the dew drops
Clinging to the leaves of native stems
That rise from roots extending far into the soil,
Roots that pump carbon into the soil,
Carbon that must be removed from our air,
Carbon that has become unbalanced,
A balance that can be restored if we plant
More and more acres of native grasses,
For in the restoration of nature's cycles
Lies the hope for the future.
Hope found watching a bird of the savannah
On the Stringfellow Wildlife Management Area
In Brazoria County on a cold winter's day.

THE COOT

In the Sacahuista sloughs
On the Texas coastal prairie
East of 281 near Encino.

The coots dot the surface
Of a flooded grass meadow—
Sparkling green shoots of cellulose
Embraced by sweet blue water
That flows ever so slowly
Eastward under the ground
Toward the Laguna Madre.

Watching the black duck-like bird
With the white slash across its forehead,
It becomes clear why men of the age
Of me and my friends are called "old coots."
As we drive up, the coots run
Across the water surface
Not quite able to get airborne—
Vacillating between flying and lighting.
And when their footsteps
No longer crease the smooth flat surface,
They just chug along—not fast, not hurried,
Just grazing and gazing.

But most of all they murmur to each other non-stop,
As if talking under their breath,
Commenting upon the way of the day,
Commenting on the newest issue to pass before
Their collected wisdom,
Offering comments and quips,
Basking in friendships formed long ago.
Old coots living through another good day.

So for now, good-bye from this old coot. And don't forget to learn that new dance, which should include a bit of poetry.

References

Introduction

Blackburn, James. *The Book of Texas Bays*. College Station: Texas A&M University Press, 2004.

Daly, Herman. *Beyond Growth*. Boston: Beacon Press, 1996

Daly, Herman, and John B. Cobb Jr. *For the Common Good*. Boston: Beacon Press, 1989.

Figure I.3. Developed areas: Texas Natural Resources Information System (TNRIS), 2009; Google Earth, 2012. Industrial areas: Google Earth, 2012. Remaining land and county boundaries: TNRIS. Waterways (lakes and bays): Texas Parks and Wildlife Department (TPWD). Protected lands: National Audubon Society; Gulf Coast Bird Observatory; US Fish and Wildlife Service (USFWS); National Park Service (NPS); Galveston Bay Foundation (GBF); National Marine Sanctuary; National Oceanic and Atmospheric Administration (NOAA); Scenic Galveston; The Conservation Fund (TCF); The Nature Conservancy (TNC); TPWD; Texas General Land Office (TX GLO); US Army Corps of Engineers (USACE) (for details on source attribution, see fig. 2.11, map of protected lands). County boundaries: TNRIS.

Figure I.4. Major rivers: Texas Water Development Board (TWDB). State boundary: TIGER / US Census (TIGER = Topologically Integrated Geographic Encoding and Referencing). Interstates: Center for Geospatial Technology, Texas Tech University. Waterways (lakes and bays): TPWD.

Chapter 1

Figure 1.2. Lakes and bays: TPWD. Major rivers: TWDB. State boundary: TIGER / US Census.

Figure 1.3. Precipitation data from Natural Resources Conservation Service (NRCS). NRCS precipitation data generated by Prism (climate group, Oregon State University). Waterways (lakes and bays): TPWD.

Figure 1.4. River basins and major rivers: TWDB. Interstates: Center for Geospatial Technology, Texas Tech University. Waterways (lakes and bays): TPWD.

Figure 1.5. Elevation data: USGS 3DEP National Elevation Dataset; digital elevation models (DEMs). Data varies by county in methodology: (i) LIDAR in Harris, Nueces, Kleberg, Kenedy, Willacy, Cameron, and southeastern Jefferson Counties; (ii) complex linear interpolation in all other counties, including Jefferson County, other than the southeastern segment. Latest date of digital models was 2008 or as follows: 2010 Harris; 2009, 2012 Willacy; 2008, 2012 Calhoun, Nueces; 2005, 2008 San Patricio; 2008, 2009 Kleberg, Kenedy; 2003, 2008, 2009 Cameron; 2004 Orange. Major rivers: TWDB. Lakes and bays: TPWD.

Figure 1.8. Wetlands data: USFWS, National Wetlands Inventory, 2015. Developed areas: TNRIS, 2009; Google Earth, 2012. Lakes and bays: TPWD.

Figure 1.10. Seagrasses: NOAA and TPWD. Oyster reefs: GLO and Coastal Atlas, Texas A&M University (TAMU) (based on TPWD data). Oyster reef data source attribution varies by county: GLO for Chambers, Galveston, Refugio, lower Calhoun County bays. TAMU for Orange County (Sabine Lake area; consolidated, unconsolidated, and exposed reef); Matagorda County, upper Calhoun County bays. GLO and TAMU for Aransas and Nueces Counties. Lakes and bays: TPWD.

Figure 1.11. Protected lands: National Audubon Society; Gulf Coast Bird Observatory; USFWS; National Parks and Wildlife Service (NPW); GBF; National Marine Sanctuary; NOAA; Scenic Galveston; TCF; TNC; TPWD; TX GLO; USACE (for details on source attribution, see legend). Lakes and bays: TPWD.

Chapter 2

Figure 2.3. Fairways, channels, and Intracoastal Waterway: NOAA. Lakes and bays: TPWD.

Figure 2.5. Channels and Intracoastal Waterway: NOAA. Industry areas: Google Earth. Railroads: TNRIS. Lakes and bays: TPWD.

Figure 2.6. Channels and Intracoastal Waterway: NOAA. Industry areas: Google Earth. Railroads: TNRIS. Pipelines: US Energy Information Administration (US EIA). Lakes and bays: TPWD.

Figure 2.7. US EIA and USGS (wind turbines, to 2014). Lakes and bays: TPWD.

Figure 2.9. Major and minor roads: TIGER / US Census. Interstates: Center for Geospatial Technology, Texas Tech University. Lakes and bays: TPWD.

Figure 2.10. Developed areas: TNRIS, 2009; Google Earth, 2012. Industry areas: Google Earth, 2012. Remaining land (private lands) and county boundaries: TNRIS.

Figure 2.16. City points: TPWD. City boundaries: TIGER / US Census. Exceptions: locations of points for "Census-Designated Places" (CDPs) from TIGER / US Census for Port O'Connor CDP and Matagorda CDP; city of Sargent from Google Earth. TIGER file includes both incorporated places (legal entities) and CDPs (statistical entities). Roads and highways: TIGER / US Census. Major rivers: TWDB. Lakes and bays: TPWD.

Chapter 3

Costanza, Robert, Ralph d'Arge, Rudolf de Groot, Stephen Farber, Monica Grasso, Bruce Hannon, Karin Limburg, et al. "The Value of the World's Ecosystem Services and Natural Capital." *Nature* 387 (May 15, 1997): 253.

Nueces Bay Environmental Flows Recommendation Report, BBEST Study, Texas Commission on Environmental Quality.

Figure 3.2. River Authorities: TWDB. Lakes and bays: TPWD.

Figure 3.3. Groundwater Conservation Districts: TWDB. Lakes and bays: TPWD.

Figure 3.4. Water transmission lines: for Sabine River area, Sabine River Authority of Texas; for Galveston and Causeway, City of Galveston Public Works (via GCWA); for Coastal Bend Water Supply System (includes Mary Rhodes Waterlines and Evangeline Aquifer), San Patricio Municipal Water District; for Mary Rhodes, Phase II (to the north), City of Corpus Christi; for Formosa line (Mary Rhodes area), Formosa Plastics; for South Texas and lower Rio Grande Valley area, TAMU, Irrigation Technology Center (via Harlingen Public Utilities Board; Harlingen Irrigation District); for Angelina Neches Dam B, USACE and Stephen F. Austin State University (SFA ScholarWorks Faculty Publications in Forestry, 2009, "Habitat Use of American Alligators in East Texas"). Pumping Stations: GCWA. Purification Plants: City of Houston, Public Works Department. Desalination: TWDB. Other waterlines as shown (as defined in legend): CWA, GCWA, LCRA, NHCWA, SJRA, SJWA. Major reservoirs and rivers: TWDB. Note: to the north at Trinity Bay, "Region H" = GCWA, Reg. H. To the west of Mary Rhodes are two vertical pipelines: at north, Beeville; at south, Alice pipelines. Lane City Reservoir: LCRA. Lakes and bays: TPWD.

Figure 3.5. 2012 Texas Water Plan, TWDB. Regional water planning areas: TWDB. Lakes and bays: TPWD.

Figure 3.6. TWDB data: 2012 State Water Plan, Texas water planning areas.

Chapter 4

Figure 4.2. Sources (by region): Houston-Galveston Area Council (H-GAC), July 2015 (Brazoria, Chambers, Galveston, Harris, and Matagorda Counties); Texas Department of Emergency Management (TDEM), 2013 (Sabine Lake area); TDEM, 2002 (Calhoun, Jackson, and Victoria Counties); TDEM, 2008 (Coastal Bend Area, including Aransas, Kenedy, Kleberg, Nueces, Refugio, and San Patricio Counties); TDEM, 2001 (Valley Area, including Willacy and Cameron Counties). Lakes and bays: TPWD.

Figure 4.5. Graphic produced by Ben Bass, SSPEED Center, Rice University, based on computer modeling of a projected storm like Ike but with 15 percent greater wind speed coming ashore at the worst place for surge in the region near San Luis Pass.

Figure 4.6. Historical hurricane tracks: NOAA, 2014. Lakes and bays: TPWD.

Figure 4.7. Elevation data: USGS 3DEP National Elevation Dataset, digital elevation models (DEMs). Data varies by county in methodology: (i) LIDAR in Harris, Nueces, Kleberg, Kenedy, Willacy, Cameron, and southeastern Jefferson Counties; (ii) complex linear interpolation in all other counties, including Jefferson County, other than the southeastern segment. Latest date of digital models was 2008 or follows: 2010 Harris; 2009, 2012 Willacy; 2008, 2012 Calhoun, Nueces; 2005, 2008 San Patricio; 2008, 2009 Kleberg, Kenedy; 2003, 2008, 2009 Cameron; 2004 Orange. Lakes and bays: TPWD.

Figure 4.8. 100-year floodplain: FEMA and TAMU (developed from FEMA data). For five-county area of Chambers, Harris, Galveston, Brazoria, and Matagorda, and for Refugio: FEMA. For all other counties: TAMU, developed from FEMA data (most recent year varies). Lakes and bays: TPWD.

Figure 4.9. Developed areas: TNRIS, 2009; Google Earth, 2012. Elevation: USGS 3DEP National Elevation Dataset. 100-year floodplain: FEMA and TAMU (developed from FEMA data). For five-county area of Chambers, Harris, Galveston, Brazoria, and Matagorda, and for Refugio: FEMA. For all other counties: TAMU, developed from FEMA data (most recent year varies). Preserved lands: various sources; see figure 2.11 for preserved lands data sources. Acreage of preserved lands excludes 57 sq mi of Flower Garden area. Lakes and bays: TPWD.

Figure 4.10. Rijkswaterstaat Beeldbank, Netherlands. http://www

.cityguiderotterdam.com/fileadmin/_migrated/pics/Maeslantkering_Rotterdam2.jpg.

Figure 4.11. Rijkswaterstaat Beeldbank, Joop van Houdt, Netherlands. http://www.dutchwatersector.com/news-events/news/14556-tocardo-to-place-tidal-energy-turbines-in-eastern-scheldt-storm-surge-barrier.html.

Figure 4.12. SSPEED Center, Rice University.

Figure 4.13. USACE (Port Arthur, Matagorda, and Freeport areas); SSPEED Center at Rice University (Galveston and Texas City areas); Gulf Coast Community, Protection and Recovery District (Orange County area). Lakes and bays: TPWD.

Chapter 5

Hansen, James, Makiko Sato, Paul Hearty, Reto Ruedy, Maxwell Kelley, Valerie Masson-Delmotte, Gary Russell, et al. "Ice Melt, Sea Level Rise and Superstorms: Evidence from Paleo-Climate Data, Climate Modeling, and Modern Observations that 2° C Global Warming Could Be Dangerous." *Atmospheric Chemistry and Physics* 16 (2016): 3761.

Intergovernmental Panel on Climate Change (IPCC). *Fifth Assessment Report*. 2013. http://www.ipcc.ch/report/ar5/wg1/.

Pacala, Stephen, and Robert Socolow. "Stabilization Wedges: Solving the Climate Problem for the Next 50 Years with Current Technologies." *Science* 305 (August 13, 2004): 968.

Schmidheiny, Stephen. *Changing Course: A Global Business Perspective on Development and the Environment*. Cambridge, MA: MIT Press, 1992.

Smart, B. *Beyond Compliance: A New Industry Review of the Environment*. Washington, DC: World Resources Institute, 1992.

Union of Concerned Scientists. *Oil Refinery CO_2 Performance Measurement, September 2011*. File No. COMMBETTERENVFY11103.

Figure 5.1. Elevation data: USGS 3DEP National Elevation Dataset; digital elevation models (DEMs). Data varies by county in methodology: (i) LIDAR in Harris, Nueces, Kleberg, Kenedy, Willacy, Cameron, and southeastern Jefferson Counties; (ii) complex linear interpolation in all other counties, including Jefferson County other than the southeastern segment. Latest date of digital models was 2008 or as follows: 2010 Harris; 2009, 2012 Willacy; 2008, 2012 Calhoun, Nueces; 2005, 2008 San Patricio; 2008, 2009 Kleberg, Kenedy; 2003, 2008, 2009 Cameron; 2004 Orange. Major rivers: TWDB. Lakes and bays: TPWD.

Figure 5.2. Carbon footprint calculated by staff of the Blackburn and Carter law firm.

Chapter 6

Costanza, Robert, Ralph d'Arge, Rudolf de Groot, Stephen Farber, Monica Grasso, Bruce Hannon, Karin Limburg, et al. "The Value of the World's Ecosystem Services and Natural Capital." *Nature* 387 (May 15, 1997): 253.

Hale, Courtney, Avantika Gori, and Jim Blackburn. "Ecosystem Services of the Mid-Texas Coast." Prepared for the SSPEED Center, September 2014.

Roan, Sharon. *Ozone Crisis*. New York: John Wiley and Sons, 1989.

Figure 6.2. Courtesy of the SSPEED Center and Dr. Henk Mooiweer.

Figure 6.4. Ecosystem data: Houston Wilderness (Big Thicket, Piney Woods, Prairie Systems); Texas Tech (Crops; based on USDA data); Houston Wilderness (Bottomlands upper coast), Texas Tech (Bottomlands lower coast). Wetlands: USFWS, National Wetlands Inventory; and Houston Wilderness to the north. Lakes and bays: TPWD.

Figure 6.8. Protected lands: National Audubon Society; Gulf Coast Bird Observatory; USFWS; National Park Service (NPS); GBF; National Marine Sanctuary; NOAA; Scenic Galveston; TCF; TNC; TPWD; TX GLO; USACE (for details on source attribution, see legend). Lakes and bays: TPWD.

Chapter 7

National Parks Conservation Association. *Opportunity Knocks: How the Lone Star Coastal National Recreation Area Could Attract Visitors, Boost Businesses, and Create Jobs*. Washington, DC: National Parks Conservation Association, 2011.

Outdoor Industry Association. *The Outdoor Recreation Economy*. 2012. https://outdoorindustry.org/images/researchfiles/OIA_OutdoorRecEconomyReport2012.pdf.

US Fish and Wildlife Service. *2011 National Survey of Hunting, Fishing and Wildlife-Associated Recreation—Texas*. FHW/11-TX. May 2013.

———. *Birding in the United States: A Demographic and Economic Analysis*. 2013. https://www.fws.gov/southeast/economicimpact/pdf/2011-birdingreport--final.pdf.

Figure 7.1. Aerial map: Google Earth. Location of Christmas Bird Count circle: National Audubon Society.

Figure 7.4. Christmas Bird Count data as of 2014: National Audubon Society. Lakes and bays: TPWD.

Figure 7.6. Rookery data: TX GLO. Lakes and bays: TPWD.
Figure 7.8. Birding Trail data: TPWD. Lakes and bays: TPWD.
Figure 7.9. Protected lands: National Audubon Society; Gulf Coast Bird Observatory; USFWS; NPS; GBF; National Marine Sanctuary; NOAA; Scenic Galveston; TCF; TNC; TPWD; TX GLO; USACE (for details on source attribution, see legend). Lakes and bays: TPWD.
Figure 7.13. Birding Trail data: TPWD. World Birding Center locations: World Birding Center (in association with TPWD, USFWS, and nine valley communities). Protected lands: National Audubon Society; Gulf Coast Bird Observatory; USFWS; NPS; GBF; National Marine Sanctuary; NOAA; Scenic Galveston; TCF; TNC; TPWD; TX GLO; USACE. NWRs: USFWS, National Marine Sanctuary, NOAA. State Wildlife Management Areas: TPWD; TNC; TCF. Lakes and bays: TPWD.

Chapter 8

Mississippi State University Coastal Research and Extension Service. "Economic Impacts of Natural and Technological Disasters." http://gomos.msstate.edu/txannualcommerciallandings.html.
Outdoor Industry Foundation. *The Active Outdoor Recreation Economy.* http://www.outdoorfoundation.org/pdf/ResearchRecreationEconomy.pdf.
US Fish and Wildlife Service. *2011 National Survey of Fishing, Hunting and Wildlife-Related Recreation—Texas.* FHW/11-TX. May 2013.
Figure 8.7. Boat ramps: TPWD (via TX GLO). Major and minor roads: TIGER / US Census.
Figures 8.9, 8.10, and 8.11. Catch rates: TPWD, 2013. Lakes and bays: TPWD.

Chapter 9

Figure 9.4. Hand-drawn map by Tom Stehn.

Chapter 10

Cesaretti, C. A., and Stephen Commins, eds. *Let the Earth Bless the Lord: A Christian Perspective on Land Use.* New York: Seabury Press, 1981.
Delio, Ikia, Keith Douglass Warner, and Pamela Wood. *Care for the Creation*, Cincinnati: Franciscan Media, 2007.
Leopold, Aldo. *A Sand County Almanac.* New York: Oxford University Press, 1949.

Pope Francis. "Encyclical Letter Laudato Si' of the Holy Father Francis on Care for Our Common Home." http://w2.vatican.va/content/francesco/en/encyclicals/documents/papa-francesco_20150524_enciclica-laudato-si.html.

Presbyterian Eco-Justice Task Force. *Keeping and Healing the Creation*. Committee on Social Witness Policy, Presbyterian Church (USA), 1989.

White, Lynn, Jr. "The Historical Roots of Our Ecological Crisis." *Science* 155 (March 10, 1967): 1203–7.

Figure 10.2. Association of Religion Data Archives.

Chapter 12

Figure 12.2. Developed areas: TNRIS, 2009; Google Earth, 2012. Elevation: USGS 3DEP National Elevation Dataset. 100-year floodplain: FEMA and TAMU (developed from FEMA data). For five-county area of Chambers, Harris, Galveston, Brazoria, and Matagorda, and for Refugio: FEMA. For all other counties: TAMU, developed from FEMA data. Most recent year of data varies. Preserved lands: various sources; see figure 2.11, map of preserved lands. Lakes and bays: TPWD. Acreage of preserved lands excludes 57 sq mi of Flower Garden area. Levee systems: USACE (Port Arthur, Matagorda, and Freeport areas); SSPEED Center at Rice University (Galveston, Texas City areas); Gulf Coast Community Protection and Recovery District (Orange County area).

Index

Note: Page numbers in *italics* indicate illustrations, tables, or figures; page numbers in **bold** indicate maps. All locations are in Texas unless otherwise indicated.

Other Books in the Gulf Coast Books Series

Lighthouses of Texas
T. Lindsay Baker

Laguna Madre of Texas and Tamaulipas
John W. Tunnell and Frank W. Judd

Fishing Yesterday's Gulf Coast
Barney Farley

Designing the Bayous: The Control of Water in the Atchafalaya Basin, 1800–1995
Martin Reuss

Life on Matagorda Island
Wayne H. McAlister and Martha K. McAlister

Book of Texas Bays
Jim Blackburn

Plants of the Texas Coastal Bend
Roy L. Lehman and Tammy White

Galveston Bay
Sally E. Antrobus

Crossing the Rio Grande: An Immigrant's Life in the 1880s
Luis G. Gómez, translated by Guadalupe Valdez Jr.

Birdlife of Houston, Galveston, and the Upper Texas Coast
Ted Eubanks Jr., Robert A. Behrstock, and Ron J. Weeks

Formation and Future of the Upper Texas Coast: A Geologist Answers Questions about Sand, Storms, and Living by the Sea
John B. Anderson

Finding Birds on the Great Texas Coastal Birding Trail: Houston, Galveston, and the Upper Texas Coast
Ted Eubanks Jr., Robert A. Behrstock, and Seth Davidson

Texas Coral Reefs
Jesse Cancelmo

Fishes of the Texas Laguna Madre: A Guide for Anglers and Naturalists
David A. McKee and Henry Compton

Louisiana Coast: Guide to an American Wetland
Gay M. Gomez

Storm over the Bay: The People of Corpus Christi and Their Port
Mary J. O'Rear

After Ike: Aerial Views from the No-Fly Zone
Bryan Carlile

Kayaking the Texas Coast
John Whorff

Glory of the Silver King: The Golden Age of Tarpon Fishing
Hart Stilwell

River Music: An Atchafalaya Story
Ann McCutchan

Del Pueblo: A History of Houston's Hispanic Community
Thomas H. Kreneck

Letters to Alice: Birth of the Kleberg-King Ranch Dynasty
Jane Clements Monday and Francis Brannen Vick

Hundred Years of Texas Waterfowl Hunting: The Decoys, Guides, Clubs, and Places, 1870s to 1970s
R. K. Sawyer